MCSE Test Success:
NT Workstation 4

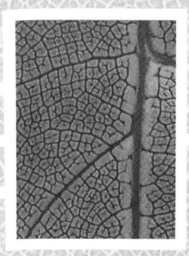

MCSE Test Success™:
NT® Workstation 4

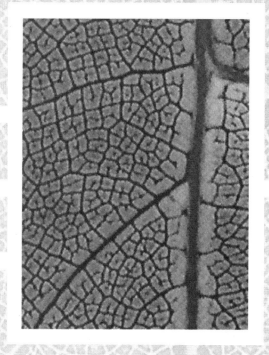

Todd Lammle
Lisa Donald

San Francisco • Paris • Düsseldorf • Soest

Associate Publisher: Guy Hart-Davis
Contracts and Licensing Manager: Kristine Plachy
Acquisitions & Developmental Editor: Bonnie Bills
Editor: Dana Gardner
Project Editors: Brenda Frink and Lori Ash
Technical Editor: Ron Reimann
Book Designer: Patrick Dintino
Desktop Publisher: Maureen Forys, Happenstance Type-O-Rama
Production Coordinator: Eryn L. Osterhaus
Indexer: Ted Laux
Cover Designer: Archer Design
Cover Photographer: FPG International

November 1, 1997

Dear SYBEX Customer:

Microsoft is pleased to inform you that SYBEX is a participant in the Microsoft® Independent Courseware Vendor (ICV) program. Microsoft ICVs design, develop, and market self-paced courseware, books, and other products that support Microsoft software and the Microsoft Certified Professional (MCP) program.

To be accepted into the Microsoft ICV program, an ICV must meet set criteria. In addition, Microsoft reviews and approves each ICV training product before permission is granted to use the Microsoft Certified Professional Approved Study Guide logo on that product. This logo assures the consumer that the product has passed the following Microsoft standards:

- The course contains accurate product information.
- The course includes labs and activities during which the student can apply knowledge and skills learned from the course.
- The course teaches skills that help prepare the student to take corresponding MCP exams.

Microsoft ICVs continually develop and release new MCP Approved Study Guides. To prepare for a particular Microsoft certification exam, a student may choose one or more single, self-paced training courses or a series of training courses.

You will be pleased with the quality and effectiveness of the MCP Approved Study Guides available from SYBEX.

Sincerely,

Holly Heath
ICV Account Manager
Microsoft Training & Certification

MICROSOFT INDEPENDENT COURSEWARE VENDOR PROGRAM

I would like to dedicate this book to Richard Mumper who gave me my start in 1981 by believing in me when no one else would take the chance with an 18-year-old kid.

—Todd Lammle

For Alvin Tan and Cindy Osborne, thanks for the great start!

—Lisa Donald

ACKNOWLEDGMENTS

This Test Success Book has been a great project to work on. It has been made possible by associate publisher Guy Hart-Davis and acquisitions and developmental editor Bonnie Bills. Bonnie is always willing to lend a helping hand and has been instrumental in developing the scope and content of the Test Success books.

Thanks to Dana Gardner for all of her editing expertise and Ron Reimann who did an excellent job as the technical editor (as always!). Lori Ash and Brenda Frink helped coordinate the project from the Sybex end, thanks for the hard work.

Finally, thanks to Maureen Forys, desktop publisher; Eryn Osterhaus, production coordinator; and Ted Laux, indexer.

This book would not have been possible without the great team contribution.

CONTENTS AT A GLANCE

TABLE OF CONTENTS

INTRODUCTION

One of the greatest challenges facing corporate America is finding people who are qualified to manage corporate computer networks. One of the most common operating systems is Windows NT, which requires skill and knowledge to manage. Microsoft has a certification program that shows employers that a candidate is capable of managing complex NT networks. The most highly coveted certification is MCSE or Microsoft Certified Systems Engineer.

Why become an MCSE? The main benefit is that MCSE carries high industry recognition and gives you much greater earning potential. Certification can be your key to a new job, a higher salary—or both.

So what's stopping you? If it's because you don't know what to expect from the tests or are worried that you might not pass, then this book is for you.

Your Key to Passing Exam 70-073

This book provides you with the key to passing Exam 70-073: Implementing and Supporting Windows NT Workstation 4.0. You'll find all the information relevant to this exam, including information on some of the "picky" questions on less frequently used options, and hundreds of practice questions.

Understand the Exam Objectives

This book is structured according to the MCSE NT Workstation 4.0 objectives. At-a-glance review sections and more than 400 review questions bolster your knowledge of the information relevant to each objective and the exam itself. You learn exactly what you need to know without wasting time on tangents that are not covered by the exam—this book prepares you for the exam in the shortest amount of time possible.

Get Ready for the Real Thing

More than 200 sample test questions prepare you for the test-taking experience. These are multiple-choice questions that resemble actual exam questions—some are even more difficult than what you'll find on the exam. If you can pass the Sample Tests at the end of each unit and the Final Exam at the end of the book, you know that you're ready.

Is This Book for You?

This book is intended for those who already have some experience with Microsoft NT. It is especially well suited for:

- Students using courseware or taking a course to prepare for the exam who need to supplement their study material with test-based practice questions.

- Network engineers who have worked with the product but still need to fill in some holes.

- Anyone who has studied for the exams—using self-study guides, computer-based training, classes, or on-the-job experience—and wants to make sure that they're adequately prepared.

Understanding Microsoft Certification

Microsoft offers several levels of certification for anyone who has or is pursuing a career as a network professional working with Microsoft products:

- Microsoft Certified Professional (MCP)

- Microsoft Certified Systems Engineer (MCSE)

- Microsoft Certified Professional + Internet

- Microsoft Certified Systems Engineer + Internet

- Microsoft Certified Trainer (MCT)

The one you choose depends on your area of expertise and your career goals.

Microsoft Certified Professional (MCP)

This certification is for individuals with expertise in one specific area. MCP certification is often a stepping stone to MCSE certification and allows you some benefits of Microsoft certification after just one exam.

By passing one core exam (meaning an operating system exam), you become an MCP.

Microsoft Certified Systems Engineer (MCSE)

This is the certification for network professionals. By becoming an MCSE you differentiate yourself from an MCP. This certification is similar to a college degree in that it shows that you can make a commitment to complete all of the steps required for certification and that you meet the high standards required to successfully complete all of the required exams.

To become an MCSE, you must pass a series of six exams:

1. Networking Essentials (waived for Novell CNEs)

2. Implementing and Supporting Microsoft Windows NT Workstation 4.0 (or Windows 95)

3. Implementing and Supporting Microsoft Windows NT Server 4.0

4. Implementing and Supporting Microsoft Windows NT Server 4.0 in the Enterprise

5. Elective

6. Elective

The following list applies to the NT 4.0 track. Microsoft still supports a track for 3.51, but 4.0 certification is more desirable because it is the current operating system.

Some of the electives include:

- Internetworking with Microsoft TCP/IP on Microsoft Windows NT 4.0

- Implementing and Supporting Microsoft Internet Information Server 4.0

- Implementing and Supporting Microsoft Exchange Server 5.5

- Implementing and Supporting Microsoft SNA Server 4.0

- Implementing and Supporting Microsoft Systems Management Server 1.2

- Implementing a Database Design on Microsoft SQL Server 6.5

- System Administration for Microsoft SQL Server 6.5

Microsoft Certified Trainer (MCT)

As an MCT, you can deliver Microsoft certified courseware through official Microsoft channels.

The MCT certification is more costly because in addition to passing the exams, it requires that you enroll in the official Microsoft courses. You also have to submit an application that must be approved by Microsoft. The number of exams you must pass depends on the number of courses you want to teach.

For the most up-to-date certification information, visit Microsoft's Web site at www.microsoft.com/train_cert.

Understanding Microsoft's Exam Objectives

To help you prepare for certification exams, Microsoft specifies a list of exam objectives for each test. This book is based on the objectives.

For this exam the objectives were designed to measure your ability to design, install, configure, administrate, and troubleshoot NT Workstation 4.0 when it is part of an enterprise network.

Scheduling and Taking an Exam

Once you think you're ready to take an exam, call Prometric Testing Centers at (800) 755-EXAM. They'll tell you where to find the closest testing center. Before you call, get out your credit card because each exam costs $100. (If you've used this book to prepare yourself thoroughly, chances are you'll only have to shell out that $100 once!)

You can schedule the exams at your convenience. The exams are downloaded from Prometric to the testing center, and you take the exam on a computer at your scheduled time. When you complete the exam, you find out whether you passed and you receive a score report that lists the seven areas you were tested on and how you performed. Each unit in this book corresponds to one of the seven main objectives. If you do not pass the exam, you'll know from the score report where you did poorly, so you can study that particular unit in the Test Success book more carefully. If you passed the exam, you don't need to do anything else—Prometric uploads the test results to Microsoft.

Test-Taking Hints

The hints discussed in this section will help you to be a more effective test-taker.

Get There Early and Be Prepared This is your last chance to review. Bring your Test Success Book and review any areas you feel unsure of. Also be prepared to show two forms of ID. If you need a quick drink of water or a visit to the restroom, take the time before the exam—you cannot pause the exam in the middle.

What You Can and Can't Take with You The MCSE exams are closed book. The only thing that you can use is scratch paper provided by the testing center. Use this paper as much as possible to diagram the questions; many times, diagramming a question helps make its answer clear. You have to return the scratch paper to the test administrator at the end of the exam.

Many testing centers are very strict about what you can take into the testing room. Some testing centers have gone so far as to forbid you to even take in a zipped-up purse. If you feel tempted to take in any outside material, beware that many testing centers use monitoring devices such as video and audio equipment. (So don't swear, even if you are alone in the room!)

Prometric Testing Centers take the testing process and test validation very seriously.

What to Expect When you arrive for your exam, you're asked to present your ID. You're also asked to sign a piece of paper that specifies that you understand the testing rules; for example, you agree not to cheat on the exam.

Before you start the exam you have an opportunity to take a practice exam. It is not related to NT; it used only so that you get a feel for the exam process.

When you're done with the exam, you receive your score report. You also have an opportunity to evaluate your exam and the testing center.

Best Way to Approach the Test   This really depends on the type of test taker you are. I'm of the school that believes you either know the answer or you don't. If you know the answer, answer the question and move on. If you're not sure of the answer, mark your best guess, then mark the question. At the end of the exam, you can view all of your answers or only the questions you have marked—make the decision based on how much time you have left. I always like to double-check all my answers because sometimes I misread the question on the first pass. I also find that a related question might provide the answer for a question that I may have been unsure of.

Be sure to answer all questions. Unanswered questions are scored as incorrect and count against you. Make sure you keep an eye on the remaining time so you can pace yourself accordingly.

One piece of advice: If you have narrowed down the answers to two options, always go with your gut reaction—it is usually correct.

If you do not pass the exam, write down everything you can remember while the exam is still fresh in your mind. This will help you prepare for your next exam. Many times the questions overlap; you don't want to miss the same questions again.

After You Become Certified

Once you become an MCSE, Microsoft kicks in some goodies, including:

- A one-year subscription to Microsoft Technet, a valuable CD collection that contains Microsoft support information.

- A one-year subscription to the Microsoft Beta Evaluation program, which is a great way to get your hands on new software. Be the first kid on the block to play with new and upcoming software.

- Access to a secured area of the Microsoft Web site that provides technical support and product information. This certification benefit is also available for MCP certification.

- Permission to use the Microsoft Certified Professional logos (each certification has its own logo), which look great on letterhead and business cards.

- An MCP certificate (you get a certificate for each level of certification you reach), suitable for framing or copying and sending to Mom.

- A one-year subscription to *Microsoft Certified Professional Magazine*, which provides information on professional and career development.

Preparing for the MCSE Exams

To prepare for the MCSE certification exams, you should try to work with the product as much as possible. In addition, there are a variety of resources from which you can learn about the products and exams.

Courses

Instructor-Led   Be very careful when choosing instructor-led courses. The Microsoft training materials do not always have a high correlation with the exam objectives. If your primary goal is to pass the certification exams, this book is an excellent resource because it will fill in holes left by the Microsoft courseware.

Online   Online training is an alternative to instructor-led training. This is a useful option for people who are prevented geographically from attending instructor-led training.

Self-Study Guides

If you prefer to use a book to help you prepare for the MCSE tests, you'll find a wide variety available, from complete study guides (such as the Network Press MCSE Study Guide series, which covers the core MCSE exams and key electives) through test-preparedness books similar to this one.

Sybex Web Site

For more MCSE information, point your browser to the Sybex Web site, where you'll find information about the MCP program, job links, and descriptions of other quality titles in the Network Press line of MCSE-related books. Go to http://www.sybex.com and click on the MCSE logo.

How to Use This Book

This book is designed to help you prepare for the MCSE exam. It reviews each objective and relevant test-taking information, then gives you a chance to test your knowledge through Study Questions and a Sample Test. For each unit:

1. Review the exam objectives list at the beginning of the unit. (You may want to check the Microsoft Train_Cert Web site to make sure the objectives haven't changed.) There are seven main objectives. They include:

   - Planning

   - Installation and Configuration

   - Managing Resources

   - Connectivity

   - Running Applications

   - Monitoring and Optimization

   - Troubleshooting

2. Depending on your level of expertise, read through or scan the reference material that follows the objectives list. Broken down according to the objectives, this section helps you brush up on the information you need to know for the exam.

3. Review your knowledge in the Study Questions section. These are straightforward questions designed to test your knowledge of the specified topic. Answers to Study Questions are listed in the Appendix at the back of the book.

4. Once you feel sure of your knowledge of the area, take the Sample Test. The Sample Test is formatted in content and style to match the real exam. Instead of asking the "cut-and-dry" questions, you are presented with more scenario-based questions. This will help prepare you for the real exam. Sometimes, half of the battle is in trying to figure out exactly what the question is asking you. Set a time limit based on the number of questions: In general, you should be able to

answer 20 questions in 30 minutes. When you've finished, check your answers with the Appendix in the back of the book. If you answer at least 85 percent of the questions correctly within the time limit (the first time you take the Sample Test), you're in good shape. To really prepare, you should note the questions you miss and be able to score 95-100 percent correctly on subsequent tries.

5. After you successfully complete Units 1-7, you're ready for the Final Exam in Unit 8. Allow yourself 90 minutes to complete the test of 55 questions. If you answer 85 percent of the questions correctly on the first try, you're well prepared. If not, go back and review your knowledge of the areas you struggled with and take the test again.

6. Right before you take the test, scan the reference material at the beginning of each unit to refresh your memory.

At this point, you are well on your way to becoming certified!
Good Luck!

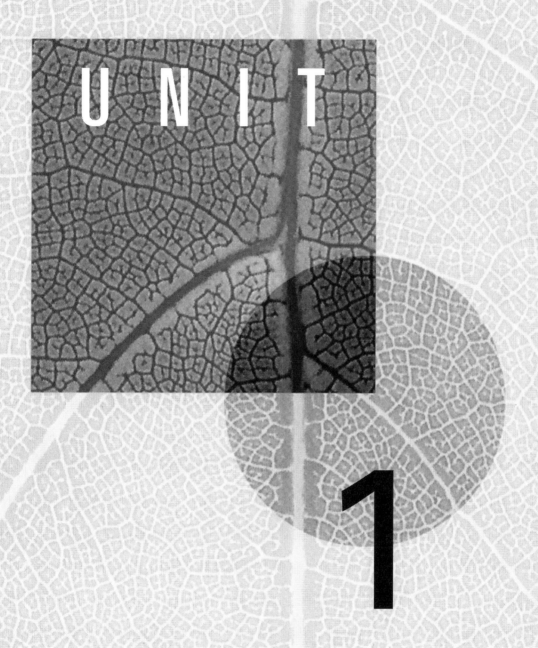

UNIT

1

Planning

Test Objectives: Planning

■ Create unattended installation files.

■ Plan strategies for sharing and securing resources.

■ Choose the appropriate file system to use in a given situation. File systems and situations include:

- NTFS
- FAT
- HPFS
- Security
- Dual-boot systems

Exam objectives are subject to change at any time without prior notice and at Microsoft's sole discretion. Please visit Microsoft's Training & Certification website (www.microsoft.com/Train_Cert) for the most current exam objectives listing.

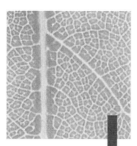

In this unit, I'll go through the objectives for planning on an NT Workstation. These objectives cover in detail exactly how to set up and configure an unattended installation, as well as how to share and secure shares on the workstation when connected to a network. Additional attention is given to the different types of file systems available with NT Workstation 4.0, and how to implement and secure the resources on different types of file systems.

Create Unattended Installation Files

You can configure NT installations so you don't have to respond to any prompts from the installation program while you're installing the OS. This feature makes upgrading a large number of machines easier. For the unattended installation to work, you first must configure both UNATTEND.TXT answer files and UDF customization files. These files contain the information you would normally have to type into dialog boxes and at installation prompts.

- UNATTEND.TXT: This file, which has a template located on the NT Workstation CD-ROM, lets you either upgrade from NT 3.5*x* or create simple installations.

- SETUPMGR.EXE: This executable file, located on the NT Workstation CD-ROM, creates the unattended answer files. SETUPMGR.EXE lets you configure the General Setup, Networking Setup, and Advanced Setup portions of the unattended installation text file.

The General Setup screen (shown in Figure 1.1), contains the following tabs:

- **User Information:** User's name; organization; NetBIOS name; and product ID.

- **General:** Hardware settings; run the program during setup; type of upgrade and specific instructions, if upgrading.

- **Computer Role:** Determine what computer role version, if installing; workstation group or domain; PDC or DBC (server only); domain or workgroup name; optional computer name.

- **Install Directory:** Default installation directory, or custom.

- **Display settings:** Display graphics configuration.

- **Time Zone:** Time zone information.

- **License Mode:** Only for server, configure per seat or per server.

FIGURE 1.1

General setup screen

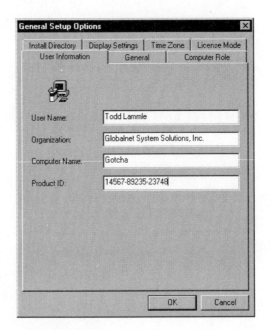

The Networking Options screen (shown in Figure 1.2) contains the following tabs:

- **General:** Specify whether you'll install networking during the installation process, or from the Setup Manager program.

- **Adapters:** Select the Adapter card; specify communications protocol. You can select only one Network Interface Cards (NICs) during NT installation, but additional NICs can be installed subsequently.

- **Protocols:** Specify the protocols installed and their parameters.

- **Services:** Specify the network services to be installed and set the parameters.

- **Internet:** Specify which Internet services to install and where to store information (servers only).

- **Modem:** Configure modem type and configuration. Available only if RAS is installed and configured.

F I G U R E 1.2

Networking Options screen

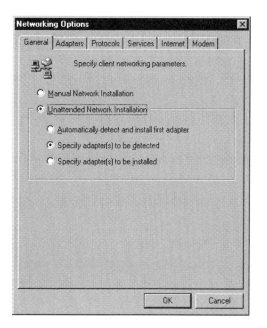

Figure 1.3 shows the Advanced Options screen. The advanced options include a number of settings that you shouldn't change unless you have a good understanding of the install process, and a need to perform an unorthodox installation. One setting is the Convert to NTFS option in the File Systems tab. Check this option if you wish to format the hard drive partition that NT will be installed on to use the advanced NTFS features.

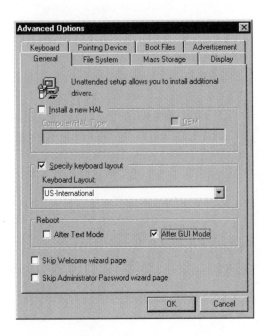

Using the Unattended Answer File with WINNT and WINNT32

The /U:answer_file option in WINNT and WINNT32 allows you to specify an unattended answer file for a Windows NT installation. The /U option requires that the /S option is also selected, specifying the source directory for the Windows NT installation files. Unattended installations should also explicitly specify the /B switch to suppress default creation of the three installation diskettes when installing from network shares or CD ROM. The answer file provides the answers to some or all of the prompts that the user would otherwise need to respond to during setup.

Answer Files (UNATTEND.TXT)

You can create different unattended answer files for various setup configurations used in your company. You can use UDF files (explained below) to further customize the unattended answer files as needed. For example, you can create one answer file for each remote location, or for each department. To tailor the information to individual users, you then create a UDF file with a section for each user. The administrator then has to specify both the answer file and the UDF when installing NT using either WINNT.EXE or WINNT32.EXE.

Creating an Unattended Answer file

You can create unattended answer files by editing a copy of the UNATTEND.TXT file that's included with the Workstation 4.0 CD-ROM or by using the NT 4.0 Workstation Resource kit, or by using the Setup Manager utility. Use any text editors to modify the file, then save the modified copy as a text file.

The Uniqueness Database File (UDF)

Uniqueness Database File (UDF) identifies differences between installations, such as the computer name and the user name for that installation. UDFs are used to provide specific replacements for sections of the answer file, or to supply additional sections as required to customize installs. The use of a UDF requires the use of an Unattended Answer file.

You can create UDF files using a text editor. You also need to provide settings for the computer name for each installation.

To specify a Uniqueness Database File during setup, run WINNT.EXE or WINNT32.EXE with the following parameters:

WINNT /U: answer_filename /UDF: ID[udfdatabase_filename]

Answer_filename is the full path name of the UNATTEND.TXT Unattended Answer file. Replace ID with the uniqueness ID to use while installing Windows NT on the computer, and database udf_filename with the file name, including the full path of the UDF.

The Sysdiff Utility

Sysdiff records the difference between a normal Windows NT installation and an installation to which you've added applications and data files. The Sysdiff utility is a powerful tool you can use to automate the distribution of both operating system and application software to a large number of users.

Sysdiff can perform in the following modes:

- **Snap:** Sysdiff takes a snapshot of the state of the Windows NT operating system Registry, and the state of the file system and files and directories. This information is written to a snapshot file. The snapshot establishes a baseline NT install picture from which customized installations can be built.

- **Diff:** Sysdiff records the differences between the state of a previous snap-shot of a Windows NT installation and the state of the installation at the time Sysdiff is run again. Sysdiff/Diff create a difference file.

- **Apply:** Sysdiff/Apply applies the data in the difference file to a Windows NT installation. Apply can be used as part of an unattended answer file or run separately.

- **Inf:** Sysdiff creates an inf file and installation data from the difference file. This can be placed in a server share so the differences captured with the Diff command are automatically applied to installations of Windows NT made from the server share.

- **Dump:** This produces a readable text file that details the contents of the difference file.

Plan Strategies for Sharing and Securing Resources

In a network environment, you often need to share information that resides on your Windows NT workstation. You can implement this by creating shared directories. A hand underneath the directory identifies the directory share, as shown below.

For your computer to share directories, several network components must be in place:

- The Server Service must be started on your computer. If you've installed the networking components of Windows NT, this service should start automatically when Windows NT starts.

- The user creating the network share of the directory must have access permissions to create the share. The default local user groups that are allowed to create shares are Administrators and Power Users. In NT Workstation, only Administrators and Power Users can share folders/ resources.

- The user attempting to view the share must have at least list permissions for that directory if it is on an NTFS partition (and therefore subject to NTFS file permissions).

You can share any directory on your NT Workstation, regardless of the file system or media type. NT Workstation allows you to set the sharing of the files and directories from several places, including NT Explorer and My Computer on the desktop.

The share name does not have to be the same as the directory name. You can make the name up to 255 characters, but some DOS-based systems may not be able to handle it if it's longer than eight characters.

Figure 1.4 shows the dialog, accessed from the property menu of a directory, that lets you share the directory.

FIGURE 1.4

Sharing a directory

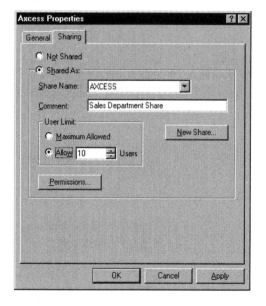

You can set the share two ways, as shown in Figure 1.4.

- **Not Shared:** Disables the sharing of a directory, keeping it available for local use only.

- **Shared As:** Enables sharing on the directory and uses the following fields (Share Name, Comment, User Limit, New Share, and Permissions) to configure the share.

  - **Share Name:** The resource name the other remote users computers will see when accessing the shared volume.

  - **Comment:** Additional description visible to the browsing computers.

  - **User Limit:** Allows you to set the maximum number of connections.

  - **New Share:** Allows you to make multiple names or aliases for the same share.

  - **Permissions:** Opens the Share Permissions window (discussed below).

Shares can also be hidden from the browser if you use a $ behind the name. For example, sales$ is a shared directory, but it doesn't show up in the network browser and you can only use it if you were told about it.

Shared Directory Permissions

Directories shared over a network are protected by share permissions. These permissions are not the same as NTFS permissions, rather they're in addition to the NTFS permissions. In the case of overlapping permissions, the most restrictive permission prevails.

The four permissions for shared directories are No Access, Read, Change, and Full Control.

- **No Access:** Users can connect to the resources but cannot access the directory or list its comments.

- **Read:** An individual with Read access can:

  - Display the files and subdirectories contained by the shared directory.

  - Run program files from the shared directory.

- Access subdirectories of the shared directory.

- Read and copy files from the shared directory.

- **Change:** In addition to having read capabilities, a user with Change permissions can:

    - Create subdirectories and files.

    - Delete files and subdirectories.

    - Read and write to files in the directory.

    - Change file attributes.

- **Full Control:** In addition to having read and change capabilities, a user with Full control of a share can:

    - Change file permissions.

    - Take ownership of files on an NTFS volume. However, Administrators can *always* take ownership of files, even when Administrators are specified to have No Access.

Choose the Appropriate File System to Use in a Given Situation

A file system is a method of organizing files on a physical storage device. In Windows NT this method is implemented as an operating system module that controls the storage and retrieval of data to the disk. Possible file systems include NTFS, FAT, VFAT, HPFS, Security, and Dual Boot Systems.

NTFS

New Technology File System (NTFS) was created by Microsoft specifically to work with Windows NT. NTFS implements many protective features to ensure the reliable storage and retrieval of data:

- **Fault tolerance:** Log-based file system allows recovery of files if they're corrupted or if there's an emergency shutdown.

- **Security:** Supports security on all files and directories. Maintains the permissions and auditing features implemented by the NT security model.

- **File and partition sizes:** NT can store up to 16 exabytes. An exabyte is 2^{64}. The recommended minimum partition size is 50MBs.

- **File compression:** NT provides real-time file compression. NTFS can compress or expand an individual file or all the files in a directory.

- **POSIX support:** Windows NT supports POSIX standard network naming conventions, such as case sensitivity, last-access time, and hard links, which are two directory entries that point to the same file.

- **Performance:** To decrease fragmentation, Windows NT always attempts to save files in contiguous blocks. NT uses the B-Tree directory structure found in OS/2 High Performance File System (HPFS), rather than the linked list directory structure used by FAT, speeding searches and reducing missing links that result in data loss.

FAT

The FAT system has been around since 1981, a long time in computer time. Almost all computer operating systems support the FAT file system in some way. Below are some advantages of the FAT file system:

- It supports files and partitions as large as 2GB.

- It's accessible by many operating systems, including MS-DOS, Windows NT, Windows 95, OS/2, MacOS, and many variants of the UNIX family of operating systems.

- It has the least file system overhead of any file system, which makes it better than NTFS for small partitions (smaller then 50MBs).

- It's the only PC-compatible file system that can be used on a floppy.

- It's suitable for removable hard disks, many of which are too small to efficiently use NTFS.

VFAT

MS-DOS version 7, Windows 95, and Windows NT versions 3.51 and 4.0 support the long filenames feature found in VFAT. VFAT is not the same as FAT 32 which is now offered on Windows 95 OEM installs. FAT 32 is not compatible with NTFS or FAT (now called FAT 16).

The main difference between FAT and VFAT is the naming convention. Table 1.1 shows the differences between FAT and VFAT.

	FAT	VFAT
TABLE 1.1 These are the differences between the FAT and VFAT files systems.	Name must be eight characters, with a three letter extension	Name can be up to 255 characters
	Must start with either a letter or number	Must start with either a letter or number
	Can contain all characters except "/\[]:;|=,^*?	Can contain all characters except "\[]:;|=,^*?
	Not case sensitive	Not case sensitive
	Only one period is allowed	The name can contain multiple periods, but the text after the last period is still considered the extension.
	Does not preserve case	Preserves case
	CON, AUX, COM1 through COM 4, LPT1 through 3, PRN and NUL are reserved	None

HPFS

Up to version 3.51, Windows NT supported read and write access to OS/2 High Performance File System (HPFS) partitions. This support has been removed in Windows NT version 4.0. You should convert existing NT Workstation 3.51 installations to NTFS prior to upgrading to NT Workstation 4.0.

If the computer that contains the HPFS partition is not running a previous version of NT, you will need to backup the data, delete the HPFS partition, and create and format a FAT partition. After the NT installation is complete the data can be restored and the partition converted to NTFS.

Security

When using the NTFS file system under Windows NT, you have many security options that do not exist in a DOS FAT file system. Some of the NTFS security features are:

- **Permissions:** NTFS compares Access Tokens (generated during user log-on) to NTFS resource Access Control Lists (ACLs) maintained by the SAM to determine if and at what level access should be granted.

- **Auditing:** Windows NT can record NTFS access-related events to a log file that can be viewed using the Event Viewer. The system administrator can specify which events, accesses, actions, and files will be audited and to what degree of detail, and can review the information collected later. Auditing is configured in User Manager. The System, Security, and Application Log can be viewed by Administrators only using the Event Viewer.

- **Transaction logging:** NTFS is a log-based file system, which means that it records changes to files and directories as they happen, and also records how to undo the changes in case of a system failure.

- **Ownership:** NTFS tracks ownership of files. The creator of a file or directory is automatically the owner, and only the administrator or user with Full Control can take ownership of a file or directory. Ownership can only be taken, it cannot be given.

Dual-Boot Systems

You can install several different operating systems on your computer and use the Windows NT boot loader to select which operating system you wish to boot at boot time. As you install operating systems on your computer, the new boot menu options are added to the menu automatically. These are kept in the Boot.INI file and can be edited by any text editor. However, this file is read-only, so you must remove the read-only attribute before editing it. BOOT.INI has Archive, System, and Read-Only flags set. You have to remove all three before editing it.

Keep in mind that if you have Windows 95 on your computer prior to loading NT workstation or server using the NTFS file system, you won't be able to load Windows 95. This is because Windows 95 can't read or use NTFS. Likewise, if your installation of Windows 95 (OEM SR-2) has the FAT32 filing system, NTFS will not be able to access those drives. Make sure you create separate partitions to load the operating systems, or use the FAT file system.

S T U D Y   Q U E S T I O N S

Create Unattended Installation Files

1. True/False: An answer file allows you to automate an NT Workstation installation by providing installation program responses and configuration parameter settings in a text file.

2. What file enables you to supply machine specific installation information such as computer name during an unattended installation?

_____

3. Where would you find the UNATTEND.TXT file?

_____

4. What does the SETUPMGR.EXE executable do?

_____

5. True/False: The General Setup tab in the SETUPMGR.EXE program allows you to choose the hardware settings.

6. Using the SETUPMGR.EXE program, what tab allows you to enter Users name, organization, NetBIOS name, and product ID?

_____

7. In the General Setup screen, where do you choose the workgroup or domain, PDC or BDC, domain or workgroup name, and optional computer name?

_____

8. What does the Display Settings information box in the SETUPMGR.EXE program General Setup screen allow you to configure?

_____

9. True/False: The License Mode information in the General Setup screen is for both Server and Workstation.

10. What information does the General tab in the Networking Screen allow you to specify?

_____

11. Which tab in the SETUPMGR.EXE program allows you to specify the protocols installed and their parameters?

_____

12. True/False: The Adapter tab in the Networking screen lets you specify the communication parameters for the adapter cards chosen.

13. In which screen and tab do you set the Change to NTFS file system?

_____

14. True/False: You only need one Answer file for various setup configurations.

Using the Unattended Answer File with WINNT and WINNT32

15. What does the /U option allow you to specify when running WINNT or WINNT32?

_____

16. True/False: When choosing the /U option when running WINNT or WINNT32, the /D option must also be selected, specifying the source directory for the Windows NT installation files.

Answer Files (UNATTEND.TXT)

17. True/False: The answer file provides the answers to some or all of the prompts that the user would not usually need to respond to during setup.

18. In what circumstance would the user have to specify both the answer file and the UDF when running WINNT or WINNT32?

_____

Creating an Unattended Answer File

19. What two methods can you use to create unattended answer files?

_____

The Uniqueness Database File (UDF)

20. True/False: The UDF identifies the similarities between installations.

21. When would you use a UDF file?

_____

22. You can create the UDF files using a text editor. You also need to provide settings for at least the _____ for each installation.

23. What is the command line format you would use to specify an unattended text file and uniqueness data file ID during a NT setup?

_____

24. True/False: To specify a uniqueness ID during setup, you can only run WINNT.EXE. WINNT32.EXE only works for NT server.

The SYSDIFF Utility

25. What would you use the Sysdiff utility for?

_____

26. True/False: Sysdiff allows you to install applications software.

27. When using the Sysdiff /Diff command, what happens?

_____

28. True/False: Sysdiff /Snap takes a snapshot of the state of the Windows NT operating system Registry, but not the file system, files, and directories.

29. When would you use the Sysdiff /Dump command?

_____

30. What command creates a difference file?

_____

Plan Strategies for Sharing and Securing Resources

31. What icon identifies a network share?

_____

32. Which service must be running on your NT Workstation in order for your computer to share directories or printers?

33. True/False: the Server service on your NT Workstation is started through the device manager in control panel.

34. What two default groups are allowed to create shares?

_____

_____

35. The user creating the network share of the directory must have which permission to create the share?

_____

36. The user attempting to view the share must have at least _____ permissions for that directory if it is on an NTFS partition.

37. True/False: You can share both files and directories, regardless of the file system.

38. List two places from which you can set a network share.

_____

_____

39. True/False: The share name must be the same as the directory name.

40. How long can a share name be?

_____

41. True/False: There are no consequences to making a share name longer than eight characters.

42. What is the maximum number of connections to a share on an NT workstation at any one time?

_____

43. True/False: You can't change the maximum number of connections to a network share at any one time.

44. In what field do you set the maximum connections?

_____

45. True/False: You can only set one share per directory.

46. In which field do you create a different share for the same directory?

_____

Shared Directory Permissions

47. True/False: Share permissions are part of the NTFS partition permissions.

48. True/False: NTFS permissions always override the share permissions when on a NTFS partition.

49. List the four share permissions below and what their functions are:

Permission	Function
_____	_____
_____	_____
_____	_____
_____	_____

Choose the Appropriate File System to Use in a Given Situation

50. True/False: A file system is a way of organizing files.

NTFS

51. True/False: The New Technology File System was created by IBM specifically to work with OS/2 and Microsoft licensed it for Windows NT.

52. What is the main fault tolerant feature of NTFS?

_____

_____

53. True/False: When on an NTFS partition, you cannot use share permissions; you must use NTFS permissions.

54. What is the maximum partition size in an NT partition?

_____

55. What is the recommended minimum size of an NT partition?

_____

56. True/False: File compression is only available on NTFS partitions.

57. True/False: NTFS can compress only by directory, compressing all files inside the directory. It cannot compress individual files.

58. When referring to POSIX support, what is meant by hard links?

_____

FAT

59. List five advantages of the FAT file system.

_____

_____

_____

_____

_____

VFAT

60. Under what platforms is VFAT used?

_____

61. True/False: The main difference between FAT and VFAT is the naming convention.

62. True/False: The FAT file system must start with either a letter or number.

63. True/False: VFAT names can be up to 255 characters.

64. How long can a FAT name be?

_____

HPFS

65. True/False: HPFS was created by IBM.

66. True/False: HPFS is used only in OS/2.

Security

67. What is the main purpose for permissions in an NTFS partition?

_____

68. Windows NT can record NTFS security-related events to a log file for later review using the

_____.

69. What are two purposes of Transaction logging?

_____

_____

Dual-Boot Systems

70. True/False: You can install as many operating systems on your NT Workstation as you want, but you must have an NTFS volume.

71. What is the filename for the Windows NT boot loader?

_____

72. True/False: Windows 95 can share an NTFS partition with Windows NT Workstation, but not NT Server.

SAMPLE TEST

1-1 Select the files required to perform an automated unattended installation of Windows NT Workstation 4.0 on 40 identical units, assigning each machine its own NetBIOS computer name and installing MS Office 97.

Select all that apply:

A. WINDIFF.EXE

B. Uniqueness Database File (UDF)

C. ACMESETUP.EXE

D. SYSDIFF.EXE

E. AUTOSETUP.EXE

F. UNATTEND.TXT

G. SETUP /B

1-2 Your corporate engineering department needs to upgrade five existing Windows NT 3.51 computers to NT 4 to use enhanced DirectDraw graphics capabilities. The machines are Pentium 166 MHz desktops with 64MB of RAM and 2GB Hard Disk Drives. The drives are partitioned as single HPFS primary partitions. Some existing files have 30-character file names. How should you best handle the situation?

A. Run CONVERT.EXE and convert the HPFS partition to FAT, install NT 4 and enable VFAT to handle the long filenames.

B. Install NT 4, HPFS supports long filenames.

C. Run CONVERT.EXE and convert the HPFS partition to NTFS, install NT 4.

D. These computers cannot be upgraded to NT 4.

S A M P L E   T E S T

1-3   Joel is a Power User on his NT 4 Workstation computer. Julie's NT account is a member of the Finance Group and the Users Group. Joel needs to let Julie access some spreadsheets on his computer. He shares the NUMBERS directory and assigns permissions as follows:

Administrators	Full Control
Power Users	Full Control
Creator-Owner	Full Control
Finance	Change
Users	No Access

What can Julie do with the files in Joel's NUMBERS directory?

A. Julie can't read the files in the directory.

B. Julie can read and write to the directory.

C. Julie can delete files in the directory.

D. Joel does not have adequate authority to share the directory.

1-4   Jim is a member of the Payroll group. He accesses a shared directory on an NTFS partition that is configured to grant the Payroll group CHANGE permissions. What can Jim do with the files in this directory?

Select all that apply:

A. Jim can read the files.

B. Jim can write files to the directory.

C. Jim can delete the files.

D. Jim can take ownership of the files in the directory.

Questions 1-5 through 1-7 use the same scenario and objective, but the proposed solution varies.

1-5 You must deploy 50 identically configured new computers as part of a corporate expansion. You need to install Windows NT Workstation 4.0, MS Office 97, Visio 5 Professional and Attachmate Extra! 3270 emulation software.

Required Result: Automated installation of the Operating System.

Optional Result 1: Each computer is configured with a specific Computer Name and User Name.

Optional Result 2: Automated installation of the application software.

Proposed Solution: Create a baseline NT installation on one computer. Run SYSDIFF /SNAP. Install all application software, and run SYSDIFF /DIFF. Create an UNATTEND.TXT file that incorporates SYSDIFF /APPLY. Place all files in the shared network directory. Boot to a DOS network access diskette, and connect to the network share as a logical Z:\ drive. Run WINNT /U:UNATTEND.TXT /S:Z /B

    A. This solution produces the required result and both optional results.

    B. This solution produces the required result and one of the optional results.

    C. This solution produces the required result but neither of the optional results.

    D. This solution does not produce the required result.

1-6 You must deploy 50 identically configured new computers as part of a corporate expansion. You need to install Windows NT Workstation 4.0, MS Office 97, Visio 5 Professional and Attachmate Extra! 3270 emulation software.

Required Result: Automated installation of the Operating System.

Optional Result 1: Each computer is configured with a specific Computer Name and User Name.

Optional Result 2: Automated installation of the application software.

Proposed Solution: Create a baseline NT installation on one computer. Run SYSDIFF /SNAP. Install all application software, and run SYSDIFF /DIFF. Create an UNATTEND.TXT file that incorporates SYSDIFF /APPLY. Place all files in the shared network directory. Boot to a DOS network access diskette, then connect to the network share as a logical Z:\ drive. Run WINNT32 /U:UNATTEND.TXT /S:Z /B

> **A.** This solution produces the required result and both optional results.
>
> **B.** This solution produces the required result and one of the optional results.
>
> **C.** This solution produces the required result but neither of the optional results.
>
> **D.** This solution does not produce the required result.

1-7   You must deploy 50 identically configured new computers as part of a corporate expansion. You need to install Windows NT Workstation 4.0, MS Office 97, Visio 5 Professional and Attachmate Extra! 3270 emulation software.

Required Result: Automated installation of the Operating System.

Optional Result 1: Each computer is configured with a specific Computer Name and User Name.

Optional Result 2: Automated installation of the application software.

Proposed Solution: Create a baseline NT installation on one computer. Run SYSDIFF /SNAP. Install all application software, and run SYSDIFF /DIFF. Create an UNATTEND.TXT file that incorporates SYSDIFF /APPLY. Create a .UDF file with Computer Name and User Name configuration parameters for each machine. Place all files in the shared network directory. Boot to a bootable DOS network access diskette, then connect to the network share as a logical Z:\ drive. Run WINNT /U:UNATTEND.TXT /UDF:*id*[variable] /S:Z /B

> **A.** This solution produces the required result and both optional results.
>
> **B.** This solution produces the required result and one of the optional results.
>
> **C.** This solution produces the required result but neither of the optional results.
>
> **D.** This solution does not produce the required result.

1-8 Your manager has a sensitive payroll file she wants to send on a floppy disk to your accountants. She's very concerned about the sensitive salary data, so she wants to use NTFS security to safeguard it. She asks you how to prepare the disk. What is your answer?

A. From an NT command prompt, run FORMAT A: /FS:NTFS.

B. Double-click on the My Computer icon, insert the disk, right-click on the disk icon, select Properties, and check NTFS.

C. Click on START ➤ RUN, enter FORMAT A: /NTFS, and click on OK.

D. You can't do this.

1-9 Tom just purchased a new desktop computer that has Windows 95 OSR2 factory installed on it. The factory load uses FAT32 to provide the most efficient cluster allocation. For security reasons, you're asked to install NT Workstation 4.0 on this computer. What should you do?

A. Insert the NT Workstation 4.0 CD-ROM. Click on START ➤ RUN, then enter WINNT32, and click on OK.

B. Insert the NT Workstation 4.0 CD-ROM, and click on START ➤ RUN. Enter WINNT, and click on OK.

C. Insert the NT Workstation 4.0 CD-ROM, then restart the computer with the first NT installation diskette. Setup automatically configures the machine as dual-boot.

D. Insert the NT Workstation 4.0 CD-ROM, then restart the computer in MS-DOS mode. Run FDISK, delete all existing partitions, and reboot the computer with the first NT installation diskette.

1-10   Sally is a member of the Power Users group on her Windows NT Workstation 4.0 computer. She shares an existing directory on an NTFS partition and specifies everyone (which includes all user groups and administrators) as NO ACCESS. After she restarts the computer, she finds that she can no longer see the files in the shared directory. She calls you and you log on with your administrator user ID. You can't see the files in the directory either. What can you do?

    A. Create a new shared directory, assign appropriate permissions, and restore the files from a recent backup into the new directory.

    B. Boot to a DOS disk and copy the contents of the directory into another directory.

    C. Right-click on the shared folder icon, select Sharing, and Take Ownership of the directory.

    D. You can't access this directory. NO ACCESS overrides all other permissions.

1-11   Why use a UDF during automated installations?

    A. It gives specific information for individual users or computers.

    B. It gives specific information for enabling a workstation computer to join a domain or workgroup.

    C. It gives specific information for installing hardware device drivers.

    D. It gives specific information for installing a suite of applications.

1-12   What is the minimum number of answer files and UDF files required if you are installing 100 desktops and 40 laptops?

    A. One answer file and two UDF files

    B. Two answer files and one UDF file

    C. Two answer files and 140 UDF files

    D. 140 answer files and two UDF files

1-13   Why use an answer file during automated installations?

    A. It gives specific information for individual users or computers.

    B. It gives specific information for enabling a workstation computer to join a domain or workgroup.

    C. It gives specific information to some or all of the user prompts during Setup.

    D. It gives specific information for installing a suite of applications.

1-14   Why use the Sysdiff.EXE file during automated installations?

    A. It gives specific information for individual users or computers.

    B. It gives specific information for enabling a workstation computer to join a domain or workgroup.

    C. It gives specific information for installing hardware device drivers.

    D. It gives specific information for installing a suite of applications.

1-15   What files do you need to automate the installation of Win32-based applications on 100 computers with different hardware platforms?

Choose all that apply:

    A. UNATTEND.TXT (answer file)

    B. UDF

    C. SYSDIFF.EXE

    D. SETUP.INF

1-16 You want to boot either Windows 95 or Windows NT Workstation on your computer, and you have one hard drive partition that's large enough to hold both operating systems. You don't share your computer with others, so you don't need security for your files, and you want to access your files from either operating system. What's your best option?

A. Upgrade your Windows 95 installation to NT (install to the same directory) so your settings will migrate, then re-install Windows 95. Leave the hard drive as a FAT volume.

B. Install Windows NT to a different directory than Windows 95. Leave the hard drive as a FAT volume.

C. Back up your files. Divide your hard drive into two partitions, and install Windows 95 to one partition and restore your files. Install Windows NT Workstation to the other partition and convert the partition to NTFS.

D. You cannot have both Windows 95 and Windows NT on the same computer.

1-17 You currently have 100 identical Pentium-class computers, 75 identical 486-class computers, and 25 identical laptops on your network. You want to automate the installation of Windows NT Workstation on these computers. Choose your best option:

A. Install Windows NT Workstation individually to each computer.

B. Prepare an unattended answer file and a Uniqueness database file. Use these two files to install Windows NT Workstation to all of the computers.

C. Prepare an unattended answer file for each type of computer and one Uniqueness database file. Use these files to install Windows NT Workstation to the computers.

D. Prepare an unattended answer file and a Uniqueness database file for each computer on the network. Use these two files to install Windows NT Workstation to each of the computers.

E. You can't install Windows NT Workstation on the laptop computers.

1-18 Your company has a standard set of software that's used in all company sites. You want to automate the process of installing the operating system and software to the 75 identical computers on the new network. What can you do to automate the process?

    A. Install Windows NT workstation to a computer, along with the additional software. Copy the contents of the hard drive of that computer to all of the other hard drives of the other computers on the network.

    B. Install Windows NT Workstation to a computer. Run Sysdiff to take a snapshot of the installation. Install the additional software, then run Sysdiff again to obtain a difference file. Install Windows NT to all of the computers using an unattended answer file and a uniqueness database file. Use Sysdiff on each to apply the differences to each computer.

    C. Install Windows NT Workstation to each of the computers using the boot floppies and the installation CD-ROM. Place the installation files for all of the software on a server share and then install to each client over the network.

    D. You cannot automate the process of installing software to Windows NT Workstation because installing software makes changes to the Windows NT Registry.

1-19 You're installing Windows NT Workstation to 75 identical IBM-PC compatible computers. Which program helps you create the unattended answer file?

    A. User Manager for Domains

    B. Syscon

    C. Setup Manager

    D. Network Client Administrator

SAMPLE TEST

1-20   A Windows NT workstation contains a shared folder on an NTFS partition. Which of the following statements concerning access to the folder is correct?

    A. A user accessing the folder remotely has the same or more restrictive access permissions than if he accesses the folder locally.

    B. A user accessing the folder remotely has less restrictive access permissions than if he accesses the folder locally.

    C. A user accessing the folder remotely has the same access permissions as when accessing the folder locally.

    D. A user accessing the folder remotely has more restrictive access permissions than if he accesses the folder locally.

UNIT

2

Installation and Configuration

Test Objectives: Installation and Configuration

- Install Windows NT Workstation on an Intel platform in a given situation.

- Set up a dual-boot system in a given situation.

- Remove Windows NT Workstation in a given situation.

- Install, configure, and remove hardware components for a given situation. Hardware components include:
  - Network adapter drivers
  - SCSI device drivers
  - Tape device drivers
  - UPS
  - Multimedia devices
  - Display drivers
  - Keyboard drivers
  - Mouse drivers

- Use Control Panel applications to configure a Windows NT Workstation computer in a given situation.

- Upgrade to Windows NT Workstation 4.0 in a given situation.

- Configure server-based installation for wide-scale deployment in a given situation.

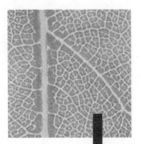

In this unit, I cover installing NT Workstation in different ways on an Intel platform, and show you how to use different operating systems in the same machine simultaneously. In addition, I demonstrate how to remove and upgrade in various situations, as well as how to install and configure NT workstation in a large, wide-scale deployment. I also explore in detail how to configure, install and remove different hardware devices in an NT workstation.

Installing Windows NT Workstation

Windows NT Workstation will not function properly if it is installed onto a computer that does not have compatible components.

You can get a list of these components from the NT Hardware Compatibility List (HCL). The Windows NT Hardware Compatibility List is part of the Windows NT documentation package that comes with Windows NT. It lists the hardware that Microsoft has tested and found to be compatible with Windows NT. It gives information on:

- Storage devices, including SCSI and RAID I/O subsystems
- Monitors, modems, Network adapters, CD-ROMs, UPS systems, keyboards, and pointing devices
- CPUs

Before you install Windows NT Workstation, you should make sure your system meets the minimum requirements to run NT. Table 2.1 shows the minimum requirements for installing NT workstation.

Microsoft's NT Hardware Qualifier Disk is a utility provided by Microsoft to inspect your computer that provides you with a detailed report of any suspected incompatibility problems.

T A B L E 2.1 Requirements for Running Windows NT Workstation	Microprocessor	486/33 or higher
	Disc Storage	120MB
	Memory	12MB (16MB recommended)
	Display	VGA or higher
	Required Additional Drive	CD-ROM, or access to files from a net-worked CD-ROM drive

Some of the common installation methods are listed below:

- Boot from floppies and install from CD-ROM: No operating system on the computer is required. By booting the boot floppies, you are actually launching WINNT.EXE with no parameters.

- Connect to network share containing i386 installation files: Typically, it's faster to install NT by connecting to a server and downloading the installation from there. An operating system is required to attach to the server with the distribution files.

- Boot from a Network Installation Startup Disk and run from the network share: If no operating system is present on the system, you can create a boot/install disk from the NT CD. This will create a DOS disk boot with networking capabilities, allowing the workstation to connect to a server network share.

- Install from existing operating system by accessing the NT Workstation CD: If you can access the CD-ROM, but the CD is not HCL compatible, you can copy the distribution files to the hard drive and start the installation with the /B switch to skip boot floppies. If installing NT Workstation on a computer that has an HPFS partition: Convert the partition with either the CONVERT.EXE or the ACLCONVERT.EXE to NTFS. The difference being that the CONVERT.EXE does not retain the file system security attribute information.

Why not use the Autoplay screen install button on the CD-ROM to start the Workstation install? You can, in fact, use this method to start the install and it will work. Bear in mind that it is the typical vice 'custom' install path. If you need to control your install in a special way, you can't do if you use this method. It's fine for a straight simple install.

Installing Windows NT by Using WINNT.EXE

The Setup program for 16-bit operating systems (WINNT.EXE) is capable of performing the following:

- Creating a set of the three Setup boot disks for Intel based systems by using the /o or /ox switches. The /x switch prevents the floppy set creation if an existing set of disks are to be used.

- Creates a temporary folder called Win_nt.~ls and copies the Workstation files to this folder. If the floppy disk boot files are to be loaded to the system hard drive from the CD-ROM or network share service using the disks, the /b switch is used.

- Prompts the user to restart the computer from the first Setup disk.

Table 2.2 explains the switches, which can be used with WINNT.EXE to control the setup process.

	Switch	Explanation
T A B L E 2.2 Switches to Control the Installation Process	/b	Installs without installation boot floppies.
	/c	Skips free space check on installation boot floppies.
	/f	Copies files from the boot floppies without verifying the copies.
	/ll	Specifies the filename (but not the path) of the setup information file. The default is DOSNET.INF.
	/o	Creates boot floppies only.
	/ox	Creates boot floppies for CD-ROM based installation.

	Switch	Explanation
T A B L E 2.3	/s	Specifies the source location of Windows NT setup files. Must be in the form WINNT /s: <Path>.
Switches to Control the Installation Process	/t	Specifies the drive to contain the temporary setup files.
	/u	Specifies unattended operation and optional script file.
	/udf	Tailored, unattended installation for installation on multiple machines.

 WINNT32.EXE is very similar to WINNT.EXE, except that it can only be used on a computer already running NT (a true 32-bit OS). This is used to upgrade or install NT into a different directory to allow dual-booting of NT Operating Systems.

System and Boot Partitions

Differentiating between the Boot and System partitions can be confusing because the names seem to be backwards. The actual files used to boot the system are on the system partition where the WINNT or %systemroot% resides, and the System files used to run NT are stored on the boot partition.

System Partition

The System partition contains the files NT uses to start itself: NTLDR, BOOT.INI, BOOTSECT.DOS, NTDETECT.COM, and, if the system is SCSI-based, NTBOOTDD.SYS. These must be in the root of the startup disk or partition—usually the C:\ drive.

Boot Partition

The Boot partition contains key files that make up NT (NTOSKRNL.EXE and HAL.DLL), which are found in the %systemroot%\System32 directory (default = c:\winnt\system32).

Therefore, if you choose to install NT on a non-default drive such as D:\, you can create a situation where NT "boots" or starts from its SYSTEM partition on C:\ and runs from its BOOT partition on D:\.

Dual-Boot Systems

Dual-boot systems are computers that have more than one operating system installed on the same computer.

Windows NT will coexist happily with other operating systems on the same computer, and Windows NT can be installed in its own partition using NTFS or with other operating systems in a FAT partition. The boot loader (BOOT.INI) which is talked about in detail in Unit 7 decides which operating system starts by default, or can allow the user to select an operating system at start up.

File Systems and Dual-Boot Configurations

You can install and run NT with the NTFS file system. However, Windows 95, Windows for Workgroups, and DOS use the FAT file system. If you want to share files between your NT operating system and any other operating system, you must format or retain at least one FAT partition in addition to the NT operating system. However, if you wanted to have security on your NT operating system you must format or convert all partitions to NTFS.

Common Dual-Boot Configurations

Dual-boot configurations are common because most people like to keep their old operating system when upgrading to NT for legacy applications. If you want to dual-boot with your old operating system—for example, Windows for Workgroups—then you must install NT in its own directory. This is C:\WINNT by default. If you wanted to upgrade from Windows for Workgroups or Windows 95, then by installing NT in the C:\Windows directory will upgrade the current operating system to NT.

Some of the common dual-boot configurations are DOS and NT Workstation, Windows for Workgroups and NT and Windows 95 and NT. There is not limit to the amount of operating systems on your computer. The only limit is your disk space.

It is not a good idea to load NT and then load Windows 95, as Windows 95 has its own boot loader and can effectively disable a Windows NT boot loader.

Configuration of Applications in a Dual-Boot System

One of the problems with installing NT and Windows 95 as a dual-boot system is that each application must be installed for each operating system. If, for example, you have Microsoft Word installed in Windows 95 then set up your system to dual-boot with Windows NT, you have to reinstall Microsoft Word while the Windows NT operating system is loaded to be able to run that application in NT and Windows 95.

Special Issues in a Dual-Boot System

OS/2 has its own boot manager. When installing NT on the same machine as OS/2, the boot manager for OS/2 is disabled in favor for NT's boot manager. To enable the OS/2 boot manager, you can go to the Disk Administrator and set active the OS/2 boot partition.

Removing Windows NT Workstation

If you have to remove NT, you must first consider what operating systems will be left on the computer:

- If NT 4.0 is the only operating system, then a replacement system should be installed before NT's removal.

- If another NT version will still be resident on the machine, you only need to delete several directories and modify the BOOT.INI file to reflect the removal of NT 4.0.

- If another installed system will be used as the primary operating system, then several directories and files must be removed. Also, the master boot record of the hard drive primary partition must be present to bypass the NTLDR, which starts the NT boot process.

Because Windows NT doesn't have a specific uninstall routine, you need to use a few tricks to remove it, and reinstall the previous operating system. Follow these three steps:

- Remove the NTFS volume if necessary.
- Change the bootstrap routing.
- Delete the Windows NT directories and files.

Removing Windows NT by Deleting the NTFS Partition

Removing an NTFS volume can indeed be difficult. Why? Because some versions of the MS-DOS FDISK program can't delete an NTFS volume, and none of the versions can remove an NTFS logical drive in an extended MS-DOS partition. The easiest way to delete an NTFS partition is:

- Boot the three floppy disks that come with NT.
- When prompted to create or choose a partition, select the NTFS partition where the Windows NT files are located.
- Press D to delete the partition, and exit setup.

 You can use Disk Administrator to delete NTFS partitions, but not the boot partition. That must be done with the FDISK DOS utility.

Removing Windows NT from a FAT Partition

Boot from a Windows 95 emergency boot disk, or from a DOS disk, and run the SYS.COM command by typing **sys c:** This resets the hard disk master boot record and bypasses NTLDR.

Restart the computer, then delete the following files:

- PAGEFILE.SYS—This is the swap file that allows NT to use more memory than is physically installed in the system.
- BOOT.INI
- NT*.*—This removes NT startup files NTLDR, ntdetect.COM, and NTBOOTDD.SYS (SCSI systems only).
- BOOTSECT.DOS

- %systemroot% directory—This is the installation directory. The default is C:\WINNT.

- C:/PROGRAM FILES/WINDOWS NT—This directory contains various utility files installed by NT 4.0.

Installing, Configuring, and Removing Hardware Components

The general procedure for installing a hardware device is described below:

- Determine the hardware settings.

- Verify the required hardware resources are unused on the Workstation.

- Configure and install the hardware using jumpers or software utilities.

- Boot the NT Workstation and add the NT driver.

- Reboot the system.

The general procedure for removing a hardware device is described below:

- Uninstall the device driver.

- Power down the computer.

- Remove the device.

- Restart the computer.

Remember to check the HCL and verify latest drivers. Again, Windows NT doesn't support Plug-n-Play, so hardware designed for both NT and 95 operating systems may have separate configuration methods.

In the following sections, I describe specific hardware components, and how to work with them.

Network Adapter Drivers

Installing a network adapter is simple. Typically the driver is included within Windows NT. If it's not, make sure you have a driver from the manufacturer.

Remember that any changes to the Control Panel ➤ Network usually require access to the original NT installation source, so have your CD-ROM or network share to the NT distribution files accessible.

To install a network adapter:

- Install the network interface card.

- Boot the NT Workstation, then open the Control Panel and click on Network.

- Select the Adapters tab, and click on Add.

- Select the driver listed or click on Have Disk.

- Click on Close and reboot the system.

To remove a network adapter:

- Open the Control Panel, click on Network, and select the Adapter tab.

- Highlight the adapter you want to remove.

- Click on Remove.

- Shut down and remove the network interface card.

SCSI Devices

SCSI stands for Small Computer Systems Interface. These adapters are used to connect devices such as hard drives, CD-ROM players, and printers.

Installing a SCSI adapter properly can be the most difficult portion of a Windows NT installation. You can minimize potential glitches by following these guidelines:

- Only use SCSI controllers that are listed in the HCL, and that are marked as WinNT compatible.

- Search the Microsoft Windows NT Knowledge base at http://www .microsoft.com, and search for the key "SCSI" to identify any compatibility issues associated with the particular SCSI controllers you're considering using with Windows NT.

- Make sure the SCSI card is terminated properly. Boot the computer once with no devices installed to ensure that the driver loads correctly.

- If installing NT on an existing system that has a SCSI interface, use the NTHQ program to identify and resolve SCSI adapter issues before attempting to install Windows NT.

- Disable the Plug-and-Play BIOS on your computer and manually assign interrupts to PCI slots.

- Enable the SCSI BIOS to boot the hard disk attached to SCSI ID 0, then install Windows NT in the first primary partition of that disk.

Tape Device Drivers

Adding tape drives to Windows NT is fairly easy for most tape devices. Open the Control Panel, click on Tape Devices, then click on the Detect button. Windows NT loads each tape driver it knows about and scans for the presence of a supported device. If found, it automatically installs the driver. You can also add and remove device drivers by using the Add and Remove buttons located on the Drivers tab. You don't even have to restart Windows NT to add or delete tape devices.

When installing IDE and SCSI tape devices, make sure to set the correct Master/Slave setting on your IDE devices and the correct SCSI number and terminators for your SCSI tape devices.

UPS

Uninterruptible Power Supplies, or UPSs, provide power to your computer in the event of conventional power loss. Advanced UPSs can communicate with your computer through a serial port using a standard RS-232 serial cable.

You must be sure and test the UPS unit after it has been configured. Upon startup of Intel-based computers, NTDETECT.COM sends test messages to all serial ports to determine whether or not a serial mouse is attached. Some UPS units misinterpret these test messages and respond by shutting down. If this happens, you can prevent your UPS unit from doing this by adding the /NoSerialMice switch to the entries in the operating system section of the BOOT.INI file.

UPS settings are controlled through the UPS program in the Control Panel, as shown in Figure 2.1.

F I G U R E   2 . 1

UPS in Control Panel

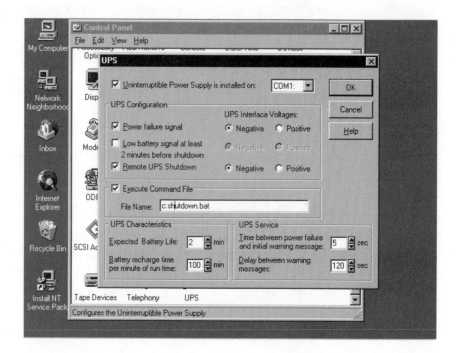

Multimedia Devices

Multimedia device drivers are added and configured from the Multimedia Control Panel applet. Multimedia devices include MIDI instruments and sound cards. Inside the Control Panel, there is also a Devices tab, with which you can view information on all the multimedia devices and drivers installed on your system.

You can't configure sound cards during an unattended installation. You can only do this after a successful installation has taken place.

Display Drivers

The initial display driver is installed when Windows NT is installed—a display driver must be present for Windows NT to operate. You can change display drivers through the Display Type button on the Settings tab of the Display Control Panel.

The Settings tab also lets you choose options for your display:

- Color Palette—Lists color options for the display adapter.

- Desktop Area—Configures screen area used by the display.

- Display Type—Allows installation of new drivers and displays options about the display device driver.

- Font Size—Configures color and desktop.

- Refresh Frequency—Sets the screen refresh rate for high-resolution drivers.

- Test—Tests changes to screen choices.

Because Windows NT must have a display driver to operate correctly, you should remove your old driver, and install the new one prior to shutting down your computer and swapping display cards. You should also set your display resolution to VGA to ensure that you can see the screen when you reboot for the first time following installation of a new display driver. Once proper operation is verified, switch display settings as required.

If the display driver installed on Windows NT Workstation is not compatible to your device, the Workstation will go directly to the Display setup when you boot the computer. Change your driver to the correct video driver and reboot.

Keyboard Drivers

You can change keyboard drivers through the General tab of the Keyboard in the Control Panel. The three Control Panel Tab choices are:

- Speed—This tab lets you control repeat character delay, character repeat rate and cursor blink speed.

- Input Locales—This one specifies international keyboard layout.

- General—Use this tab to view or change the keyboard driver.

Mouse Drivers

You can change your mouse drivers to change the behavior of your mouse through the General tab of the Mouse Control Panel. Here are some Mouse Configuration Options:

- Buttons—Use this to configure the mouse for right or left handed operation, as well as the speed of double click.

- Pointers—You can choose different pointer shapes here.

- Motion—With this, you can control pointer speed, and specify whether you want the mouse pointer to snap to the default button in dialog boxes.

- General—This is where you change or update the mouse driver.

Use Control Panel Applications to Configure a Windows NT Workstation Computer

In the previous section of this unit, I explained how to view and change many settings from icons in the Control Panel. This section shows you how to change the environment of each individual user to match that user's preferences. You can change the following items on the Control Panel on a per-user basis:

- Display

- Keyboard

- Mouse

- Regional Settings

- Sounds

Display

The Display Properties window shown in Figure 2.2 has five sections, represented by tabs at the top of the window.

- **Background**—Allows you to set the pattern or image that will appear in the background of your computer screen.

- **Screen Saver**—Allows you to select the particular screen saver you want to appear when your computer has been inactive for a period of time.

FIGURE 2.2

The Display Properties
window

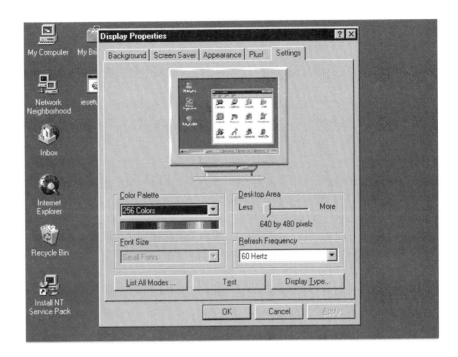

- **Appearances**—Configures the colors and sizes of Windows NT screen elements such as border windows, icons, and the desktop. You can also create and manipulate schemes. These contain predefined or user-defined settings for the screen elements.

- **Plus!**—Allows you to choose the type of icons designating certain desktop elements. It also lets you change certain characteristics of the Windows NT desktop such as the size of icons, whether windows should appear as solid, or as outline shapes when you move them, and whether icons should be shown in all possible colors or not.

- **Settings**—Here's where to configure the hardware settings of the display that can set the resolution, the number of colors, and the refresh rate. This is also where you configure the device driver that Windows NT uses to talk to your video card. These settings apply to every user.

Keyboard

The Keyboard Properties window is where you configure the keyboard speed and layout. The Speed tab allows you to set the cursor repeat delay, rate, and blink rate. The Input Locales tab provides multiple key mappings so you can remap the keyboard for other languages or preferred key placements. The General tab is a system configuration tab. You'll most likely accept the default PC/AT Enhanced Keyboard settings, but if you have an unusual keyboard attached to your computer, this is where to configure it.

Mouse

The Mouse Properties window is where you configure the buttons, pointers, and motion of the mouse. Each aspect has a tab. You can use the General tab to select the type of mouse attached to your computer.

- **Buttons**—This lets you specify whether you're left- or right-handed and how fast you have to click the mouse buttons for it to be recognized as a double-click.

- **Pointers**—This lets you customize the appearance of the mouse pointer. A different mouse icon can represent many activities of the system, and you can select which icon represents which activity.

- **Motion**—This customizes how fast the mouse pointer sweeps across the screen when you move the mouse. You can also select the Snap to Default option, which makes the mouse cursor go to the default button on a window when it appears.

Regional Settings

The Regional Settings window lets you set the default language, time zone, number currency, and time representations from pre-defined lists or by creating your own specifications. You can also input locales for the current user.

Sounds

The Sound Properties window (see Figure 2.3) allows you to associate sounds with system events, such as a window opening or the system shutting down. You can associate individual sounds with individual events, or you can select or even create a sound scheme that associates sounds with events important for you.

FIGURE 2.3

The Sound Properties
window

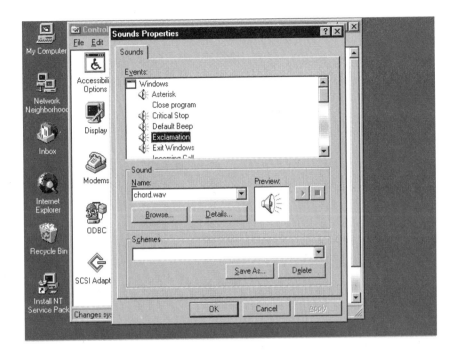

Upgrade to Windows NT Workstation 4.0

After you've prepared your hardware for Windows NT by making sure
you have met the minimum requirements, and after you have determined that the
hardware you are using is in the HCL, it's time to decide whether you'll upgrade
an existing Windows operating system to Windows NT Workstation 4.0, or perform a fresh installation of the Windows NT operating system.

If your computer already has Windows 3.x, Windows for Workgroups, or an
earlier version of Windows NT, you might want to upgrade to Windows NT
Workstation 4.0. Windows 95 does not support a direct upgrade path due prima-
rily to Registry differences, but can be adapted manually from a fresh installation.
The difference between installing and upgrading is that when you upgrade, many
of the old settings for the existing version of Windows are simply copied and used
in the new Windows NT Workstation 4.0 configuration.

If you are upgrading from a Windows NT installation, you need to use the
32-bit installation version WINNT32.EXE as explained earlier.

You may wish to upgrade when the following situations exist:

- You want to transfer desktop settings such as the wallpaper or sound settings.

- You want to transfer password files.

- You don't need to boot to the other version of Windows.

You may wish to install when the following situations exist:

- You want to be able to boot to other versions of Windows and even DOS.

- You're installing to a large number of computers, and you want all of the computers to be the same.

The upgrade process doesn't transfer all settings from your current Windows operating system to your Windows NT Workstation because some of the current settings don't apply to Windows NT Workstation 4.0. The settings that are transferred also vary from one original operating system to another. For instance, almost all of the Windows NT 3.51 settings, including security and user accounts, are transferred when you upgrade. Since NT 3.51 contains most of this data in the Registry, it can be easily utilized by NT 4.0. Much less configuration information is transferred when you upgrade to NT 4.0 from Windows or Windows for Workgroups since NT can't look for all configuration files created by applications.

Upgrading from Windows 95 requires the following steps:

- Check to see that all Windows 95 hardware and software will run under NT.

- Install NT 4.0 in a separate directory to create a dual-boot system.

- Re-install all application software.

- Delete the Windows 95 directory C:WINDOWS.

Configure Server-Based Installation for Wide-Scale Deployment

You can install NT Workstation on a number of computers using a server-based installation. There are several ways to do this:

- Using Microsoft Systems Management Server (SMS). This method is beyond the scope of this exam, but provides the most extensive control and speed.

- By modifying logon scripts on user accounts so that the unattended setup runs when the user logs on to the computer.

- By creating a .BAT file to run the unattended setup from the desktop. The .BAT file can be sent as an embedded link in an e-mail.

- Administrators can initiate the unattended setup from the workstation.

Regardless of the implementation method, the server-based installation combines a network installation with an automated installation. It requires several steps:

- Decide what parts of the operating system and application software will be installed on each computer.

- If required, install the operating system on one computer and use the SYSDIFF utility to take a snapshot of the computer using the /SNAP switch.

- If required, install the application software on the prototype computer and create a difference file with SYSDIFF using the /DIFF switch.

- Copy the operating system and application software installation files to a network share.

- Creating the unattended installation text files for each different configuration type (UNATTEND.TXT).

- Create a uniqueness database file having an individual section for unique data required for each computer (UDF).

- Run SYSDIFF/APPLY as part of the Unattended Setup to apply the difference file and install the software.

- Connect the target computer to the network, accessing the network share, and starting the automated setup.

Copying Installation Files

There are no special considerations for copying the installation files. You can simply copy the contents of the directory for your hardware platform to a shared directory on your network. For Intel-based machines, this is the i386 directory on the CD-ROM. All application software and any other items that are to be loaded as part of the automated installation must be placed in the OEM directory structure. The OEM directory structure is beyond the scope of the exam, but is an important topic in large, complex automated installs. It is discussed in detail in the Windows NT Workstation Resource Kit

Creating Unattended Installation Files

You should create an unattended installation file for each specific configuration type you need to install. You can either edit the UNATTEND.TXT file sample supplied on the NT Workstation CD-ROM, or if you have the Windows NT 4.0 Workstation Resource Kit, you can use the SETUPMGR.EXE tool to build your unattended installation file. Copy the unattended installation files to the same shared directory on your network. For more on creating unattended installation files, refer back to Unit 1.

Creating a UDF

A UDF allows you to create a file having sections that customize the installation of each individual computer. The UDF is used together with an unattended installation file to replace certain sections of the answer file with the information for the specific computer. You need to create a single UDF for all the computers on which you automate the installation of NT Workstation. Copy the UDF files to the same shared directory on your network.

Connecting to and Accessing the Network

If you have no other operating system on the computer, or you cannot access the network share from the existing operating system, you must create a Network Installation Boot Disk. A Network Installation Boot Disk is a bootable DOS disk you can use to start your system and connect to your network share (the location of the installation files). Since it's a DOS system disk, you need to create it on a DOS system using the command FORMAT A: /S, or by using the SYS command on a disk that was formatted for DOS previously. Go to your Windows NT Server computer, and double-click on the Network Client Administrator Utility in the Network Administration program group. This loads the files you need onto your DOS system disk. The network driver you need is specific to your client (target) system. You may need to copy driver files for your NIC.

Running SMARTDRV.EXE in the AUTOEXEC.BAT file on your network installation boot disk will greatly speed up the over the network installation.

Automate the Installation

Now that you have your network installation boot disk, you can edit the CONFIG.SYS and AUTOEXEC.BAT files to fully automate the installation. For example, assume that you've copied the installation files (from the \i386 directory) to a directory named SHARE on a computer named SERVER. You've created an unattended configuration file named CONFIG.TXT and a UDF for this specific computer named SYSTEM3.UDF. You want the disk to boot your target computer, connect to the SHARE directory on SERVER, and begin the automated installation. To do this, you can add the following commands to the AUTOEXEC.BAT file on your floppy:

```
NET USE Z:\\SERVER\SHARE
CD Z:
WINNT /U:CONFIG.TXT /UDF:id2,SYSTEM3.UDF /B
```

Let's examine these commands:

- NET USE instructs the computer to assign the logical drive letter Z to the SHARE shared directory on the SERVER computer. This form of notation is known as a Universal Naming Convention or UNC name.

- The CD Z: command instructs the computer to change to the Z: drive, where you execute your next command.

- With the WINNT command, the /U switch specifies the unattended configuration file name.

- The /UDF:id2,SYSTEM3.UDF specifies using the id2 data section from the system3.udf uniqueness database file for this computer.

- The /b switch suppresses the creation of the 3 NT installation disks.

Installing Windows NT Workstation

1. What is the purpose of the three floppy disks that come with the Windows NT 4.0 installation CD?

_____

2. How can you install Windows NT Workstation if you don't have the three disks?

_____

3. What are the minimum hardware requirements for Windows NT Workstation?

Microprocessor   _____

Disc Storage   _____

Memory   _____

Display   _____

Required Additional Drive   _____

4. True/False: You must have a CD-ROM drive on your computer to load and run Windows NT Workstation.

5. What should you do if you want to install NT Workstation on a PC that does not have an NT compatible CD-ROM?

_____

6. What is the purpose of the HCL?

_____

7. True/False: You must have an operating system already existing on a PC if you want to load NT Workstation.

8. True/False: If you install NT Workstation from the Autoplay screen, you can do a custom installation.

9. Windows NT default installation directory is _____.

10. True/False: It is possible for NT to boot from the system partition on a C: drive and run from the BOOT partition on a different drive.

11. What are the four files that MUST be located in the root of the startup disk?

_____

_____

_____

_____

12. True/False: Windows NT can be installed with other operating systems on the same machine, with each OS having its own directory.

13. The key files that make up NT (NTOSKRNL.EXE and HAL.DLL) are found in the:

_____

14. When using WINNT to install Windows NT Workstation, what does the /b switch do?

_____

15. True/False: You can install NT from floppies.

16. True/False: Windows NT is plug and play.

17. True/False: When upgrading from Windows NT 3.5x to 4.0, most of the registry is left intact.

18. True/False: You can do a system transfer to load NT Workstation on a PC.

19. True/False: WINNT32 is used to run a Windows NT installation from any operating system that runs in 32-bit mode.

20. True/False: The Hardware Compatibility List contains software certified by Microsoft to run on Windows NT.

21. True/False: You can install NT without a mouse.

22. List the three things that WINNT or WINNT32 does during the initial installation.

_____

_____

_____

Dual-Boot Systems

23. Which file allows you to choose the operating system you want to run at system startup?

_____

24. Windows NT can be installed and run with the FAT operating system and the _____
_____ file system.

25. List the six operating systems that NT can dual-boot with.

_____

_____

_____

_____

_____

_____

26. You are running Windows for Workgroups. What must you do to load NT and still be able to
run Windows for Workgroups?

_____

27. You load NT in its own directory on an existing Windows 95 installation, but you cannot run
your applications when booting NT. What is the problem?

_____

28. You have OS/2 installed on your PC and want to dual-boot with NT Workstation but keep the
OS/2 boot loader. How can you do this?

_____

29. You set up to dual-boot on your existing Windows 95B machine with NT Workstation. You install the FAT file system on NT, but cannot view the files that where created on Windows 95. What is the problem?

_____

30. Your system is running DOS and you want to upgrade the system to dual-boot both Windows 95 and NT Workstation. How should you do this?

_____

Removing Windows NT Workstation

31. What is the easiest way to delete a NTFS partition?

_____

32. If you had installed the NT operating system on a NTFS partition, after removing the NTFS partition and changing the bootstrap routing, what is the last thing you need to do to remove NT from your computer?

_____

33. True/False: When removing a copy of NT that has been installed on a NTFS partition, copying the data from an NTFS partition to a FAT partition is an effective and fast way to make certain the data will be available to your new operating system.

34. True/False: FDISK can always remove an NTFS volume with a logical drive.

35. True/False: MS-DOS FDISK can remove an NTFS logical drive in an extended MS_DOS partition.

36.   True/False: Removing the NTFS partition in which Windows NT is installed automatically removes the Windows NT files.

37.   What is the easiest way to reset the Master Boot Record when removing NT from your computer?

_____

38.   What is the PAGEFILE.SYS file used for in Windows NT?

_____

Installing, Configuring, and Removing Hardware Components

39.   True/False: When installing a new NIC card in your system, NT will determine all free resources and set the NIC card accordingly.

40.   True/False: You can install a NIC card driver on Windows NT at any time, even if the card is not physically in the system.

41.   How many NIC cards can you install in Windows NT during the initial installation?

_____

42.   List the order for the general procedures from 1 to 4 for removing a hardware device:

   A. Remove the device.

   B. Power down the computer.

   C. Restart the computer.

   D. Uninstall the device driver.

43. List the order to follow when installing a new NIC card:

    A. Boot the NT Workstation and then open the Control Panel and click on Network.

    B. Install the network interface card.

    C. Click on Close and reboot.

    D. Select the driver listed or click on Have Disk.

    E. Select the Adapters tab, and click on Add.

44. List the order to follow when removing a NIC card:

    A. Open the Control Panel, click on Network and select the Adapter tab.

    B. Highlight the adapter you want to remove.

    C. Close and shutdown.

    D. Click on Remove.

    E. Remove NIC.

45. When installing SCSI devices you must be sure to check the terminator and the SCSI ID settings. What do you check for IDE devices?

46. List at least three devices that can be connected with SCSI adapters.

_____

_____

_____

47. True/False: Installing a SCSI adapter properly can be the most difficult portion of a Windows NT installation.

48. True/False: You should only use SCSI controllers listed in the HAL.

49. Where should you look on the Microsoft Web site for problems with SCSI controllers?

_____

50. What is typically the most common problem associated with SCSI devices?

_____

51. True/False: NT can detect most tape devices by scanning for the presence of a supported device.

52. True/False: If NT finds a tape drive, it will automatically install the driver for the device.

53. True/False: UPS devices communicate with your computer using a parallel cable.

54. Where are the settings for the UPS program found in Windows NT?

_____

55. What two kinds of devices are added and configured from the Multimedia applet?

_____

_____

56. Where do you change the display drivers?

_____

57. True/False: Windows NT can operate without a display driver.

58. If you're having display problems, to what resolution should you set your display driver to ensure you can see the screen when you reboot?

_____

59. Where can you set the keyboard driver?

_____

60. What two settings can you set for your keyboard?

_____

_____

61. What is the General tab of the Mouse control panel found in the Control Panel used for?

_____

Use Control Panel Applications to Configure a Windows NT Workstation Computer

62. True/False: The Background tab in the Display property window allows you to set the pattern or image that will appear in the background of your computer screen.

63. What are the three main functions set in the Settings tab in the Display Control Panel?

_____

_____

_____

64. True/False: The Keyboard Properties window is where you configure the keyboard speed and layout.

65. True/False: The Mouse Properties window is where you configure the buttons, pointers, and motion of the mouse.

66. What four things does the Regional Settings allow you to configure?

_____

_____

_____

_____

67. What Control Panel applet can you use to associate sounds with system events?

_____

68. What Control Panel applet would you use to create a roaming profile?

_____

69. What applet should you use to remove a Network Interface Card?

_____

70. True/False: When installing a new piece of hardware in NT, you should use the Add New Hardware applet in Control Panel.

Upgrade to Windows NT Workstation 4.0

71. The difference between upgrading and installing is _____.

72. True/False: You should upgrade if you want to transfer password files.

73. True/False: You should simply install NT Workstation when you don't want to be keep the current version of Windows on the computer.

74. True/False: Much less information is transferred when you upgrade to NT 4.0 from Windows for Workgroups than from Windows NT 3.5x.

Configure Server-Based Installation for Wide-Scale Deployment

75. True/False: The server-based installation combines a network installation with an automated installation and requires several steps.

76. What directory do you need to copy from the Windows NT CD to a shared directory on your network if you are running Intel based machines?

_____

77. For each type of specific hardware configuration type, what file should be created?

_____

78. Which file allows you to customize the installation of each individual computer?

_____

2-1 Your manager asks you to install a new internal US Robotics Sportster 56Kbps modem on her NT Workstation desktop computer. She will be taking the desktop to her home office and connecting to her ISP with the modem. The modem is jumpered to use COM 2 and IRQ 3. You install the modem adapter in an available ISA slot and replace the machine covers. What should you do next?

Select the best answer:

  A. Boot NT Workstation and let Plug-and-Play autoconfigure the modem.

  B. Boot NT Workstation, click on the Start button, then click on Settings ➢ Control Panel, and double-click the MODEMS applet.

  C. Boot NT Workstation, click on the Start button, then click on Settings ➢ Control Panel, and double-click on the Telephony applet.

  D. Boot NT Workstation, click on the Start button, then click on Settings ➢ Control Panel, and double-click on the Add New Hardware applet.

2-2 Your department needs to upgrade some older machines. You have a Windows NT 3.51 Workstation computer with the following configuration:

> One physical hard disk drive—540 MB SCSI, partitioned with a primary FAT partition of 200MB as C: and a secondary extended HPFS partition of 340MB. The machine has 64MB of RAM, an Intel 80386-33MHz processor and a single speed SCSI CD-ROM.

What must you consider before you upgrade this computer to NT Workstation 4.0?

Select all that apply:

  A. You must upgrade the single speed CD-ROM.

  B. You must run CONVERT.EXE to convert the HPFS partition to NTFS.

  C. You must run CONVERT.EXE to convert the FAT partition to NTFS.

  D. You cannot upgrade this computer to NT Workstation 4.0.

2-3 A remote branch office has two computers, a Windows 95 desktop and an NT Workstation 4.0 desktop. The hard disk drive on the NT machine fails, so you're dispatched with a replacement hard disk drive, an NT Workstation 4.0 CD-ROM, and the three NT installation disks. Your mission is to install the new hard disk drive and load NT Workstation. Both machines are equipped with CD-ROM drives. You install the replacement hard disk drive and start to load NT when you discover that NT installation diskette #2 is corrupted. What can you do?

Select the best answer:

   A. Obtain a replacement disk from your home office.

   B. Run DISKCOPY.EXE on the Windows 95 machine to make a new disk.

   C. Put the NT CD in the Windows 95 machine's CD-ROM drive and run WINNT /OX to create a set of installation disks.

   D. Use the Windows 95 browser to download the disk from the Microsoft FTP site.

2-4 You have purchased a new SoundBlaster AWE-32 sound card for your Windows NT Workstation 4.0 computer. After installing the hardware, what must you do to configure your computer to use the sound adapter?

Select the best answer:

   A. Run the Add New Hardware applet in the Control Panel.

   B. Select Audio Devices and click on the Add button on the Devices tab of the Multimedia applet in the Control Panel.

   C. Click on the Devices applet in the Control Panel.

   D. Click on the Devices tab of the Sounds applet in the Control Panel.

2-5 You must install a Tape Backup Unit to your Windows NT Workstation computer. How do you configure the Operating System to recognize this device after you install the hardware?

Select the best answer:

   A. Click on Start ➤ Settings ➤ Tape Devices.

B. Run WINCONFIG and click on the Have Tape check box.

C. Click on Start ➤ Settings ➤ Control Panel ➤ Tape Devices.

D. In the Control Panel, click on the Devices applet.

2-6 You want to install Windows NT Workstation 4.0 on a computer currently running Windows NT Workstation 3.51 and HPFS. You want to maintain all of the existing customization and user preferences, along with long file names and existing file security settings. What installation steps must you perform?

Select all that apply:

A. During the character mode portion of the installation, delete existing partitions.

B. During the character mode portion of the installation, specify upgrade.

C. Run the CONVERT utility on the HPFS partition.

D. Insert the CD-ROM and run WINNT /b.

E. Boot from the Windows NT Workstation 4.0 Installation Setup disk.

F. Insert the CD-ROM and run WINNT.

G. Format the partition as NTFS.

2-7 Your manager wants an Uninterruptable Power Supply installed on her NT Workstation computer to protect the computer when a power outage occurs. In the box the UPS came in there is a data cable and a power cable. What steps must you perform to configure the UPS?

Select all that apply:

A. Connect the data cable to an external SCSI-2 interface port.

B. Connect the data cable to a PS/2 port.

C. Connect the data cable to a serial port.

D. Connect the data cable to a parallel port.

E. Configure the UPS from the command line: START UPS.

F. Configure the UPS using the UPS applet in the Control Panel.

S A M P L E   T E S T

2-8 What operating systems can NT Workstation co-exist on the same computer with?

   A. Windows 95

   B. NT Server

   C. Windows for Workgroups

   D. OS/2

2-9 You installed Windows NT Workstation and Windows 95 dual boot on your home computer. You selected the FAT file system and used default settings to install the Operating Systems. Now you determine that NT will not properly support all the games you run on your system. You want to free some space, so you decide to remove the unneeded NT installation. How can you do this?

Select all that apply:

   A. Boot to the NT installation floppies and delete the NT partition.

   B. Reinstall Windows 95. This overwrites the NT installation.

   C. Boot your Windows 95 Emergency Recovery disk, and run FDISK /MBR.

   D. Boot your Windows 95 Emergency Recovery Disk, and run SYS C:

   E. Change attributes and DELETE NTLDR, BOOT.INI, BOOTSECT.DOS and NTDETECT.COM.

   F. Erase the C:\WINDOWS directory.

   G. Erase the C:\WINNT directory.

2-10 What step(s) should you take to make sure your hardware is compatible with NT before you install NT Workstation?

   A. Call the PC manufacturer and ask them.

   B. Check the HCL.

   C. Run the NTHQ.

   D. You can't. Try it and find out.

SAMPLE TEST

2-11   Where would you install drivers for a MIDI device in Windows NT?

    A. Control Panel, Network

    B. Drivers Applet

    C. Multimedia applet

    D. System applet

2-12   What is the minimum memory requirement for NT Workstation on an Intel chip?

    A. 8MBs

    B. 12MBs

    C. 16MBs

    D. 24MBs

2-13   When running the WINNT32.EXE installation program, what switch can you use to make the three boot floppies?

    A. /o

    B. /udf:

    C. /f

    D. /b

2-14   You want to install Windows NT Workstation on your computer running Windows 3.1. What should you do to make sure you could boot both operating systems?

    A. Install NT in the same root directory as Windows 3.1.

    B. Install NT into a separate directory.

    C. Install NT into the root directory, but manually update the BOOT.INI to dual-boot.

    D. You cannot boot both operating systems.

```
S A M P L E   T E S T
```

2-15   You have a computer running both Windows NT and Windows 95. NT was loaded into a NTFS partition. You want to remove NT but keep Windows 95 intact. What steps should you take?

    A. Boot the three boot floppies and delete the NT partition.

    B. Boot the three boot floppies and reformat the NT partition as FAT.

    C. Reset the C: drive Master Boot Record.

    D. Delete the NT root directory and files.

2-16   If you want to upgrade from Windows 3.1 to Windows NT Workstation, which installation program should you use?

    A. Install.EXE

    B. WINNT.EXE

    C. WINNT32.EXE

    D. WINNT.EXE /u:path to source files

2-17   You have a UPS installed in the serial port of your computer. Whenever you boot your system, the UPS automatically shuts it down. What could the problem be?

    A. The UPS configuration is faulty.

    B. The UPS hardware is faulty.

    C. The system thinks there is a serial mouse in the port.

    D. NT did not detect the UPS device.

2-18   Which applet in the Control Panel would you use to install the drivers for a new sound card?

    A. Devices

    B. Add/Remove programs

    C. Multimedia

    D. Sounds

2-19   Which applet in the Control Panel allows you change the international settings for your keyboard?

  A. System

  B. The General tab in the Keyboard applet

  C. The Input Local tab in the Keyboard applet

  D. Multimedia

2-20   Your system boots NT Workstation by default. Windows 95 is also installed on the system. How can you make the system default to Windows 95 whenever it boots?

  A. Edit the Registry.

  B. Via Control Panel ➤ Network.

  C. Via Control Panel ➤ System.

  D. You can't.

UNIT

3

Managing Resources

Test Objectives: Managing Resources

- Create and manage local user accounts and local group accounts to meet given requirements.

- Set up and modify user profiles.

- Set up shared folders and permissions.

- Set permissions on NTFS partitions, folders, and files.

- Install and configure printers in a given environment.

Exam objectives are subject to change at any time without prior notice and at Microsoft's sole discretion. Please visit Microsoft's Training & Certification website (www.microsoft.com/Train_Cert) for the most current exam objectives listing.

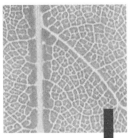

In this unit I take a look at how to create and manage user and group accounts on Windows NT Workstation. I also create and modify profiles, including user, roaming, and mandatory profiles, then go in depth on permissions for both FAT and NTFS partitions for both share and file level permissions. Installing and configuring printers in a local and networking environment is my last discussion.

Create and Manage Local User Accounts and Local Group Accounts

User accounts maintain the privacy of information on a shared computer and keep track of users' personal preferences. Every user who uses Windows NT must have a user name and password to gain access to the workstation. Remember the user account name and password are just attributes of the SID and can be changed.

Windows NT creates two accounts by default: the Administrator account and the Guest account.

- **Administrator**: Manages the overall configuration of the computer. You can use it to manage security policies, create or change users and groups, set shared directories for networking, and for other hardware maintenance tasks. You can rename this account, but you can't delete it. This ensures that at least one user account will always be available.

- **Guest**: Enables one-time users with low or no security access to use the computer in a limited fashion. The Guest account won't save user preferences or configuration changes, so any changes a guest user makes are lost when the user logs off. You install the Guest account with a blank password. You can rename it, but not delete it. By default, it is disabled.

Creating User Accounts

You can add user accounts to your NT workstation in two ways: By creating new user accounts, or making copies of existing user accounts. In either case, you can make changes in two areas:

- User account information

- Group membership information

You create and manage accounts and groups through the Windows NT Workstation utility called User Manager. To add a new user account, you use the New User dialog box, as shown in Figure 3.1, which is administered through the User Manager administrative tool. Table 3.1 describes the properties of the user account that are accessible from the New User dialog box.

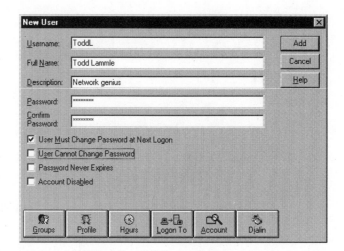

FIGURE 3.1

The New User dialog box

TABLE 3.1	Field	Value
User account properties	User Name	A required text field of up to 20 characters. Uses both uppercase and lowercase characters except "" / \ [ ]: ;	= , + * ? < > but it's not case sensitive. This name must be unique among workstation users or among network domain members if attached to a network.
	Full Name	An optional text field typically used for the complete name of the user.

	Field	Value
T A B L E 3.1 *(cont.)* User account properties	Description	An optional text field used to more fully describe the user, his or her position in the firm, home office, etc. This field is limited to 48 characters.
	Password	A required text field of up to 14 characters—it's case sensitive. This field displays asterisks, rather than the character typed, to keep your password secure.
	Confirm Password	A required text field used to confirm the password field. This avoids typing errors.
	User Must Change Password at Next Logon	A check box field used to force a password change at the next logon. Windows NT does not allow you to apply changes to a user account if this field and User Cannot Change Password field are both checked. The default for this is to leave it checked.
	User Cannot Change Password	A check box field that makes it impossible for users to change their own password. Typically not used.
	Password Never Expires	A check box that prevents a password from expiring according to the password policy. This setting is normally used for automated software services that must be logged on as a user.
	Account Disabled	A check box field that, when set, prevents users from logging on to the network with this account.
	Account Locked Out	This option is checked if the account is currently locked out due to failed logon attempts. You can clear it to restore access to the account, but it can't be set.
	Groups button	Assigns Group membership.
	Profile button	Activates the user profile information and home directory.
	Dial-In button	Allows users to dial into this computer using RAS and sets the RAS Callback options.

Copying User Accounts

If you need to create accounts for a large number of users, you can minimize the tedium by creating a few basic user accounts templates, then copying them as needed. A user account template is a generic user account that provides all the features new users need, and has its Account Disabled field enabled. When you need to add a user account, you can simply copy the template.

Windows NT copies these values from the template to the new user account:

- Description
- Group Account memberships
- Profile Settings
- User Cannot Change Password
- Password Never Expires

Windows NT leaves the following field blank in the new User account dialog box:

- User Name
- Full Name
- User Must Change Password as Next Logon
- Account Disabled
- Password

Groups

Setting permissions is more manageable with the security groups concept, where permissions are assigned to groups, rather than to individual users. Users that belong to a certain group have all the permissions assigned to that group. Windows NT has two types of groups:

- **Local groups:** Used to assign rights and permissions to resources on the local machine. Remember that these resources consist of drive space and printers on the specific computer, and that the local group only exists on that particular computer, in its local SAM database.

- **Global groups:** A collection of user accounts within the domain. These global groups have no inherent access or power by themselves—they must be assigned to local groups to gain access to the local resources. You can use a global group as a container of users, and then insert the global group into a local group.

The Built-In Groups

NT Workstation creates six local groups at installation that are meant to provide convenient group features for a basic workstation. The built-in groups are:

- **Administrators:** Can fully administrate the workstation.
- **Users:** Have normal user rights and permissions.
- **Guests:** Have guest user rights and permissions.
- **Power Users:** Have user rights, plus they can share directories and printers.
- **Backup Operators:** Can bypass security to perform backup and restore operations.
- **Replicator:** Used to supports file replication service in a network domain.

Creating Groups

You create groups much like you create users. Select New Local Group from the User menu in the User Manager window (see Figure 3.2.) Then, you can enter the Group Name, Description, and Members in the New Local Group dialog box (see Figure 3.3). The Group Name field identifies the local group. The group name has the same restrictions as a User Name.

You can highlight more then one user in the User Manager by using the standard Windows Shift and Control key operations. Then, when you create a new local group, these selected users are placed into this new local group automatically.

You cannot rename a local group account, and if you delete a local group, all rights and permissions are gone forever. You can't delete any of the six default local groups.

Remember that group membership changes do not take effect until the user logs out and logs back in to the workstation to create a new access token.

FIGURE 3.2

Selecting a New Local
Group from the User
Manger window

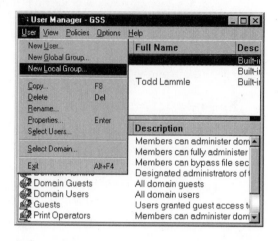

FIGURE 3.3

The New Local Group
dialog box

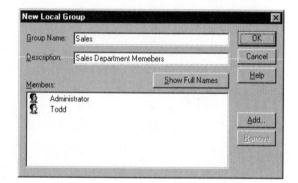

Granting Dial-In Permission

You can also set, on a per-user basis, Dial-in Permissions. You must give rights
to users that need dial-in access, or they won't be able to log on remotely. The
call back options are:

- **No Call Back**: This disables any call back requirement for a particular
  account. The user only calls in and connect to the RAS Server.

- **Set by caller**: The user can tell the server which number the RAS server
  should use to call the user back, so travelers don't have to pay toll charges.
  It also allows tracking of the numbers that the connections were made to.

- **Preset to:** The RAS server calls the user back, but only to a pre-set number set by the administrator. This is most effective for Callbacks to sites that are stationary, such as telecommuters or remote office sites.

Managing User Accounts

It's important to understand how to modify, rename, or delete user accounts on NT Workstation. To modify user accounts, double-click on the user name from within User Manager to bring up the User Properties Window. All properties are accessible from the dialog box and are the same as when you're creating a new user, with one exception. The account name is changed from the User menu, not in the User Properties window. Remember that when you create a user, a SID (Security Identifier) is created for that user. You can rename a user account, and keep all the rights, permissions, and group associations for that user account, but deleting and recreating the user creates a new SID, and all existing rights and permissions are deleted, even if the account name is exactly the same.

Generally, you should disable an account, rather than delete it, because deleting a user account deletes the entire SID. By simply disabling the account, you can just rename the disabled account for the user's replacement, enable it, and all the rights, permissions and group associations would still be in place. On the other hand, if you delete the account, you'd have to recreate all the rights, permissions and group assignments. If you're administrating a large, multi-domain network, this could eat up a lot of time!

Setting Account Policies

Account policies are a way to administrate users globally, meaning you can make one change, and it affects all users. Account policies are managed within the User Manager utility, as shown in Figure 3.4. The polices you can set are Password Restrictions and Account Lockout. The options are listed below:

Password Restrictions: By default, the following Password Restrictions are enabled with the listed default values:

- **Maximum Password Age:** This allows you to set whether and for how long a password is valid before users must change it. The default is 42 days.

- **Minimum Password Age:** This sets the minimum amount of days that must pass before users can change their password. The default is to Allow Changes Immediately.

- **Minimum Password Length:** You can set this to zero and allow blank passwords, or you can set it to 14, the maximum for a password in Windows NT. The default is to permit blank passwords.

- **Password Uniqueness:** This keeps users from using the same password over again within a specified time. For example, if you enter 8 into this field, users can't return to an old password until they have changed their password eight times. The default is Do Not Keep Password History.

Account Lockout Options: Unlike Password Restrictions, you can enable or disable Account Lockout features in aggregate. While they are disabled by default, you can activate them with the following default values:

- **Lockout After Bad Logon Attempts:** The default number of bad logon attempts is five. If you accept the default, when a user attempts to log on to the account after five unsuccessful tries, the account is disabled.

- **Reset Count After:** This specifies how long the account is disabled after the number of bad logon attempts has been reached. The default is 30 minutes.

- **Lockout Duration:** This specifies how long in minutes the account should remain locked out if the lockout counter is exceeded. It can also remain locked forever—until unlocked by an administrator using User Manager. This value is set to a default duration of 30 minutes.

- **User Must Log On in Order to Change Password:** This requires a user to log on successfully before changing the password. If a user's password expires, that user can't log on until the administrator changes the password for them. The default value for this is off.

Template Accounts

Templates make it easier for an administrator to set up user accounts. For example, an administrator can set up a user account named "Marketing," and fill in all the property values needed for the Marketing department. The administrator can then copy that user account whenever the need arises to create a new user. That new user will have all the properties the template affords. Don't forget to disable user accounts used as templates!

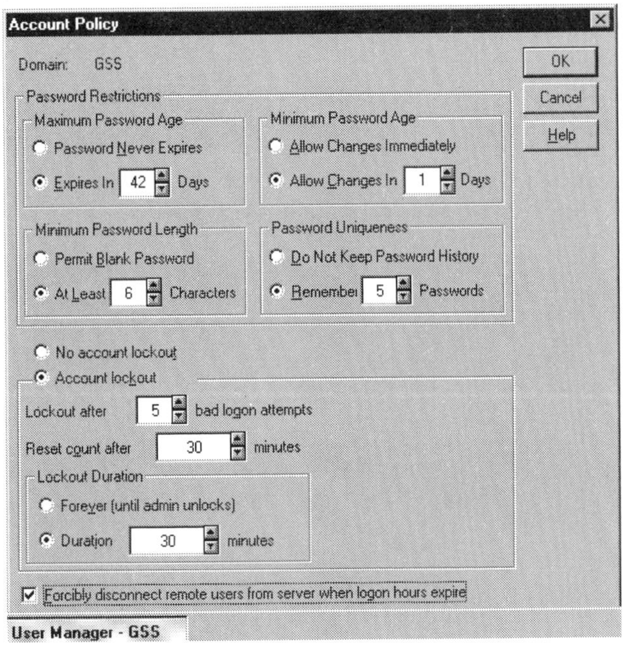

FIGURE 3.4

The Account Policy
dialog box

FIGURE 3.4

The Account Policy dialog box

Set Up and Modify User Profiles

User preferences are stored in a user profile, which is created from the default user profile the first time the user logs on. Any personal changes that user makes are saved in the user profile, so that the next time the user logs on, the changes take effect.

Profiles contain quite a number of items, including:

- Settings for the user-specific Control Panel entries

- Persistent network drive connections

- Personal program groups

- User environment variables

- Bookmarks in Help

- Preferences for Win32 applications

- Most recently accessed documents in Win32 applications

There are a couple of files that make up the users personal profile, located in the %systemroot%\profiles directory:

- `Ntuser.DAT`: contains Registry information.

- `Ntuser.DAT.LOG`: fault tolerant, log-based file for `ntuser.DAT`.

- **Miscellaneous files:** A series of folders containing other items, such as shortcuts and application-specific profile data.

The two different types of profiles are:

- **Local profiles:** When a user logs on for the first time, Windows NT creates a profile for that user from the default profile and stores it in the %systemroot%/profiles directory—typically C:\WINNT\PROFILES. Windows NT creates a new user profile on initial logon from the new local user profile. The saved user profile is then loaded the next time a user log on at the workstation.

- **Roaming profiles:** These are normally stored on a Windows NT Domain Controller server, but can also be stored on a Novell 4.11 server. By storing one profile on the server, instead of storing a local profile on each of the Windows NT Workstations you use, changes to your environment are in effect for all workstations you use, rather than just the one on which you make the change. You create a roaming profile by specifying a path to the profile in User Manager for Domains, as shown in Figure 3.5. You then can copy an existing local profile from the NT Workstation to the Domain Controller's roaming profile path.

F I G U R E   3.5

Setting a path to a roaming profile

Administrating Profiles

Administrators can set a *Mandatory profile* by preconfiguring a roaming profile that a user can't change. To create a mandatory profile, begin by creating a roaming profile subdirectory, and specify the path to that directory in the User Manager for Domains on an NT Server. Then, just after copying the user profile to the roaming profile subdirectory, rename `ntuser.DAT` to `ntuser.MAN`. Remember, this prevents the user from changing any aspect of the profile. If the Domain Controller is unavailable, it also prevents the user from being able to log on to the Domain.

Hardware profiles are a collection of hardware information about a certain workstation. These were specifically designed for laptops that change configuration when mated to a docking station, since the hardware can change each time the user goes to the office or home. Hardware profiles are displayed at startup—the user then chooses which hardware profile to use. Some examples are docked or undocked, and networked or stand-alone. Enabling or disabling a device for a given hardware profile is done through the Control Panel ➤ Devices.

Set Up Shared Folders and Permissions

In a networked environment, you often need to share information that resides on your Windows NT Workstation. You can implement this by creating shared directories. Sharing can only be done at the folder level—you can't share individual files. Also remember that by default all subdirectories inherit the share access level of the parent directory. For your computer to share directories, several network components must be in place:

- The Server Service must be started on your computer. If you've installed the networking components of Windows NT, this service should start automatically when Windows NT starts.

- The user creating the network share of the directory must have permissions to create the share. The default local user groups that are allowed to create shares are Administrators and Power Users.

- The user attempting to view the share must have at least list permissions for that directory if it is on an NTFS partition (and is therefore subject to NTFS file permissions), in addition to having the share permissions required.

Assuming you're a member of the Power Users or Administrators local groups, you can share any directory on your NT Workstation, regardless of the file system or media type. NT Workstation lets you set the sharing of the files and directories from several places, including NT Explorer and My Computer on the desktop.

The share name does not have to be the same as the directory name. The name can be up to 255 characters, but keep in mind that DOS-based systems may not be able to read the full name if it's longer than eight characters.

You can set the share two ways, as shown in Figure 3.6.

F I G U R E   3.6

Setting up a share

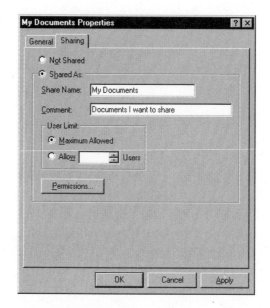

• **Not Shared:** Disables the sharing of a directory, keeping it available for local use only.

• **Shared As:** Enables sharing on the directory and uses the following fields to configure the share:

  • **Share Name:** The resource name the other remote users' computers see when accessing the shared volume.

  • **Comment:** Additional description visible to the browsing computers.

  • **User Limit:** Allows you to set the maximum number of connections to a certain value, or keep the default maximum allowed.

- **New Share:** Allows you to make multiple names or aliases for the same share.

- **Permissions:** Opens the Share Permissions window (discussed below).

Shared Directory Permissions

As mentioned in Unit 1, you can set a network share to any directory on an NT Workstation, Server, or Windows 95 machine, but you can only share a directory, not individual files, and all files and subdirectories (also known as a folder) will be accessible. Remember that these permissions are not the same as NTFS permissions—rather, they're in addition to the NTFS permissions, and in the case of overlapping permissions, the most restrictive permission prevails.

The four permissions for shared directories are: No Access, Read, Change, and Full Control. Figure 3.7 shows the permissions screen on a share.

FIGURE 3.7

Setting permissions on a network share

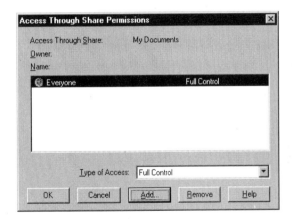

- **No Access:** Users can connect to the resources, but can't access the directory or list its comments.

- **Read:** An individual with Read access can:

  - Display the files and subdirectories contained by the shared directory

  - Run program files from the shared directory

  - Access subdirectories of the shared directory

  - Read and copy files from the shared directory

- **Change**: In addition to having read capabilities, a user with Change permissions can:

  - Create subdirectories and files

  - Delete subdirectories and files

  - Read and write to files in the directory

  - Change file attributes

- **Full Control**: In addition to having read and change capabilities, a user with Full control of a share can:

  - Change file permissions

  - Take ownership of files on an NTFS volume. Administrators can *always* take ownership of files, even when they're specified to have No Access.

Hidden shares are directories that are shared, but not made visible to users by the browsing service. You can create hidden shares by placing the $ sign at the end of a share name.

Sharing from the Command Prompt

You can use the net share command if, for some reason, you want to set shares from Windows NT command prompt. The syntax for the net share command is:

```
Net share <share_name> =<drive_letter>: path /REMARK /USERS
```

For example, to share the sales folder in the C:\business directory, type:

```
Net share Sales=C:\Business /REMARK: "Sales Leads" /USERS:8
```

If you do not use the /USERS switch, the default is unlimited. (Remember, the maximum connections on a workstation at any one time is 10.) To stop a share from the command prompt in Windows NT, use the /DELETE switch:

```
Net share sales /DELETE.
```

Administrative Shares

Windows NT, by default, always creates the following two hidden shares on all NT computers for operating system use:

- **C$:** This shares the root of the computer's C: drive.

- **ADMIN$:** Shares the root of the system drive, regardless of where it is located.

Set Permissions on NTFS Partitions, Folders, and Files

When using an NTFS partition, you can assign file and directory rights that are not available if you're using the FAT file system. These NTFS file system permissions (sometimes just called file permissions) are always in effect to all users and processes. Directory-level permissions are listed in Table 3.2. There are six basic permission actions you can perform to a directory:

- Read (R)

- Write (W)

- Execute (X)

- Delete (D)

- Change Permissions (P)

- Take Ownership (O)

T A B L E 3.2 Directory-level permissions	**Permission**	**Explanation**	**Directory Permissions**
	No Access	Users can't access the directory.	None
	List	Users can view the contents of a directory, but can't access the contents.	RX
	Read	Users can access the files in a directory, but can't save changes.	RX

T A B L E 3.2 *(cont.)*

Directory-level permissions

Permission	Explanation	Directory Permissions
Add	Users can add files to the directory, but can't read existing files.	WX
Add & Read	Users can view and read existing files and also save new files in the directory, but can't modify existing files.	RXW
Change	Users can view and read existing files in the directory, and also save new files in the directory. Users can also modify and delete existing files and change attributes.	RXWD
Full Control	Users can save, read, save, modify, or delete the directory and its contents.	RXWDPO

In addition to the Directory-level permissions that NTFS security offers, it gives File-level permissions also. These are listed in Table 3.3.

T A B L E 3.3

File-level permissions

Permission	Explanation	File Permission
No Access	Users can't access this file, but the file name and basic attributes appear in File Manager.	None
Read	Users can read this file, or execute it, but can't modify it.	RX
Change	Users can read, modify, execute or delete the file.	RXWD
Full control	Users can read, write, execute, or delete the file. Also, they can change permission, and take ownership.	RXWDPO

Setting Permissions

The default for NTFS directories is that the Everyone group has Full Control. This lets any user make changes to permissions. Depending on how you configure your security model, this may be something you want to change!

You can use Windows Explorer or My Computer to set permissions for a file or directory. Chose File ➤ Properties on the file for which you want to change permissions, and then click on the Permissions button on the Security tab of the File properties dialog box. Click on the Add button to get to the Add Users and Groups dialog box, where you can add users or groups. Figure 3.8 shows the Add users and Groups dialog box.

FIGURE 3.8

Add Users and Groups
dialog box

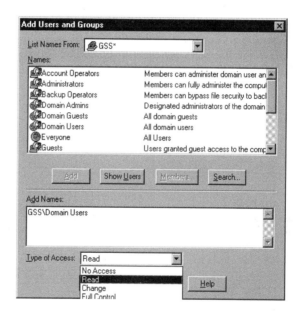

Taking Ownership of Files and Folders

A user who creates a file or folder is the owner of the file or folder by default, and has full control permissions. To take ownership of the file or folder, you must have the Take Ownership (O) permission or be a member of the Administrators local group. If a user removes everyone but himself from the permission list, only an administrator can take ownership of the file or folder. The administrator can take ownership even if the administrator's effective rights are No Access.

You must give a user Full Control, Take Ownership, or Change Permissions for that user to take ownership of a file or folder.

Moving and Copying Files

You must understand the difference between copying a file and moving a file, and what happens to the NTFS permissions when you do these things.

- When you copy a file form one folder to another, the file receives the permissions of the folder it is being copied into.

- When you move a file from one folder to another, the file maintains its original permissions. However, if you move a file to a folder on a different partition, the file receives the permissions of the folder the file was moved into.

Install and Configure Printers in a Given Environment

Windows NT workstation gives you flexible and powerful printing support. You can attach printers directly to your computer, or you can print to printers over the network.

To install a printer, you must be logged on with an account that has the appropriate permissions. The groups that have permission to install printers in Windows NT Workstation are Administrators and Power Users.

Printing Devices

Printing devices are the physical parts of the printing system. Typically, you would call these printers, but Microsoft calls them printing devices. The term "Printer" actually refers to a software construct that translates print requests and forwards the resulting print jobs to the appropriate printing device.

The NT Print Architecture

Each portion of the Windows NT printing system has a specific purpose and well-defined interfaces to other components of the system. The modular architecture makes Windows NT printing flexible, because you can install different versions of the modules for different purposes, and you only need to load the versions of the modules you need. This is very different from the print models of DOS and Windows 3.x. Application software now relies on the operating system to handle all printing jobs.

NT comes with installed print drivers for Windows 95 and all NT versions 3.x and later (for all processor types). You must install print drivers for other operating systems on the print servers.

When one printer services more than one printing device, the printing devices form a printer pool. All the printing devices in the printer pool must use the same print driver, and the print server assigns documents to be printed to whichever printing device is free in the printer pool. Print devices in a pool should be physically near one another.

You need to be familiar with the different components of the Windows NT printing process. Figure 3.9 displays Windows NT print architecture. The components work together to form the following process:

- A user sends a print job from an NT Workstation. If the driver is not installed, or is older than the one on the print server, Windows NT downloads a new version of the printer driver to the client machine.

- The print driver sends the data to the client spooler, which spools the data to a file, then makes a remote procedure call (RPC) to the server spooler.

- The server spooler sends the data to the Local Print provider.

- The Local Print Provider passes the data to a print processor where it's rendered into a format that matches the printer device. You can add a separator page in this process if needed or requested. Lastly, the Local Print Provider passes the rendered data to the print monitor.

- The print monitor points the rendered data to the printer port, and it, in return, passes the data on to the appropriate printing device.

Graphics Device Interface (GDI)

The graphics device interface provides Windows programs with a single unified system for presenting graphical information to the user. This way, the program can ignore the specific details of the device's resolution, color depth, coordinate system, bits per pixel, available fonts, and so on. The GDI translates the generic print requests of the application into a device driver request that's specific to the printing characteristics of that device.

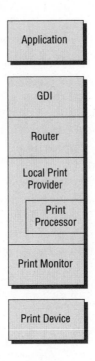

Print Driver

The print driver is the software component that translates the printer-generic Device Driver Interface (DDI) calls into the printer-specific command that's passed on to the actual printer. You must have a print driver for the type of printer your workstation is connected to when you print.

The printer driver consists of three parts:

- **Printer Graphics Driver DDL:** This part of the printer driver does the actual DDI-to-printer-language conversion. It is always called by the Graphics Device Interface (GDI). There are three default DDLs in NT for PostScript, raster, and HPGL print devices.

- **Printer Interface Driver DDL:** This is the user interface or management portion of the printer driver, which can be used to configure a printer. The three default DDLs match the PGD DDLs above.

- **Characterization Data File or Minidriver:** This is used to keep information specific for the printer. This component is used by the other two DLL whenever they need specific information about a printer.

Printer manufactures can supply all three components of the printer driver, but usually they only need to provide the minidriver for one of the three Microsoft-supplied printer graphics and printer interfaces.

Print Router

The print router receives the job from the print spooler and directs it to the appropriate print provider. The router can also download a printer driver for the printer if that printer is on a remote computer. The remote computer is configured to provide a printer driver for the specific type of computer the router is running on.

Print Provider (Spooler)

The spooler for a local printer accepts print jobs from the router, calls the print processor to perform any final modifications to the print jobs, and transfers the jobs one by one to the print monitor. Print providers can accept jobs while a print job is printing; the spooler also adds separator pages to print jobs if the user has requested them in the Print Manager.

When print jobs gets jammed in the spooler, you can stop and start the spooler in the Service Manager applet found in the Control Panel. Any current jobs that have already been spooled are deleted when the spooler service is stopped.

By default, the C:\%systemroot%\system32\spool\printers directory is used by the spooler service to print jobs. To modify the directory location, open the Printers folder, click on the File menu, select Server Properties, and use the Advanced tab.

Print Processor

The print processor performs any modifications (called rendering) to the print job before passing it on to the print monitor. The print processor recognizes the following data types:

- **Raw data:** Data that is ready to send to the printer. No more processing needs to be done.

- **Enhanced Metafile (EMF)**: The GDI generates the EMF information before spooling, instead of the raw printer data being generated by the driver.

- **Text**: Raw text that needs minimal formatting. Typically ASCII text that the printing device won't accept.

Print Monitor

The print monitor is the software component that transmits the print job, which has by now been transformed into the language of the printer, to the printing device. Windows NT provides several print monitors, the most important of which are LOCALMON.DLL for local print devices, HPMON.DLL for HP networked print devices, and LPRMON.DLL for UNIX line printer devices.

The local print monitor communicates with the printing device through serial and parallel ports, remote print shares, and named pipes, and can store the print file in a file, instead of sending it to a printer.

The print monitor is responsible for:

- Tracking print job status

- Monitoring print device status (out of paper\toner)

- Releasing the port when printing is complete

The HP print monitor sends the print jobs to an HP printer that's connected directly to the network, instead of attached through a computer.

The LPR (Line Printer) printer monitor sends the print job to UNIX LPD (Line Printer Daemon) printer server.

Installing Printers

The Printers folder is the Windows NT printing system's primary user interface. You can install, configure, administrate, and delete local and network printers from the print folder. The print queues are also available from the print folder. They allow you to pause, purge, and restart print jobs. The Add Printer Wizard in the print folder allows you to set up a printer share and set the printer defaults. Figure 3.10 portrays the printer folder.

FIGURE 3.10

Printer folder

Connecting to a Local Printer

From the printers folder, double-click on the Add Printer icon. This opens the Add Printer Wizard, shown in Figure 3.11.

FIGURE 3.11

The Add Printer Wizard

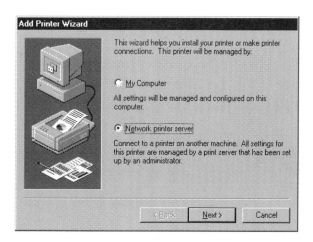

After choosing to use a Local or Network printer, select what port or ports you want to use to connect to the device. If you have more then one printer on different ports, they must use the same printer driver and configuration. Figure 3.12 depicts the Available Ports screen.

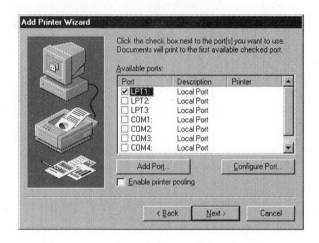

Next, specify a printer name (up to 32 characters long) and decide whether the printer will be shared. If so, supply the share name. You must then specify the operating systems being used by all computers that are sharing the printer. Figure 3.13 lists the operating systems that can print to a shared printer.

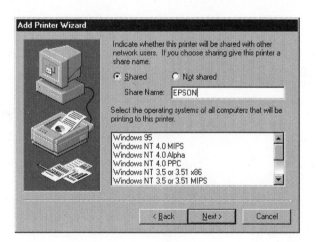

The Add Printer Wizard installs the printer driver and asks to print a test page.

Connecting to a Remote Printer

To print to a remote printer, choose the Network print server option in the first screen of the Add Printer Wizard screen (see Figure 3.10). The Add Printer Wizard opens the Connect to Printer dialog box, which asks for the name of the shared printer. Click on Browse to select from available printers.

The Add Printer Wizard then asks you if you want to make this your default printer, and finishes the installation.

Printer Configuration

To configure your printer, right-click on the printer icon in the Printers folder and choose Properties. The Properties window has six tabs across the top. Figure 3.14 portrays a Printer Properties screen.

- **General:** This tab lets you enter a comment about the printer, describe the location, and select the printer driver. The three buttons on the bottom are:

  - **Separator page:** This is where you enter a separator page or file.

F I G U R E 3.14

Printer Properties
screen

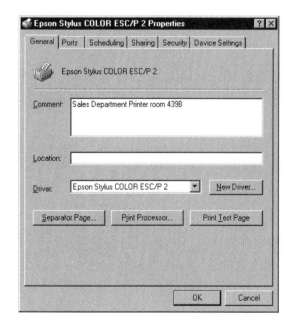

- **Print Processor:** Here's where you change the print processor.

- **Print Test Page:** Prints a test page.

- **Ports:** The ports tab shows a list of ports you can use. If you have several printers attached to your computer, configure this printing selection to print to whichever port isn't busy. Several printing devices that work together are called a print pool. All the print devices in a print pool must use the same driver.

- **Scheduling:** The scheduling tab controls when the printer is available, as well as how print jobs are presented to the printer. You can set the printer to be always available, or to be available only certain hours of the day. You can also set the priority of print jobs from this printer in the Priority section of the window. This only impacts print jobs from other printers to the same print device. Higher priority printers print first. The Spooling options allow you to set the printer to either spool, or not to spool jobs to disk. If you choose not to, the jobs are stored on the hard disk until the print monitor is ready to accept them.

- **Sharing:** Sharing allows you to control the availability of your printer on the network. By selecting the Not Shared option, you restrict printing to a certain printer to your computer. If you enable sharing, you must provide a share name. You may also configure your workstation to automatically download print drivers to computers that access your printer over the network.

- **Security:** The Security tab contains three buttons:

  - **Permissions:** This displays a window from which you can set user permissions and manage documents.

  - **Auditing:** This allows you to track the printing activities of users and groups.

  - **Ownership:** With this button, you can take ownership of the printer.

- **Device Settings:** This contains a hierarchical view of device-specific settings such as the default tray assignments, loaded printer fonts, available printer memory, etc.

Create and Manage Local User Accounts and Local Group Accounts

1. What are the two accounts that NT Workstation creates by default during installation?

_____

_____

2. True/False: The two default user accounts can be deleted.

3. What are the two ways to add user accounts on an NT Workstation?

_____

_____

4. What administrative tool allows you to create and administrate user accounts?

_____

5. What does the Dial-in button allow the administrator to configure?

_____

6. True/False: The Full Name field is optional.

7. True/False: The Password field is optional.

8. The User Name is a required text field for up to_____ characters.

9. True/False: The Account Locked-Out check box can be checked or unchecked only by an Administrator.

10. True/False: Creating a template in NT is done through the File ➤ Create ➤ Template command in User Manager.

11. True/False: For security purposes, a user account that is used as a template should have its Account Disabled field enabled.

12. Next to each of the 10 values listed below, indicate which five fields Windows NT copies from a template to a user account, and which five are left blank when using a template to create a user.

Property	Copied	Left Blank
Group Account memberships	_____	_____
Full Name	_____	_____
Description	_____	_____
User Must Change Password as Next Logon	_____	_____
Account Disabled	_____	_____
Profile Settings	_____	_____
User Cannot Change Password	_____	_____
Password Never Expires	_____	_____
User Name	_____	_____
Password	_____	_____

13. What is a benefit of using groups?

_____

14. True/False: Users that belong to groups have most of the permissions assigned to that group.

15. What are the two different types of groups?

_____

_____

16. Which one of the two types of groups can go into the other group?

_____

17. Match up the numbers and the letters between the built in group and the definition.

A. Administrators _____ 1. Can share directories and printers.

B. Power Users _____ 2. Supports automatic file copying in a network domain.

C. Users _____ 3. Have very basic user rights and permissions.

D. Guests _____ 4. Can fully administrate the workstation.

E. Backup Operators _____ 5. Have normal rights and permissions.

F. Replicator _____ 6. Can bypass security to backup and restore files.

18. What are the two steps to take to create a group?

_____

_____

Set Up and Modify User Profiles

19. True/False: Profiles store user data and workstation information.

20. True/False: A user profile is created for a user from the default user profile the first time the user logs on.

21. The two minimal files that make up a personal profile are:

_____

_____

22. Where is a local profile stored?

_____

23. Where are roaming profiles stored?

_____

24. Why would you decide to use a roaming profile?

_____

25. How do you create a roaming profile?

_____

26. What four steps do you take to create a Mandatory profile?

_____

_____

_____

_____

27. What are hardware profiles?

_____

Set Up Shared Folders and Permissions

28. What service must be started on your NT Workstation for your computer to share directories?

_____

29. What are the two default local groups that are allowed to make shares?

_____

_____

30. True/False: NTFS permissions are irrelevant when sharing a directory on a FAT partition.

31. True/False: You can only share files on an NTFS partition.

32. How long can a share name be?

_____

33. True/False: The share name does not have to be the same as the directory name.

34. What are the maximum actual connections to a shared file on Windows NT Workstation?

_____

35. True/False: You can create multiple share names or aliases for the same share.

36. True/False: Share permissions are the same as NTFS permissions.

37. What are the four permissions for shared directories?

_____

_____

_____

_____

38. True/False: NTFS permissions always prevail over Share permissions.

39. True/False: Hidden shares can be created by placing the "&" sign at the end of a share name.

40. What command would you use to share the Sales folder located in the C:\Business directory from a DOS prompt?

_____

41. What switch do you use to remove a share name from a DOS prompt?

_____

42. What are the two default hidden shares that NT creates (and the administrator has rights to by default)?

_____

_____

Set Permissions on NTFS Partitions, Folders, and Files

43. What rights does the Add & Read directory permissions on a NTFS partition give a user?

_____

44. What rights does the Change directory permissions on a NTFS partition give a user?

_____

45. The six basic permissions actions that are performed to a directory are:

_____

_____

_____

_____

_____

_____

46. The Read file level permission is used to do what for a user?

_____

47. The Read file level permission is notated as RX. What is the Change level permission known as?

_____

48. In what two ways can you set permissions for a file or directory?

_____

_____

Install and Configure Printers in a Given Environment

49. What does Microsoft call what is typically known as a printer?

_____

50. When you have more then one printer being serviced by the same printer server, it is said you have a printer _____.

51. What happens when a workstation tries to print to a printer and the client doesn't have the correct print driver?

_____

52. After the correct printer driver is either loaded or found on the workstation, where does the print driver send the data?

_____

53. The three parts of the print driver are:

_____

_____

_____

54. How do you stop the Spooler service?

_____

55. What happens to jobs in the spooler if you stop and start the spooler?

_____

56. What is the default directory that the spooler uses to spool print jobs?

_____

57. True/False: The print processor is responsible for rendering the print job into a format that the selected printer can use.

58. True/False: The print processor tracks print job location.

59. True/False: The print monitor tracks the print device status.

60. True/False: The only way to add printer in Windows NT is through the Add Printer Wizard.

61. How can you share a printer after it already has been created?

3-1   What should you do to the default users (Administers and Guest) created if you are concerned about security?

   A. Delete the accounts.

   B. Put hard-to-guess passwords on both account.

   C. Delete just the Guest account and put a hard-to-guess password on the Administrators account.

   D. Rename both user accounts.

3-2   You have a user that is going on maternity leave. What should you do with her account?

   A. Delete it and recreate it when she returns.

   B. Rename the account and rename it back when she returns.

   C. Disable the account and re-enable it when she returns.

   D. Do nothing.

3-3   What information must you supply when creating a new user account?

   A. Password

   B. User name

   C. Description

   D. Full Name

3-4   What is the default minimum password length in Windows NT?

   A. Eight characters

   B. Five characters

   C. Six characters

   D. None

3-5 By default, when is a user's profile created?

    A. When the administrator creates the user account

    B. When the user logs on for the first time

    C. When the user logs off for the first time

    D. When the administrator creates the profile

3-6 Where are the user profiles stored?

    A. %systesmroot%\system32\profiles

    B. %systesmroot%\profiles

    C. %systesmroot%\system32\users\profiles

    D. %systesmroot%\users\profiles

3-7 What utility do you use to assign a roaming profile for a user?

    A. User Manager

    B. Network applet in control Panel

    C. Server Manager

    D. Profile Manager

3-8 You need both Share and NTFS partitions on your NT Workstation with one FAT partition. What should you do?

    A. Set the NTFS permissions before the Share permissions.

    B. Set the Share permissions before the NTFS permissions.

    C. Convert the FAT to NTFS. You can only set Share permissions on an NTFS partition.

    D. Convert the FAT to NTFS. You can only set NTFS permissions on an NTFS partition.

SAMPLE TEST

3-9   What are the default permissions on a Shared folder?

    A. Everyone: Change Permissions

    B. Everyone: Full Control

    C. All local groups have Full Control

    D. Creator has Full Control

3-10   What are the permissions you can apply to a file on an NTFS partition? Choose all that apply:

    A. Read

    B. Write

    C. No Access

    D. Accept Ownership

    E. No permissions

3-11   What permissions can you apply to a file on a FAT partition? Choose all that apply:

    A. Full control

    B. Write

    C. Read

    D. No Access

    E. No permissions

3-12   What is a Print Device (in Microsoft's terms)?

    A. A directory on a hard disk that stores files until the printer is ready

    B. The DLL files that control the output to the printer

    C. A piece of hardware that output to an output medium

    D. A print driver

3-13 How many inbound printer connections does Windows NT Workstation support?

    A. 10

    B. 6

    C. 20

    D. 256

3-14 By default, which local groups can take ownership on a share that has the default permissions?

    A. Domain Users

    B. Power Users

    C. Administrators

    D. Everyone

3-15 Which modules in Windows NT Workstation can be used to help create a roaming user profile for a user? Choose all that apply:

    A. Network Control Panel

    B. System Control Panel

    C. User Manager for Domains

    D. User Manager

3-16 What is the maximum length of a NetBIOS (computer) name?

    A. 10 characters

    B. 15 characters

    C. 36 characters

    D. 256 characters

┌──────────────────────────────────────┐
│   **S A M P L E   T E S T** │
└──────────────────────────────────────┘

3-17   Users are trying to print to a printer attached to your workstation. It worked earlier in the day, and the jobs are in the queue and cannot be deleted. How do you resolve the problem?

   A. Delete all files from the spool folder on your computer.

   B. Select Services in the Control Panel on your computer, stop the spooler service, then restart it.

   C. Reboot the computer.

   D. Delete the printer and create a new printer.

3-18   What is the difference between mandatory user profiles and roaming user profiles?

   A. There are more restrictive permissions on a mandatory user profile than on a roaming user profile.

   B. A mandatory user profile must reside on a domain controller, while a roaming user profile can reside on a domain controller, member server or workstation.

   C. The suffix of a mandatory user profile is .man, while the suffix of a roaming user profile is .dat.

   D. Mandatory user profiles can only be created by members of the Administrators group, while roaming user profiles can be created by members of the Power Users group.

3-19   Your NT Workstation shares a printer for your department. You have received an updated driver for the printer. What is the best way to update the driver on all computers that print to your printer?

   A. Update the driver on all client computers; there is no need to update the driver on your computer.

   B. Update the driver on your computer and do nothing more.

   C. Create a separate printer with the updated driver on your computer, and instruct all client computers to print to the new printer.

   D. Update the driver on your computer and instruct all client computers to download the updated driver from your computer.

3-20   Where do you specify a separator page for a printer?

    A. In the General tab of the printer's property sheet

    B. On the Ports tab of the printer's property sheet

    C. On the Device Options tab of the printer's property sheet

    D. On the sharing tab of the printer's property sheet

U N I T

4

Connectivity

Test Objectives: Connectivity

- Add and configure the network components of Windows NT Workstation.

- Use various methods to access network resources.

- Implement Windows NT Workstation as a client in a NetWare environment.

- Use various configurations to install Windows NT Workstation as a TCP/IP client.

- Configure and install Dial-Up Networking in a given situation.

- Configure Microsoft Peer Web Services in a given situation.

Exam objectives are subject to change at any time without prior notice and at Microsoft's sole discretion. Please visit Microsoft's Training & Certification website (www.microsoft.com/Train_Cert) for the most current exam objectives listing.

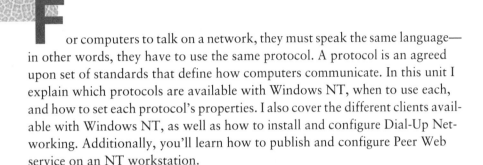

For computers to talk on a network, they must speak the same language—in other words, they have to use the same protocol. A protocol is an agreed upon set of standards that define how computers communicate. In this unit I explain which protocols are available with Windows NT, when to use each, and how to set each protocol's properties. I also cover the different clients available with Windows NT, as well as how to install and configure Dial-Up Networking. Additionally, you'll learn how to publish and configure Peer Web service on an NT workstation.

Adding and Configuring the Network Components of Windows NT Workstation

During the installation of NT Workstation, you'll have the opportunity to configure all your network protocols and clients. You can do this at anytime, not just during the installation. You can view your installation or make any changes by going to the Control Panel ➤ Network applet.

Microsoft Network Component Architecture

You don't need to understand how NT protocols map to the OSI reference model, but there are a few terms you should keep in mind when facing the NT Workstation exam.

Application Programming Interfaces (APIs) communicate between the file system and the network drivers. These include:

- **NetBIOS:** The default network operating system interface used in NT. All basic network communications are performed through NetBIOS.

- **Windows Sockets:** A standard for application communication with transport protocols such as TCP or SPX.

- **Remote Procedure Calls (RPCs):** Handles any IPCs (Interprocess communications).

- **Network Dynamic Data Exchange (NetDDE):** Developed by Microsoft; supports any DDE application over the network.

Listed below are the default components installed when NT Workstation is installed:

- **NetBIOS :** The basic network interface used in NT and Windows.

- **TCP/IP and NetBEUI:** One of the two default protocol loaded. However, you can also load NWLink at any time.

- **Workstation service:** Allows the computer to access a network share.

- **Server Service:** Allows the workstation to create a network share.

- **Computer Browser:** Allows the workstation to find a network share.

- **Network Card Driver:** Allows the Network card to communicate on the network.

- **RPC Service:** Manages the IPCs.

Redirectors

Redirectors intercept request for resources and direct those requests to a server, or share, on the network. Four different redirectors exist on NT. They are:

- Workstation Service

- Server Service

- Universal Naming Convention (UNC)

- Multi-Protocol Router (MPR)

Network Configuration

Most of the network configurations are done through the Network applet in the Control Panel. Figure 4.1 shows the Network applet plus the different tabs available for configuration.

F I G U R E 4.1

The Network applet

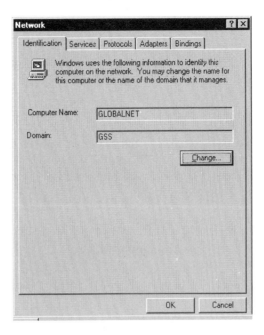

F I G U R E 4.1

The Network applet

Identification Tab

The first tab is the identification tab. It shows you the computer name and the Workgroup, or Domain name. Click on the Change button (shown in Figure 4.2) to change the computer name (up to 15 characters) or to join a workgroup or domain. (The maximum number of characters allowed for a workgroup or domain name is 15 characters.)

F I G U R E 4.2

The Identification Change dialog box

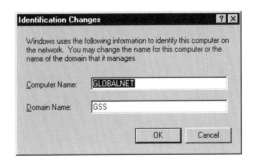

If the workstation does not have a existing computer account in the domain, you can input the name of the Administrator account and the password to create a computer account within the domain. You can switch back from a workgroup or domain at any time without affecting the SID of the workstation.

Services Tab

The services tab is where you load, remove, or configure any service for your NT Workstation. I cover specific services that are important to understand for the test later on in this unit.

Protocols Tab

This tab lets you add, remove, or configure protocols. I talk about installing and configuring protocols in greater detail later in this unit.

Adapters Tab

The adapters tab is where you install, remove and view properties for a network adapter. Very little actual configuration can take place here.

 If you don't have a network adapter installed on your system, you can still load the protocols by loading the MS Loopback adapter. This allows you to load the NIC card later.

Bindings Tab

This tab configures how the bindings of installed network components are listed, in the order of upper-layer services and protocols to lower-layer network adapter drivers.

The most frequently used protocol should be bound first or highest in the list. For example, if your network uses both TCP/IP and NetBEUI, but most computers are using TCP/IP, the bindings should be set to TCP/IP first, then to NetBEUI.

Using Various Methods to Access Network Resources

You can connect to network resources through your NT Workstation by using any of the methods on the following page.

Universal Naming Convention

The Universal Naming convention (UNC) is a way to specify share names on a computer or printer, for example *computer_name\share_name*.

When creating a share name, you can add a $ sign at the end of it if you want it to be a hidden share.

Network Neighborhood

By double-clicking on the Network Neighborhood icon, you can view all domains, workgroups, and network resources that you have access to.

The Network Neighborhood actually shows a graphical view of all computers found in the browse list. You can double-click on any computer in the network neighborhood to see the list of resources that are shared or available from it.

Command Prompt

You can view the browse list from a command prompt by typing:

```
C:\Net view
```

You can use the net share command if you want to set shares from the Windows NT command prompt. The syntax for the net share command is:

```
Net share <share_name> =<drive_letter>: path /REMARK /USERS
```

For example, to share the sales folder in the C:\business directory, type:

```
Net share Sales=C:\Business /REMARK: "Sales Leads" /USERS:8
```

If you don't use the /USERS switch, the default is unlimited. (Remember, the maximum connections allowed on a workstation at any one time is 10.) To stop a share from the command prompt in Windows NT, use the /DELETE switch:

```
Net share sales /DELETE.
```

Implement Windows NT Workstation as a Client in a NetWare Environment

Even if you don't have NetWare servers on your network, the exam is full of NetWare questions. Make sure you understand the different clients and protocols involved, and how they relate to a situation where Novell devices exist in an NT network environment.

NetWare Protocols

Novell's proprietary networking protocol is called IPX/SPX. Novell's servers run IPX/SPX, and for the most part, you cannot communicate with Novell servers without IPX/SPX.

That's why Microsoft created its own IPX/SPX protocol called NWLink. It's virtually the same protocol, and is compatible with any Novell server running IPX/SPX.

You don't have to have Novell servers in your network for NT to run the NWLink protocol. Actually it's a faster protocol than TCP/IP, and is recommended in smaller networking environments because it's so easy to administrate. Why? Because it offers self-addressing of hosts.

Ethernet Frame Types

Novell utilizes the Ethernet_802.2 frame type by default on all their servers starting with version 3.12 and above. NetWare 3.11 and below used the Ethernet_802.3 frame type. All IPX clients and servers must run the same frame type in order to communicate.

Keep the following in mind when dealing with NWLink and Novell:

- If your server is configured for 802.2 frame type and your client is running 802.3, they will not be able to communicate. They must run the same frame type to communicate.

- It's not critical to know the differences between Ethernet frame types, just which frame type goes with which NetWare Server version.

- When configuring NWLink on NT servers configured as routers, you must configure the network number because it's not self-addressing, and must be unique on each network segment. Think of this like naming a street.

- You don't have to have a Novell client (clients are explained below) if you are running client/server applications on a Novell server. However, you must install NWLink to communicate with the application.

Gateway Services for NetWare (GSNW)

You install GSNW on a NT Server from the Network ➤ Services ➤ Gateway (And Client) Services For NetWare. GSNW is not available on NT Workstation.

Basically, GSNW allows users to attach to an NT Server. That NT Server then makes a connection to the Novell server. This function was created for transition periods only—things move very slowly through the NT Server to the Novell server if more than a couple people are accessing resources by this method. Microsoft assumes you're transitioning away from your Novell server, and the main purpose of GSNW is to reducing licensing requirements in an environment where minimum access to a NW server is required.

If you install GSNW and you have not installed NWLink, it will automatically load NWLink for you.

Client Services for NetWare

CSNW works with NT computers to allow them to log on to a Novell server as an ordinary Novell client. It can run on both NT Server (part of GSNW) and NT Workstation.

CSNW is installed through Network ➤ Services. Once CSNW is installed, a new icon in Control Panel appears called Client Service for NetWare.

Novell 3.x servers run a bindery based database to hold network resources. To connect to a NetWare 3.x server, enter the server name in the Preferred Server option in Client Service for NetWare.

The CSNW can also connect to Novell NetWare 4.x servers, using Netware Directory Services (NDS). To connect to a NetWare 4.x server select the Default Tree and Context in Client Service for NetWare.

Two NetWare utilities that you can run from an NT command prompt to keep in mind for the test are:

- **Setpass:** Used to change passwords from a command prompt in bindery based servers (3.1x). If your NT client's running CSNW, you can do a Ctrl+Alt+Del in Windows NT, and then click on the Change Password button to change your password on the NetWare 3.11 server.

- **Syscon:** System Console is used to connect to NetWare 3.x bindery based servers. It is used to configure network resources (users, printers) on the NetWare 3.11 server.

While most NetWare utilities are supported through NT, some aren't. In these cases, NT has other utilities you should use. These are:

NetWare	Instead use
Attach	Net Use
Capture	Net Use
Login	Net Logon
Logout	Net Logoff
Slist	Net View

Printing in CSNW

The Printing Options for Client Service for NetWare main window allows a user to set three printing options:

- **Add Form Feed:** The Add Form Feed option should be set if a user wants a form feed command sent after each print job. This usually is not required by modern applications and usually results in a blank page being ejected.

- **Notify When Printed:** If a user wants notification that their print jobs have printed successfully on the NetWare printer, they should check the Notify When Printed option on this window

- **Print Banner:** The Print Banner option should be set if a user wants a banner page with their user account information printed at the start of every print job.

To use a separator page (that contains information about each print job at the start of each job), you should check the Notify When Printed option. You should then check the Print Banner option in Client Services for NetWare on your machine.

File and Print Services for NetWare (FPNW)

FPNW, also called Services for NetWare, makes a Windows NT Server appear like a NetWare 3.x server to native NetWare clients on a network. This is an optional service, and must be purchased separately.

Using Various Configurations to Install Windows NT Workstation as a TCP/IP Client

TCP/IP is one of the two default protocols added when installing Windows NT. It's very important to understand the network settings, protocols and tools available when using TCP/IP.

TCP/IP Protocols and Definitions

- **IP Address:** A 32-bit (4 byte) address used to identify a TCP/IP host. Every host (PCs, Macs, LAN printers, routers) must have a unique IP address. IP addresses can be between 0 and 255 for each byte. For example: 10.254.110.39 is a valid IP address

- **Subnet Mask:** Subnet masks help hosts and routers determine on which network, or subnet, the remote host is located. All hosts on the same subnet must have the same subnet mask. Subnet masks can look like the following: 255.255.255.0.

- **Default Gateway:** This is the address for the router on the network. If the information the host is trying to send is on a different network, it must be sent to the default gateway(router) to be routed to the appropriate network.

- **DHCP (Dynamic Host Configuration Protocol)**: Used to simplify TCP/IP administration of hosts. Automatically assigns IP protocol data, including IP addresses and subnet masks, to DHCP clients. This service can be run on an NT Server. NT Workstation can only be a DHCP client.

- **WINS (Windows Internet Naming Service)**: Used to resolve NetBIOS names to IP addresses. WINS is a dynamic service that can be run on an NT Server. NT Workstation can be a WINS client.

- **DNS (Domain Name System)**: Provides name resolution and a hierarchical naming system called Fully Qualified Domain Name (FQDN). This is used for resolving IP addresses to FQDs, identifying TCP/IP hosts on the Internet and on private networks.

- **SLIP (Serial Line Internet Protocol)**: Originally used in UNIX hosts for dial-up. SLIP is still available, but does not provide advanced features such as dynamic IP addressing, error-checking, flow-control, or security. NT Workstation supports the SLIP protocol that is available for connecting to UNIX hosts only.

- **PPP (Point-to-Point Protocol)**: A follow-on to SLIP. The biggest difference between SLIP and PPP is dynamic addressing of hosts, error checking, flow-control, and security.

- **PPTP (Point-to-Point Tunneling Protocol)**: Used to create secure connections between otherwise private networks over the Internet. It is the mechanism to establish Virtual Private Networks (VPNs).

Configuring TCP/IP

In configuring your TCP/IP hosts, you must have:

- A unique IP address
- A Subnet mask for the subnet the host is located on
- A Default gateway, if you have a router in your network

Optionally, you can have:

- A DNS server, if available
- A WINS server, if available

All of the above information can be provided or "leased" to a TCP/IP host automatically through a DHCP server.

TCP/IP Tools

After you install and configure TCP/IP to run on your network, you can use the handful of utilities available with NT. There are two types of utilities, status and connectivity.

You can get help for most of the utilities by typing **/?** at the end of the command. For example, NBTSTAT /? gives you all the options available for NBTSTAT.

Status These are used for determining the configuration of networks or perform diagnostic and troubleshooting efforts:

- **HOSTNAME:** Displays the name of the host.

- **ARP (Address Resolution Protocol):** Used to display and modify the ARP tables showing IP addresses to MAC addresses (physical network interface card addresses).

- **IPCONFIG:** Displays all the currently loaded TCP/IP information of the workstation.

- **LPQ(Line Printer Queue:)** Displays the print queue of a TCP/IP printer.

- **LPD (Line Printer Daemon):** A TCP/IP print service that runs on UNIX hosts and NT. To connect to a printer that uses the LPD service, you need to know the IP address of the print server and the printer name as it is defined on the LPD print server.

- **NBTSTAT:** Displays the names and IP addresses of NetBIOS hosts that the workstation has resolved to an IP address.

- **NETSTAT:** Displays protocol statistics and TCP/IP connections and packet information.

- **PING (Packet Internet Groper):** Used to test if a host is responding to TCP/IP requests.

- **ROUTE:** Adds or modifies IP routing tables.
- **TRACERT:** Used to test and display results of the route that an IP packet can take through an internetwork to a remote host address.

Connectivity

- **Finger:** Can display user information
- **FTP (File Transfer Protocol):** Used to transfer files between two hosts.
- **RCP (Remote copy):** Used to copy files between a client and a server running the remote shell service.
- **REXEC (Remote Execute):** Can execute commands on a remote system.
- **RSH (Remote Shell):** Used to execute commands on a remote system.
- **Telnet:** Used to emulate a dumb terminal session with another host or server.
- **TFTP (Trivial File Transfer Protocol):** Used to transfer files like FTP, but without any authentication.

Resolving Names

For success on the test, you must understand the difference in the way names are resolved using TCP/IP. Below are the options available:

- **WINS:** This service is used in a Windows-based network to resolve NetBIOS names to IP addresses. This is a dynamic name resolution method and is recommended to supplement DNS services and allow full host name resolutions for all Windows hosts.

- **DNS:** Used to resolved FQDN host names to IP addresses. Since DNS uses a hierarchical naming database to resolve names, you can use DNS to resolve names in subdomains within your organization and the Internet.

- **LMHOST:** A static table available in Windows-based workstations. Works like a HOSTS table for UNIX, which resolves host names to IP addresses, only LMHOST is used to resolve NetBIOS names to IP addresses. A problem with the LMHOSTS table is that it is a static file and must be updated on all computers by hand.

- **HOSTS:** Originally developed for use on UNIX stations to resolve hosts names to IP addresses, it can also be used in Windows-based systems. Like LMHOSTS, this is a manual file and it must be updated on all computers by hand.

Configuring and Installing Dial-Up Networking (DUN)

Dial-Up Networking (DUN) is the method for establishing connections to external computer hosts. It works with the Remote Access Service (RAS) server service to extend network connectivity to external clients. DUN can run on both NT Server and NT Workstation.

Remote Access Service (RAS)

RAS is an NT service that runs on either NT Workstation or NT Server. A remote RAS client can access and operate everything a standard network-attached client can, except slower. NT Server can support 256 simultaneous RAS connections, but NT Workstation can only run a single RAS connection, whether inbound or outbound.

RAS can communicate between servers and clients with:

- Public Switched Telephone Network (PSTN)
- Integrated Service Digital Network (ISDN)
- X.25 packet switching network

Protocols

Network protocols such as NetBEUI, NWLink, and TCP/IP must be encapsulated when being sent over a phone line, and then de-encapsulated on the other end. The protocols are encapsulated in what are called LineProtocols.

SLIP

Serial Line Internet Protocol (SLIP) is the oldest line protocol. SLIP has some limitations, and can only be used on an NT Workstation when dialing out over a data line. Usually used for connections with older UNIX hosts, SLIPs limits are listed below:

- Only supports TCP/IP
- Requires static IP address information
- Does not support password encryption
- Uses a script file

Windows NT Server and Windows NT Workstation include a variety of script files for connecting to different servers using Dial-Up Networking. The best way to establish connections with your Internet service provider's server is to use a standard script file, or a custom script file (standard script file with some minor modifications). The script file must be executed after a connection has been established. You can also use a terminal window after a connection has been established. Remember, SLIP can only be used for dialing out: "You can't SLIP into NT."

PPP

Because of the limitations of SLIP, a newer protocol called PPP was designed to replace it. Some advantages of PPP include:

- Support of TCP/IP, IPX and NetBEUI

- Dynamic addressing

- Password encryption

- No logon script needed

- Header compression

PPTP

Point-to-Point Tunneling Protocol was designed to let a DUN client create a secure session with a RAS server over the Internet. PPTP also supports TCP/IP, IPX, and NetBEUI, which makes it possible to run a secure corporate network over the Internet.

Installing and Configuring the RASNetworking Client

You can install both RAS and DUN during set up of NT or anytime after. To set up RAS after NT is configured, add the RAS service from the Network applet in Control Panel. Figure 4.3 shows the Modem installer that is invoked after adding the RAS service.

F I G U R E 4.3

Modem Installer screen

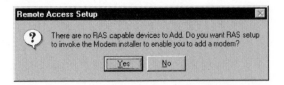

NT will then try and detect your modem, as shown in Figure 4.4.

FIGURE 4.4

NT Modem detect
screen

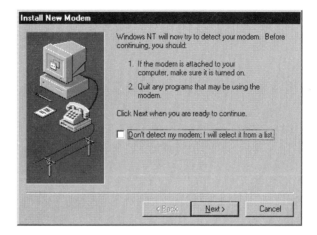

If NT successfully finds your modem, it will ask you to fill in location information as shown in Figure 4.5.

FIGURE 4.5

Location information
screen

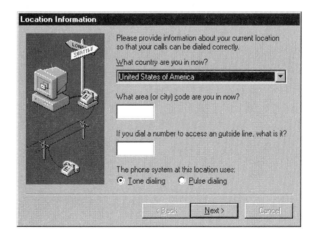

The NT will ask to add a RAS device (see Figure 4.6); this is your modem. Click OK to continue.

F I G U R E 4.6

Add RAS device screen

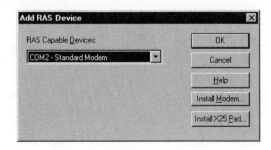

It will then go to the RAS Setup screen. Click Network to configure RAS networking (see Figure 4.7).

F I G U R E 4.7

RAS Networking
Screen

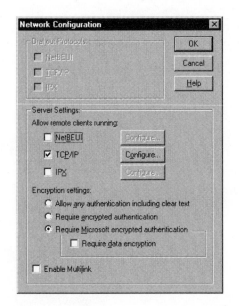

At this point you must specify how RAS should use the phone line. The default is Dial-Out only, but you can set it for Receive Calls Only or Dial-Out and Receive Calls. You can then configure the TCP/IP, IPX, or NetBEUI protocols, or just click continue.

Notice at the bottom is where you enable Multilink, which is discussed later.

Telephony API (TAPI) Properties and Phonebooks

The TAPI is a standard method of controlling communications over voice, data, and PBX. TAPI is automatically installed when you install a modem or RAS on your workstation.

The dial-out capabilities of RAS are controlled through the RAS phonebook. Phonebook entries include:

- Name, phone number, modem

- Server type, protocols

- Connection scripts

- Security

- X.25 settings, if used

Troubleshooting RAS Problems

For the NT Workstation exam, you need to remember there are two ways to troubleshoot connection problems with RAS: Dial-Up Networking Monitor and Device.Log file.

Dial-Up Networking Monitor

The DUN Monitor provides generic information about RAS connections and is generally a good place to start when troubleshooting a connection problem. DUN Monitor provides:

- Information regarding the speed at which you are connected

- The duration of the connection

- The names of the users connected to a RAS server

- The protocols used during the connection

- Which devices are part of the connection

Device.Log

If you cannot determine what is causing your problem using Dial-Up Networking Monitor, then activating the Device.Log file will provide a more detailed analysis of what is occurring when you are connecting.

The Device.Log file must be enabled through the registry, and the file is stored in the %SYSTEMROOT%\SYSTEM32\RAS directory.

Multilink (MP)

New in Windows NT 4.0, Multilink (MP) includes the capability to combine the bandwidth of multiple physical links. This can increase the total bandwidth that could be used for a RAS connection. Multilink connections are established when a client machine uses two or more modems to establish a connection to a RAS server.

MP Configuration

MP is enabled through the Dial-up Networking's Phonebook configuration window. Below is a list of how to configure multiple phone numbers in one phone book entry:

1. Create a single phone book entry and configure this entry to dial using all the modems you have. This can be accomplished in Dial-Up Networking by clicking the More button from the main window and choosing the Edit Entry and Modem Properties option.

2. Click Dial using: Multiple Lines.

3. Click configure.

4. Click Phone Number. You can then enter multiple phone numbers to dial with (see Figure 4.8).

For the test, ISDN and dedicated phone lines can work together to run MP. In a real networking situation all phone lines must be the same types in order to run MP.

Since RAS callback is limited to calling back only one number per user, configuring a RAS server for enforced callback will normally disable multilink dial-ups. This is because only one of the client's modem lines can be called back by the RAS server.

F I G U R E 4.8

Adding multiple
phone numbers

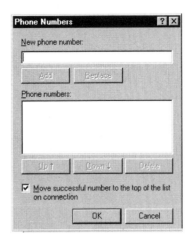

Configuring Microsoft Peer Web Services

Peer Web Services (PWS) is NT Workstations equivalent of NT Servers Internet Information server (IIS). That means it gives you the ability to publish information on private intranets. The biggest difference between PWS and IIS is that PWS is limited to 10 simultaneous connections.

PWS support the following industry standard Internet services:

- **File transfer Protocol (FTP):** Used to transfer files between TCP/IP computers

- **Hypertext transport protocol (HTTP):** Used to transfer web pages on the Internet

- **Gopher:** Hierarchical searching of for files and directories. This is no longer supported in the PWS supplied in NT Option Pack 4.

World Wide Web

The World Wide Web is a service based on the HTTP protocol. HTTP is a IPC protocol that employs text and graphics in HTML format as content. PWS offers many different options:

- Anonymous access

- NT user account restricted access

- Activity logging

- IP or domain name restricted/granted access

- Virtual server configuration

FTP

The File Transfer Protocol (FTP) is the service and protocol used on the Internet to transfer files from one computer to another. PWS offers this service to improve file distribution over the Internet and within large private networks.

Gopher

Gopher is a text-based, menu-like hierarchical organization of data. The Web has pretty much replaced Gopher services, but many Gopher sites and pages can still be found on the Internet.

Installing Peer Web Services

You must have TCP/IP configured and running on your workstation before installing PWS. Install the PWS from the Services tab in the Network applet. The latest version of PWS comes from the NT Option Pack 4 available for free from the Microsoft Web Site.

Configuring Peer Web Services

You configure the PWS from the Internet Service Manager that is placed on your desktop after PWS is installed.

Internet Service Manager can do the following:

- Find all PWS and IIS servers on your network

- Connect to servers and view installed services

- Start, stop, or pause any service

- Configure service properties

Adding and Configuring the Network Components of Windows NT Workstation

1. What is NetBIOS?

_____

2. What two protocols are the default network protocols on NT Workstation?

_____

_____

3. What does the Server Service on NT Workstation allow you to do?

_____

4. Which workstation service allows you to find a network share?

_____

5. Which three protocols are included with NT workstation?

_____

_____

_____

6. True/False: Redirectors intercept requests for resources and direct those requests to a server or share on the network.

7. Which applet in Control Panel is used to configure most of the networking in Windows NT Workstation?

_____

8. Which tab in the Network Properties sheet is used to view and modify the transport protocols in NT Workstation?

_____

9. Which tab in the Network properties sheet is used to set the computer name?

_____

10. True/False: The Services tab is where you would load, remove, or configure any service for your NT Workstation.

11. True/False: You must have an adapter installed to load networking protocols on your NT Workstation.

12. True/False: When binding protocols, NetBEUI should always be bound first because it is a non-routable protocol, then TCP/IP, and then NWLink.

Use Various Methods to Access Network Resources.

13. How many characters can a share name be?

_____

14. How many characters can a NetBIOS name be?

_____

15. In the space below, map F to the sales directory located on the Acme NT Server.

_____

16. How do you make a hidden share?

_____

17. What command can you run from a command prompt that will show you all the network shares?

_____

18. What command and syntax can you use to disconnect your workstation from a network share?

_____

Implement Windows NT Workstation as a Client in a NetWare Environment

19. How do you install CSNW on your NT Workstation?

_____

20. You want your NT Workstations to connect to your NT Server and then print to a printer that resides on a Novell server. What service do you need to load on your NT Server?

_____

21. You have an NT workstation and you want to log in to a NetWare 3.12 server. What two pieces of software must you load on your NT Workstation?

_____

_____

22. What service do you load on your NT Server to have your server login to a Novell server and use a printer?

_____

23. What is Microsoft's IPX/SPX equivalent protocol?

_____

24. True/False: You do not have to have a Novell server on your network in able to use the IPX/SPX Microsoft protocol.

25. What is the default frame type for NetWare 4.x?

_____

26. What is the default frame type for NetWare 3.x?

_____

27. You get a call from a customer complaining that they cannot log in to the Novell server from their Windows NT Workstation. They are running the Novell client and IPX/SPX compatible protocol. What is the first thing you should check?

_____

28. You have a NetWare 3.12 server running a client server application. What do you have to do to the clients in able to have them run the client/server application?

29. True/False: If you install GSNW and forgot to load IPX/SPX compatible protocol, it will stop the installation and have you load the IPX/SPX compatible protocol first.

30. Which Novell Server is bindery based: 3.x or 4.x?

31. True/False: If bindery emulation is being used, you should set the Preferred Server option in Client Service for NetWare.

32. True/False: If NDS is being used, you should select the Default Tree and Context in Client Service for NetWare.

33. If you want to change your password on a 3.12 server from your NT Workstation, what command line utility would you run?

34. True/False: The Novell utility ATTACH is not available with NT.

35. True/False: The Novell utility SYSCON is not available with NT.

36. What NT command is used instead of Novell's Login?

37. If you are using FPNW and users want to print a banner when they print to a Novell printer, what should they do?

_____

Use Various Configurations to Install Windows NT Workstation as a TCP/IP Client

38. True/False: 126.256.10.129 is a valid IP address.

39. Which part of the TCP/IP configuration is used to determine which network a host is located on?

_____

40. An IP address is how many bits long?

_____

41. Why would you use a default gateway?

_____

42. Which service is used to automatically assign IP addresses to TCP/IP clients?

_____

43. What dynamic name resolution service is used to resolve NetBIOS names to IP addresses?

_____

44. Which name resolution can resolve FQDN to an IP address?

_____

45. What three options are configured as IP Address properties during manual IP configuration?

_____

_____

_____

46. What does the IPCONFIG utility do?

_____

47. Which command sends sonar-like pulses to find out if a TCP/IP host is responding?

_____

48. Which utility is used to emulate a dumb terminal session with another host or server?

_____

49. What static table in NT can be used to resolve NetBIOS names to IP addresses?

_____

Configuring and Installing Dial-Up Networking

50. Which dial-up protocol creates a secure session over the Internet?

_____

51. What protocols are available to use when dialing into a RAS server?

_____

_____

_____

52. What is a disadvantage of SLIP?

_____

53. True/False: SLIP can use the IPX/SPX protocol.

54. True/False: When using SLIP, typically a script file is used to connect to network resources.

55. How many RAS sessions can Windows NT Workstation serve at one time?

_____

56. Which line protocol supports dynamic IP addressing?

_____

Configuring Microsoft Peer Web Services

57. What two Internet services does PWS support?

_____

_____

58.   Which service is used to transfer files between hosts?

_____

59.   Which service is used to support interactive Web-based applications?

_____

60.   Which utility is used to manage multiple Web servers from any location on your network?

_____

154 Unit 4 · Connectivity

S A M P L E   T E S T

4-1   Besides assigning a unique IP address to a NT Workstation client, what other parameters must you specify when running TCP/IP on a client? Choose all that apply:

    A. Default gateway

    B. DNS server

    C. Subnet mask

    D. WINS server

4-2   You are installing an NT Workstation, but have not purchased a NIC card yet. What can you do to load all the protocols and then load the NIC card driver later?

    A. Install the driver for the Microsoft Dial-up Adapter, then install other network components.

    B. Install the driver for the Novell NE2000 Compatible Adapter, then install other network components.

    C. Install the driver for the MS Loopback Adapter, then install other network components.

    D. Install the driver for the Generic Network Adapter, then install other network components.

4-3   You have an NT Workstation running CSNW and you print to a printer running off of a Novell Print Server. You want each print job to have a separator page. How should you configure your workstation to do this?

    A. In Client Service for NetWare on your NT Workstation, check the Use Separator Page option.

    B. In Client Service for NetWare on your NT Workstation, check the Print Banner option.

    C. On the General tab of the printer's Properties window, click the Separator Page button and specify a separator page.

    D. Configure this option on the NetWare server to which the printer is attached.

	S A M P L E T E S T	

4-4   What type of name resolution does a DNS server provide?

    A. NetBIOS names to IP addresses

    B. Domain names to NetBIOS names

    C. Domain names to IP addresses

    D. Domain names to hardware addresses

4-5   You have an NT Workstation running CSNW. You want to change your password on your Net-Ware 3.x server. How can you do this?

    A. Set a new password in Client Service for NetWare, log off and then log back on.

    B. Use the Setpass utility on the NetWare server.

    C. Use the Setpass utility on your Windows NT workstation.

    D. Press CTRL + ALT + DEL ➤ Change Password ➤ NetWare or Compatible Network in the Domain field ➤ enter a new password.

4-6   Which of the following NetWare utilities can be executed from Windows NT Workstation?

    A. Slist

    B. Capture

    C. Logout

    D. Syscon

4-7   Which of the following are functions of a DHCP Server? Choose all that apply:

    A. Dynamically assigns IP addressees to DHCP clients

    B. To give WINS server information to clients

    C. To resolve computer IP addresses to fully qualified domain names

    D. To give the DNS server IP address to clients

4-8 You have an NT Workstation that only logs into a Microsoft domain. You want to run a client/server application on a Novell server. What must you install on your Windows NT workstation to access the client/server application on the Novell server?

    A. NWLink

    B. NWLink and Gateway Service for NetWare

    C. NWLink and Client Service for NetWare

    D. NWLink, Client Service for NetWare, and File and Print Services for NetWare

4-9 You dial in to your ISP from you NT Workstation. What IP address should you use by default?

    A. 127.0.0.1

    B. The IP address provided by the Internet service provider's PPP server

    C. Any address, as long as it is a Class C address

    D. The IP address provided by your network's DHCP server

4-10 Your company has many different organizations that you need to build an intranet around. What must you install on your intranet to allow remote computers to access and resolve host names on the various subdomains of your company by dialing into the Internet?

    A. A BDC Server

    B. A WINS Server

    C. A DNS Server

    D. A RAS Server

4-11 You have an NT Workstation running CSNW to access a NetWare 4.11 server running bindery emulation. How should you configure your workstation so you can logon to your Workstation and the Novell server at the same time?

A. Select the Preferred Server option in Client Service for NetWare and select the Novell server as her preferred server.

B. Select the Default Tree and Context option in Client Service for NetWare and enter the server name in the Tree field and your account name in the Context field.

C. Select the Default Tree and Context option in Client Service for NetWare and enter your account name in the Tree field and the server name in the Context field.

D. Select the Default Tree and Context option in Client Service for NetWare and enter the server name in the Tree field and leave the Context field blank.

4-12 Your ISP only handles the SLIP protocol, and expects you to enter a standard set of responses to configure and start the SLIP protocol after establishing a connection. How should you do this?

A. Configure Dial-Up Networking to run the SLIP.SCP script before dialing

B. Configure Dial-Up Networking to run the SLIP.SCP script after dialing

C. Configure Dial-Up Networking to open a terminal window before dialing

D. Configure Dial-Up Networking to open a terminal window after dialing

4-13 Which of the following can be done from a Windows NT workstation? Choose all that apply:

A. Connect to NetWare print queues

B. Connect to a NetWare 4.x volume

C. Connect to a NetWare 3.x server

D. Change your NetWare password

4-14 You want to map network drive F: to a folder called Sales that resides on a server called Acme.com on the Internet. What is the correct path to use in this mapping?

    A. www.acme.com\sales

    B. Net view F: \\acme.com\sales

    C. Map F: www.acme.com\sales

    D. \\Acme.com\Sales

4-15 How do you change your Novell 4.11 password on a NT Workstation running CSNW?

    A. By setting a new password in Client Service for NetWare, logging off, and then logging back on.

    B. Use the Setpass utility on the NetWare server.

    C. Use the Setpass utility on your Windows NT workstation.

    D. Press the CTRL + ALT + DEL ➢ Change Password ➢ NetWare or Compatible Network in the Domain field ➢ enter a new password.

4-16 How do you configure on your NT Workstation running CSNW that your Novell print job has printed?

    A. Check the Notify When Printed option in Client Service for NetWare.

    B. Check the Notify When Printed option on the General tab of the printer's Properties window.

    C. Configure print job notification on the NetWare server for your user account.

    D. Turn on File and Object Access auditing in the Audit Policy window in User Manager.

SAMPLE TEST

4-17   Your NT Workstation uses TCP/IP to communicate on your LAN. You want to be able to access files on different UNIX servers by using their host names. What can you configure on your workstation to accomplish this? Choose all that apply:

   A. The host names of the DNS servers on your network

   B. The IP addresses of the DNS servers on your network

   C. The IP addresses of the WINS servers on your network

   D. An LMHOSTS file

4-18   You have 400 users all running DHCP. Which type of name resolution should you NOT use?

   A. DNS

   B. LMHOST

   C. WINS

   D. IPCONFIG

4-19   A user calls and asks how to connect to a TCP/IP printer on the network. What information must this user have before she can connect to the TCP/IP printer? Choose all that apply:

   A. The IP address of the print server

   B. The IP address of the DNS Server to resolve the name

   C. The print server name

   D. The printer name

4-20   Which Control Panel applet allows you to access the Dialing Properties Dialog box?

   A. Network

   B. Services

   C. Dial-Up

   D. Telephony

4-21 You cannot keep your RAS session from dropping. How should you troubleshoot the problem?

    A. Run Performance Monitor

    B. Look in the Event Viewer

    C. Run the Network Monitor

    D. View the connection status using Dial-Up Networking Monitor and view the contents of the Device.log file

4-22 You have an IDSN line with two B-channels plus a dedicated phone line attached to your NT workstation. Each of the B-lines has a separate phone line, which gives you a total of three modems on your workstation. You are calling a RAS server that has three modems running Multilink. How should you configure the phone book entries on your workstation?

    A. Create a single phone book entry and configure this entry to dial using all three modems. Enter the same RAS server phone number for each modem to dial.

    B. Create a single phone book entry and configure this entry to dial using all three modems. Enter a unique RAS server phone number for each modem to dial.

    C. Create two phone book entries: one entry for the modems that are using the ISDN B-channels and another entry for the modem attached to the dedicated phone line. Enter a unique RAS server phone number for each modem to dial.

    D. Create three phone book entries: one for each modem being used. Enter a unique RAS server phone number for each modem to dial.

4-23 Where is the Device.log file stored by default?

    A. %SYSTEMROOT%

    B. C:\WINNT

    C. C:\Winnt\System32 directory

    D. %SYSTEMROOT%\System32\RAS directory

4-24   You set your RAS server for enforced callback. Now Multilink does not work. What is the problem?

   A. You need to reconfigure your phonebook entries.

   B. You need to reinstall Multilink.

   C. You need to Reboot the NT RAS Server.

   D. You cannot use Multilink with enforced callback.

UNIT

5

Running Applications

Test Objectives: Running Applications

- Start applications on Intel and RISC platforms in various operating system environments.

- Start applications at various priorities.

Exam objectives are subject to change at any time without prior notice and at Microsoft's sole discretion. Please visit Microsoft's Training & Certification website (www.microsoft.com/Train_Cert) for the most current exam objectives listing.

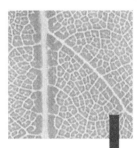

In this section, you learn how to manage applications that are run under the NT operating system. The main focus is on application support and how you can specify and control the priority that applications are run at. Support for Windows 32-bit applications is highlighted, and support for the major legacy operating DOS and Windows legacy systems is reviewed. Limited support for OS/2 and POSIX are also briefly discussed.

Starting Applications on Intel and RISC Platforms

One of the design goals of Windows NT is that it should be able to support a variety of applications that are written for different operating systems.

To provide this support, NT uses subsystems. A subsystem is a process that provides application programming interface (API) services to applications that have been written to work under specific operating systems.

Windows NT supports applications that have been written for the following environments:

- MS-DOS

- Windows 16-bit applications (Win16 applications)

- OS/2 applications

- POSIX applications

- Windows 32 applications (Win32 applications)

To support these applications, NT uses three subsystems:

- Win32 Subsystem

- OS/2 Subsystem

- POSIX Subsystem

Support for these subsystems is defined in Table 5.1.

T A B L E 5.1 NT Subsystems	Subsystem	Description
	Win32	The Win32 subsystem provides support for MS-DOS applications, Win16 applications, and Win32 applications. The MS-DOS applications and Win16 applications are supported through a DOS emulator called the NTVDM or Virtual DOS Machine. In addition, Win16 applications use the support of a service called WOW, or Win16 on Win32. Win32 applications directly access the Win32 subsystem.
	OS/2	The OS/2 subsystem is used to support OS/2 1.x character-based applications that are run from an Intel platform. There is no support for Alpha or the MIPS platform. The OS/2 Presentation Manager is not supported either.
	POSIX	POSIX is an IEEE standard that defines how applications must be compiled and executed so that they can run within different operating systems. NT supports POSIX.1 application standards through the POSIX subsystem.

MS-DOS Support

This section provides an overview of MS-DOS support, looks at the configuration of DOS applications, and specifies fault tolerance used by DOS applications running within the NT operating system.

Overview

To support DOS applications, NT uses a subsystem called NTVDM, or NT Virtual DOS Machine. You can see how this is represented in Figure 5.1.

FIGURE 5.1

MS-DOS application
support

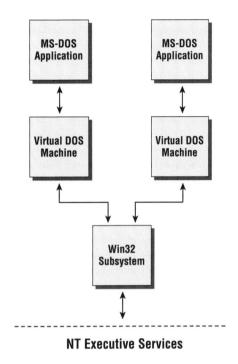

NT Executive Services

The NTVDM is a subsystem that emulates an Intel 486 DOS machine on either Intel or RISC-based platforms. It is made up of the following components, which create the Virtual DOS Machine: NTVDM.EXE, VDMREDIR.DLL, NTIO.SYS, and NTDOS.SYS.

By default, each DOS application runs in its own NTVDM memory space. The application appears to be running on a PC that has 1MB of memory installed. Each application can then access about 620 KB of RAM. The virtual computer that is created provides the following support:

- Virtual hardware support through Virtual Device Drivers (VDDs). This is required because NT does not allow applications to directly access hardware, as many DOS applications require. By using VDDs the DOS application thinks it's making a direct hardware request, but in reality, the request is passed to the VDD, which can pass the request though the Executive Services layer of the NT architectural model.

- The Intel x86 instructions, which provide DOS emulation through the Instruction Execution Unit.

- ROM-BIOS (Read-Only Memory- Basic Input Output Services) that is required for DOS emulation.
- MS-DOS Interrupt 21 services that are also required for DOS emulation.

Configuration

DOS applications normally use files called AUTOEXEC.BAT and CONFIG.SYS for configuration information. By default, NT ignores the files, with the exception of scanning the AUTOEXEC.BAT file at startup for any environment variables or path statement.

Instead, DOS applications running with NT use configuration files called AUTOEXEC.NT and CONFIG.NT. These configuration files are specifically used to store DOS application configuration information, and are stored in the %SystemRoot%\System32 folder.

In NT, you can create customized configuration files for each DOS application by editing the Program Information File (PIF) that can be associated with individual DOS applications.

Fault Tolerance

Because each DOS-based application runs in its own separate VDM and is executed as a single thread, any DOS-based application that fails does not cause any other DOS-based applications (that are running in a separate VDM space) to fail. This is the single best aspect of NT's DOS support. The concept of the VDM allows DOS applications to run without impacting any other applications outside of its own space.

MS-DOS applications that require direct access to the computers hard-ware are not supported and hang up in NT, since they violate the security system.

Win16 Support

Win16 applications are run in a different manner than MS-DOS applications. To use Win16 applications, you use the services of WOW, or Win16 on Win32. WOW basically emulates the MS-DOS and Windows 3.1x environment. Because Windows 3.1x uses MS-DOS as its underlying operating system, it is also layered on and uses the services of VDM. This section provides an overview on Win16 application execution, Win16 application configuration, and how you can configure Win16 applications to run in their own memory space.

You can see how Win16 applications are supported in Figure 5.2.

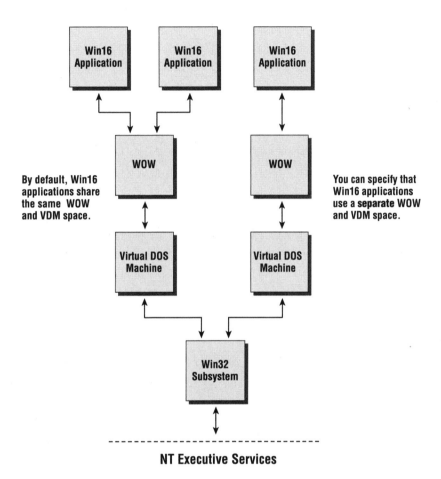

Win16 Application Execution

By default, all Win16 applications run through a single instance of WOW and VDM. The following subsections define the function of WOW and the default Win16 application execution.

WOW Overview   WOW is used to support 16-bit applications within a 32-bit environment. WOW works by translating 16-bit calls from the Win16 application to 32-bit calls that are used by the Win32 subsystem. If the Win32 subsystem must return information to the Win16 application, WOW translates the 32-bit call back to 16-bit for the Win16 application. This process is called "thunking."

Default Win16 Application Execution   By default, Win16 applications all run in a single WOW and VDM space. This brings up the following critical application execution issues:

- If you run Win16 applications in the same memory space, a Win16 application that fails can cause all other Win16 applications within the same memory space to also fail.

- By running each Win16 application in its own memory space, you improve reliability since a failed Win16 application no longer affects other Win16 applications.

- By running each Win16 application in its own memory space, you increase memory usage, which can be up to 2MB for the pagefile and 1MB of physical RAM.

- You can take advantage of multiple processors when running each Win16 application in its own memory space, since this allows a thread to execute for each separate application, as opposed to a single shared thread used when you run all Win16 applications in a shared memory space.

- If you run Win16 applications in separate memory spaces and they do not follow the OLE and DDE specifications, they can't interoperate with other Win16 applications that are run in separate memory spaces.

Win16 Application Configuration

Windows 3.1x applications are configured through the WIN.INI and SYSTEM.INI files. NT, like Windows 95, instead uses the Registry to store configuration information. If you install NT into the same folder that contains the WIN.INI and SYSTEM.INI files, the information is extracted from the .INI files and added to the NT Registry.

In addition, Win16 applications can still get configuration information from the NT equivalents to AUTOEXEC.BAT and CONFIG.SYS from a Windows 3.1x environment. NT uses the AUTOEXEC.NT and CONFIG.NT files to provide Win16 applications with configuration information.

Running Win16 Applications in Their Own Memory Space

You can specify that Win16 applications run in their own memory space in one of these four ways:

- From the Run command.

- From the command prompt using the Start command.

- By creating an association for the application through NT Explorer.

- By starting a new task through Task Manager.

Running Win16 Applications from Run   You can run Win16 applications from Start ➢ Run. By checking the "Run in Separate Memory Space" box shown in Figure 5.3, you specify that the Win16 application is run in its own memory space.

F I G U R E   5.3

Start ➢ Run dialog box

Running Win16 Applications from the Command Prompt   After accessing a DOS prompt, you can run Win16 applications in their own memory space through the START command. Assuming the program is called ABC.EXE, the syntax is as shown:

```
START /SEPARATE ABC.EXE
```

The START command lets you use a variety of optional switches, shown in Table 5.2.

T A B L E   5.2

START command switched defined

Start Command Options	Description
/separate	Forces a Win16 application to run in its own memory space.
/shared	Specifies that a Win16 application run in the shared VDM.
/min	Starts the application in a minimized window.
/max	Starts the application in a maximized window.
/low	Starts the application with a low priority.
/normal	Starts the application using the default priority structure.
/high	Starts the application using a high priority.
/realtime	Starts the application using the real-time performance priority.

Running Win16 Applications through File Association   This option works well if you call up your Win16 applications through file associations. Assume that you're using Wordpad, which is a Win16 application (WRITE.EXE). By default, a file association is set up so that by clicking on a file with a .WRI extension, you call the Wordpad application. This is how you edit the file association so that Win16 applications run in their own memory space:

Start ➤ Programs ➤ Windows NT Explorer ➤ View ➤ Options ➤ File Types tab.

Select the Write document and choose the Edit button to access the dialog box shown in Figure 5.4.

F I G U R E 5.4

Edit File Type
dialog box

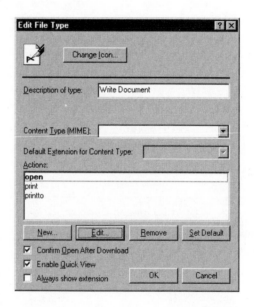

To specify that a Win16 application run in its own memory space, click on the Edit button shown in Figure 5.4, and as part of the program execution line, insert:

```
cmd /c /start /separate
```

before the path and filename.

Starting Win16 Applications in Their Own Memory Space from Task Manager   You can start new tasks through Task Manager. To access Task Manager, you press Control + Alt + Del and click on the Task Manager button.

Within the Applications tab, click on the New Task button to see the dialog screen shown in Figure 5.5.

F I G U R E 5.5

Create New Task
dialog box

Within the Create New Task dialog box, check the Run in Separate Memory Space option to have your Win16 applications run in a separate VDM session.

OS/2 Support

In addition to supporting MS-DOS and Win16 applications, NT also supports OS/2 applications. By using the OS/2 subsystem, you can use OS/2 1.x character based applications.

This option is rarely used since the following OS/2 support is NOT available:

- OS/2 2.x applications are not supported.

- NT 4.0 has no native support for Presentation Manager applications.

- You can only run OS/2 applications from Intel platforms; there is no RISC support.

POSIX Support

POSIX applications are supported through the POSIX subsystem. POSIX is not commonly used, but if you do choose to use it, it meets the IEEE 1003.1 standard. NT provides the following support:

- Case-Sensitive Naming

- Hard Links

- C Routine Library

Win32 Support

Win32 applications are designed to take advantage of NT's 32-bit memory model. These applications use the Win32 subsystem directly. You'll get better performance from Win32 applications than from any of the other application types that NT supports.

Setting Application Priority

If you're running multiple applications, the active window is considered the foreground application and the inactive windows are considered to be running background applications. By default, foreground applications are given higher processing priority than background applications.

You can specify the application priority for your foreground and background applications so that:

- Foreground applications run at priority 9 and background applications run at priority 7. This is default.

- Foreground applications run at priority 8 and background applications run at priority 7. Foreground applications still have a slight boost.

- Foreground and background applications both run at priority 7. This way all applications run at the same processing level.

This is called performance boost, and is built into NT. You can change the default application priority in two ways:

- Through Control Panel ➤ System ➤ Performance tab

- Through the START command line utility

Setting Application Priority through the Control Panel

To specify application priority through the Control Panel, use the Performance tab in the System applet. This brings up the dialog box shown in Figure 5.6.

The Application Performance slide bar allows you to set application priority. The settings are shown in Table 5.3.

F I G U R E   5.6

Control Panel ➤ System
Properties ➤
Performance tab
dialog box

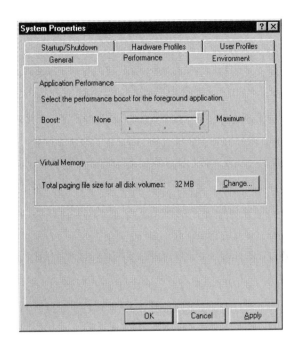

T A B L E   5.3

Application Slide Bar
Performance Options

Slide Bar Option	Foreground Performance Priority	Background Performance Priority
Maximum	9	7
Middle Position	8	7
None	7	7

Setting Application Priority through the START Command

You can also use the START command to set application priority. These options
were defined in Table 5.2.

The following example shows how you could start the ABC.EXE program
using high priority:

```
START /high ABC.EXE
```

Starting Applications on Intel and RISC Platforms

1. True/ False: MS-DOS applications run in their own memory space by default.

2. True/ False: Win16 applications run in their own memory space by default.

3. The _____ service is responsible for translating Win16 calls to Win32 calls and is also referred to as thunking.

4. The _____ service provides DOS emulation for MS-DOS applications.

5. Before accessing the Win32 subsystem, you must use _____ and _____ to support Win16 applications.

6. Which applications use the AUTOEXEC.NT and CONFIG.NT files?

   _____

   _____

7. True/ False: NT reads the AUTOEXEC.BAT and CONFIG.SYS file so configuration information about MS-DOS based applications can be extracted.

8. What is the command line utility and options that are used to start a Win16 application called XYZ.EXE in its own memory space within a minimized window?

   _____

9. True/ False: You can allow MS-DOS applications to share memory space.

10.   True/ False: You can run OS/2 2.x applications within NT.

11.   True/ False: If one MS-DOS application fails, the other MS-DOS applications that are also running are subject to failure.

12.   If you have three Win16 applications that are running in the default memory space, how many NT application threads will execute to support the Win 16 applications?

_____

13.   If you have three MS-DOS applications running in the default memory space, how many threads will execute to support the applications?

_____

14.   Your Windows NT computer is short on memory. You need to run three Win16 applications. How should you run these applications to minimize the memory that will be used?

_____

15.   Where does NT store configuration information that is required by Win16 applications?

_____

16.   List the four ways you can configure Win16 applications to run in separate memory spaces.

_____

_____

_____

_____

Setting Application Priority

17. What GUI utility should you use to set application priority so that foreground and background applications use the same priority?

_____

18. What is the command syntax to start ABC.EXE from a command prompt so that it uses high priority?

_____

19. What is the command syntax to start ABC.EXE from a command prompt so it uses low priority and is running in a maximized window?

_____

20. True/ False: By default, foreground and background applications run at the same priority.

5-1   You are running a Win16 application called ABC.EXE. Because of previous problems you have had with this application, you want to run it in its own memory space in a minimized windows. Which of the following options do you use?

   A. START /min /separate ABC.EXE

   B. CMD /min /separate ABC.EXE

   C. NET START /min /separate ABC.EXE

   D. RUN /min /separate ABC.EXE

5-2   You are using a Win16 application that has some known problems that cause it to crash occasionally. This application is part of a set of two Win16 applications that are integrated with each other. You also run three other Win16 applications that are independent of each other. You want to protect other Win16 applications from being affected if the bad Win16 application crashes. What do you do?

   A. Run all Win16 applications in their own memory space.

   B. Run the two Win16 applications that are integrated with each other in separate memory spaces. Let the known good Win16 applications run in the default shared memory space.

   C. Run the two Win16 applications that are integrated with each other in the default shared memory space. Configure all other Win16 applications to run in separate memory spaces.

   D. Let all Win16 applications run in the same memory space.

SAMPLE TEST

5-3 You are running an accounting application in the background, while using Word as a foreground application. You notice that the accounting application is running very slowly, and want to increase its performance. What do you do? Choose two answers.

A. Set the priority to high on the accounting application by launching it with the START /high command.

B. Set application priority through Control Panel ➤ System ➤ Performance tab and specify that None be used on the Application Priority slide bar. This causes foreground and background applications to use the same priority.

C. Boost the accounting application's priority through Task Manager.

D. Set the priority to high on the accounting application by launching it with the CMD / high command.

5-4 You are running a MS-DOS application called ABC.EXE. Because of previous problems you have had with this application, you want to run it in its own memory space in a minimized window. Which of the following options do you use?

A. START /min /separate ABC.EXE

B. CMD /min /separate ABC.EXE

C. NET START /min /separate ABC.EXE

D. MS-DOS applications run in their own memory space by default.

5-5 Which of the following best describes how MS-DOS applications run within an NT environment?

A. Each application runs in a shared VDM that emulates the DOS operating system.

B. Each application runs in a separate VDM that emulates the DOS operating system.

C. Each application runs in a shared VDM that emulates the DOS operating system and is supported through WOW.

D. Each application runs in a separate VDM that emulates the DOS operating system and is supported through WOW.

S A M P L E   T E S T

5-6 Which of the following best describes how Win16 applications run within an NT environment?

    A. Each application runs in a shared VDM that emulates the DOS operating system.

    B. Each application runs in a separate VDM that emulates the DOS operating system.

    C. Each application runs in a shared VDM that emulates the DOS operating system and is supported through WOW.

    D. Each application runs in a separate VDM that emulates the DOS operating system and is supported through WOW.

5-7 You need to launch a program called ABC.EXE that will run as a background application. You want the application to run at high priority. All other background applications should be running at default priority. Which of the following options can you use?

    A. Set priority for the applications through the Control Panel ➢ System ➢ Performance tab.

    B. Start the application through the START command and use the /high switch.

    C. Start the application through the CMD command and use the /high switch.

    D. Start the application through the RUN command and use the /high switch.

5-8 Which of the following files are used to provide configuration information for DOS applications running within the NT operating system? Choose all that apply.

    A. AUTOEXEC.BAT

    B. AUTOEXEC.NT

    C. CONFIG.SYS

    D. CONFIG.NT

S A M P L E   T E S T

5-9   What process is used to translate Win16 calls to 32-bit calls that are passed to the Win32 subsystem?

   A. VDM

   B. WOW

   C. WSWI

   D. NTWOW

5-10   You have an application called XYZ.EXE that you want to run with low priority in a maximized window. Which of the following commands do you use?

   A. START /max /low XYZ.EXE

   B. CMD /max /low XYZ.EXE

   C. NET START /max /low XYZ.EXE

   D. RUN /max /low XYZ.EXE

5-11   You are creating a file association that will launch files with the .abc extension with the Win16 ABC.EXE application. You want the application to run in a separate memory space. What do you need to add to the run box before the path and filename?

   A. START /c /start

   B. CMD /c /start

   C. NET START /c /start

   D. RUN /c /start

5-12 Which of the following statements are true of NT support for OS/2 applications? Choose all that apply:

A. You can run OS/2 1.x character based applications.

B. You can run OS/2 2.x applications.

C. You can run OS/2 applications using Presentation Manager services.

D. NT supports OS/2 applications on Intel or RISC platforms.

UNIT

6

Monitoring and Optimization

Test Objectives: Monitoring and Optimization

■ Monitor system performance by using various tools.

■ Identify and resolve a given performance problem.

■ Optimize system performance in various areas.

Exam objectives are subject to change at any time without prior notice and at Microsoft's sole discretion. Please visit Microsoft's Training & Certification website (www.microsoft.com/Train_Cert) for the most current exam objectives listing.

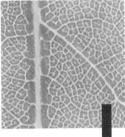

In this unit, you learn how to manage and identify performance problems using the Task Manager and Performance Monitor utilities. You also learn how you can optimize system performance for specific areas.

Monitoring System Performance

NT comes with the Task Manager and Performance Monitor utilities, which are used to monitor system performance. This section provides an overview of the Task Manager and Performance Monitor utilities. In addition, I discuss which Performance Monitor counters you should monitor and what values may indicate that you have a performance bottleneck.

Overview of Task Manager

Task Manager is a new utility in NT 4.0. The main purpose of Task Manager is to allow you to manage the programs you're running on your computer and monitor how the system resources are being used.

To access Task Manager, hit Control + Alt + Delete to access the Windows NT Security dialog box, and click on the Task Manager button. You see a screen similar to Figure 6.1.

From Task Manager, you can manage:

- Applications

- Processes

- Performance

FIGURE 6.1

Windows NT Task
Manager dialog box

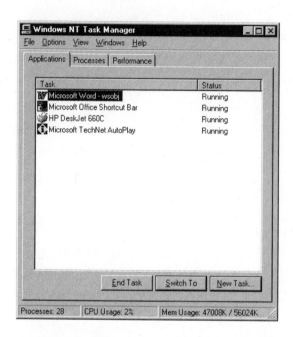

Applications Tab of Task Manager

The Applications tab shown in Figure 6.1 displays a list of any active applications. You can also end tasks, switch to a specific task, or start a new task.

Processes Tab of Task Manager

The Process tab of Task Manager is shown in Figure 6.2. This tab lists all the processes that are currently active on your computer. For each process you can see:

- The percentage of total CPU time the process uses
- Elapsed CPU time the process has used
- The amount of memory currently used by the process

By clicking on any column within the Task Manager Processes tab, you sort the active processes by that category from highest to lowest values. By using this feature, you can see which processes consume the most CPU or memory usage from highest to lowest process.

F I G U R E   6.2

Process tab of Task
Manager dialog box

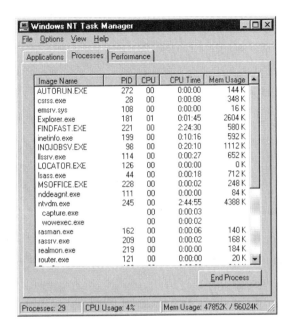

Performance Tab of Task Manager

The Performance tab of Task Manger gives you a quick and easy way to get a real-time snapshot of how your computer is currently performing. This can be seen in Figure 6.3.

This screen shows your current CPU and Memory Usage, as well as a short history in graph format. You can also see overview statistics on Totals, Physical Memory, Commit Change (memory), and Kernel Memory.

This is a quick snapshot look at computer performance and can be used as a quick method to determine if you processes are overloading the CPU or physical memory. If you require more detailed performance monitoring, you can use the Performance Monitor utility, which is covered in the next section.

Overview of Performance Monitor

Performance Monitor is a tool that ships with NT to allow you to monitor both general and specific aspects of your computer's performance. You can monitor the performance of your hardware, the NT operating system, and your applications. By monitoring the status of your computer, you can detect and eliminate system bottlenecks.

F I G U R E 6.3

Performance tab
of Task Manager
dialog box

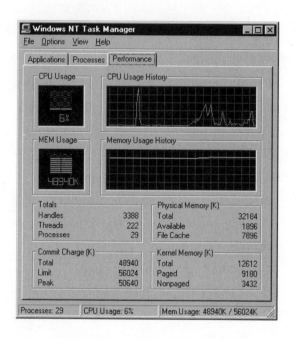

In this section, I go over the terminology used within Performance Monitor, how to monitor for common system bottlenecks, and how to enable specific counters.

Terminology Used within Performance Monitor

To understand how NT Performance Monitor works, you must first understand the following terms:

- **Object**: An object represents a specific resource on an NT computer. Objects can be a software process, a piece of physical hardware, or a section of system memory. Common objects include Memory, Paging File, Processor, Physical Disk, Logical Disk, and Processes.

- **Counter**: Each object within Performance Monitor has an associated set of counters. Counters are used to track how a specific area of the object is performing. For example, within the Processor object, you can see through specific counters how much of the processor time is spent in Privileged Mode and how much time is spent processing User Mode operations.

- **Instance:** Instances are used to track multiples of the same object. For example, if your computer has two physical hard disks, you see two instances of the object PhysicalDisk. This allows you to track how each separate disk is operating.

- **Process:** A process is created whenever an application is run. A process is a combination of an executable program, the memory the application uses, and one or more threads.

- **Thread:** A thread is the smallest unit of data that can be processed by the microkernel. An application that uses a single thread cannot take advantage of NT's multi-processing capabilities. If an application is multi-threaded, each thread can be scheduled to be processed on multiple processors simultaneously.

Monitoring for Performance Bottlenecks

While Performance Monitor allows you to track many objects, the most commonly tracked objects are processor, memory, disk access, and network access related. These areas are more likely to cause bottlenecks on your system and should be carefully monitored.

Processor

If you are using CPU intensive applications, the processor may become a bottleneck. The counters you should track are listed in Table 6.1.

	Object	Counter	Description	Desired Value
TABLE 6.1 Key Processor Counters to Track through Performance Monitor	Processor	%Processor Time	The percentage of the time the processor is busy performing useful tasks.	Below 80 percent
	Processor	Interrupts per second	This is the number of device interrupts the processor is handling each second.	Below 3,500 on a Pentium or RISC computer
	System	Processor Queue Length	The number of outstanding requests in the processor has in the queue.	Under two

If you suspect that you have a processor bottleneck, the first step is to determine which applications are causing the greatest server load, and if possible, determine whether the application is functioning properly. If the applications are functioning properly, you may need to upgrade your processor or add more processors to you computer if the computer has multi-processor capability.

If you determine that processor usage is too high, ensure insufficient physical RAM does not cause the excessive loading. Excessive page file accesses will increase processor utilization.

Memory

The most common bottleneck NT computers encounter is lack of memory. The goal is to use physical memory as efficiently as possible, and to minimize the page file usage. The counters that are most important to track are listed in Table 6.2.

	Object	Counter	Description	Desired Value
T A B L E 6.2 Key Memory Counters to Track through Performance Monitor	Memory	Available Bytes	Displays the amount of virtual RAM that is currently available.	4 MB or 10 percent of physical memory, whichever is higher
	Memory	Pages/sec	This counter is used to determine the number of pages read or written from disk because physical RAM was not able to accommodate the memory related request. This counter is used to identify if excessive paging is occurring.	20 or lower

If you determine that you have a memory bottleneck, the best solution is to add more physical RAM.

Disk Access

Disk counters are tracked through the Physical Disk and Logical Disk objects. Physical Disk relates to the physical hard drive. For example, you might have two physical hard drives, Drive 0 and Drive 1. Logical Disk refers to the disk partition. For example, Disk 0 might be broken down into Logical Drive C: and Logical Drive D:. Logical Disk counters track disk partitions.

Don't forget the special activation requirements for Disk counters, using the DISKPERF command. See the discussion in the following section. Without this activation, all Disk counters will remain at zero.

Table 6.3 defines the counters you should add to monitor your disks performance.

	Object	Counter	Description	Desired Value
TABLE 6.3 Key Disk Counters to Track through Performance Monitor	LogicalDisk	Average Disk Queue Length	This is the average number of outstanding requests that the disk is waiting to process. This number should not exceed two.	0-2
	LogicalDisk	% Disk Time	This is the percentage of time that the disk is busy processing read or write requests.	Under 50 percent

If you suspect that the disk channel is the bottleneck, you can take the following actions:

- Use RAID 0 to take advantage of disk striping (RAID 5 is only available on NT Servers).
- Add disk controllers for each physical drive.
- Use faster disks and disk controllers.
- Balance heavily used files by moving them to a less frequently used disk channel.

Network Access

You can monitor your network statistics through the NetBEUI, TCP/IP, and NWLink objects. The objects you track are dependent on the protocols you use. The discussion of each object and its associated protocol is beyond the scope of the exam.

If you suspect your network channel is the bottleneck, you should take the following action:

- Buy network adapter cards that take advantage of the full bus width on your computer.

- Segment busy networks into two or more subnets.

Enabling Specific Counters in Performance Monitor

Performance Monitor does not track all counters by default. You must run command line utilities or install additional services to see disk counters, network interface statistics, and network statistics.

Disk Counters

NT does not track disk counters by default. To enable disk counters within Performance Monitor, run **DISKPERF -y** from a command prompt, then restart the computer.

Disk counters remain enabled unless you issue the **DISKPERF -n** command and restart the computer.

Network Interface Statistics

To see the Network Interface object in Performance Monitor, you must install the Simple Network Management Protocol (SNMP) service on your NT computer.

You can use the Network Interface object to view the number of bytes that are sent or received by your computer.

You can also configure the SNMP service to send trap messages to an SNMP console. This protocol is used to manage and maintain TCP/IP network information.

Network Segment Statistics

To analyze network traffic, you must install the Network Monitor Agent service. When you install this service, you see an object called Network Segment within Performance Monitor. This object tracks the following counters:

- %Broadcast frames

- %Multicast frames

- %Network utilization
- Broadcast frames received/second
- Multicast frames received/second
- Total bytes received/second
- Total frames received/second

Optimizing System Performance

In the last section, you learned how to optimize system performance for processor, memory, disk subsystem, and the network subsystem. Two other areas you can optimize for system performance are disk performance and the page file.

Optimizing Disk Performance

To optimize NT Workstation disk performance, consider configuring multiple physical drives into a stripe set or software implementation of RAID 0. A stripe set combines disk space from multiple drives into a single logical drive. Data is written evenly across the stripe set, thus improving performance by utilizing multiple disk channels. You can see what disk striping would look like in Figure 6.4.

F I G U R E   6.4

Disk striping
illustration

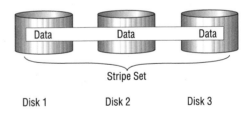

Disk 0
System
and boot partition

Stripe Set

Disk 1   Disk 2   Disk 3

The system and boot partition cannot be a part of a stripe set, and the page file cannot be stored on a stripe set.

If any drive within a stripe set fails, all drives are unavailable. Disk striping offers no fault tolerance, so make sure you maintain current backups.

Optimizing the Page File

You can optimize the page file in many ways:

- Spread the page files over multiple physical disks (but not on a stripe set or the system or boot partition).

- Place the page files on less frequently used disks.

- Place page files on high performance disk channels.

You can configure the size and location of the page file through Control Panel ➢ System ➢ Performance ➢ Virtual Memory ➢ Change button, as shown in Figure 6.5.

F I G U R E 6.5

Virtual Memory
dialog box

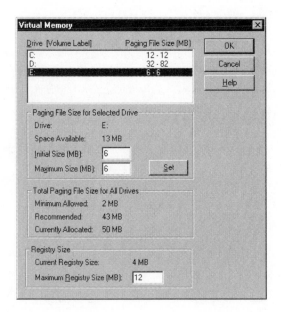

This concludes the monitoring and optimization unit.

Monitoring System Performance

1. List the two utilities that are used with NT computers to monitor memory and processor utilization.

_____

_____

2. True/False: You can start or stop applications through Task Manager.

3. True/False: You can start or stop applications through Performance Monitor.

4. You must run the _____ command to enable the disk counters within Performance Monitor.

5. If the % Processor Time counter is _____ percent or higher, a performance bottleneck may be indicated.

6. A _____ is created whenever an application is run. It is the combination of an executable program, the memory an application uses, and one or more threads.

7. A _____ is the smallest unit of data that can be executed by the microkernel.

8. If the Memory object, Pages/sec counter is over _____, a memory bottleneck may be indicated.

STUDY QUESTIONS

9. What two steps can you take to improve performance if a processor bottleneck is indicated?

_____

_____

10. What service must you install if you want to collect network segment statistics?

_____

11. What service must you install if you want to send trap messages that can be used to manage and maintain TCP/IP network statistics?

_____

12. True/False: If the System object, Processor Queue length is above two, then a processor bottleneck is indicated.

13. If the LogicalDisk object, %Disk Time counter is above _____
percent, a disk access bottleneck may be indicated.

14. What is the best solution to manage excessive paging?

_____

15. True/False: A volume set improves disk access performance.

Optimizing System Performance

16.   What disk configuration allows you to optimize disk performance on NT Workstations?

_____

17.   True/False: You can optimize disk performance by using a volume set.

18.   True/False: You can implement stripe sets with parity (RAID 5) on NT Workstations.

19.   True/False: To improve system performance, the page file should be located on the same partition as the system and boot partition.

20.   How do you configure the page files on NT computers?

_____

21.   True/False: You should place the page files on the most frequently used disk drives for best performance.

22.   True/False: If a stripe set fails on an NT Workstation, the other disks within the stripe set are not accessible.

6-1 You are running HP Openview on your NT Server. You want to capture and forward trap messages from your NT Workstation to this server. What service must you install on the NT Workstation?

    A. Network Monitor Agent

    B. SNMP

    C. Simple TCP/IP Services

    D. SAP Agent

6-2 You are trying to determine how much bandwidth is being used on your network. What service allows you to capture any packets that are transmitted to your NT Workstation?

    A. Network Monitor Agent

    B. SNMP

    C. Simple TCP/IP Services

    D. SAP Agent

6-3 Your computer is configured with four hard drives. The first hard drive contains the system and boot partition. The other drives each have a single partition and store application and data files. What is the best way to optimize the paging file for this computer?

    A. Create a single page file. Place the page file on the drive that contains the system and boot partition.

    B. Create a single page file. Configure the page file so it spans all four physical drives.

    C. Create three page files. Place the page file on each of the drives, except the drive that contains the system and boot partition.

    D. Create four page files. Place the page file on each of the four drives.

6-4   When the NT microkernel processes an application or program, what is the smallest unit that can be scheduled?

    A. A thread

    B. An object

    C. A process

    D. An operation

6-5   You notice your computer is performing slowly. What utilities can you use to view your memory and processor usage? Choose two answers:

    A. Windows NT Diagnostics

    B. Event Viewer

    C. Performance Monitor

    D. Task Manager

6-6   You use Performance Monitor to see how well your NT Workstation is performing. After running Performance Monitor for two days, you notice that excessive paging is occurring. The computer is configured with a SCSI adapter and four physical hard drives. The computer is a Pentium 120 Mhz with 32MB of RAM. What is the best solution to this problem?

    A. You need to increase the paging file size.

    B. You should create multiple page files on each hard disk, except the disk that contains the system and boot partition.

    C. You should upgrade the processor or add a second processor.

    D. You should add more memory to the computer.

6-7 What must you do to enable disk counters within Performance Monitor?

 A. You must run **DISKPERF -y** from the command prompt and restart the computer.

 B. You must install and start the DISKPERF service.

 C. You must run **DISKCOUNT -y** from the command prompt and restart the computer.

 D. You must install and start the DISKCOUNT service.

6-8 You are trying to see how your network interface is performing. After completing some research, you decide to track the Network Interface object, Bytes Received/sec and Bytes Sent/sec counters. When you try and configure Performance Monitor, this object is not listed. What service must you install on your NT Workstation?

 A. Network Monitor Agent

 B. SNMP

 C. Simple TCP/IP Services

 D. SAP Agent

6-9 When monitoring the Processor, if %Processor Utilization counter is above _____ percent, a processor bottleneck may be indicated.

 A. 25

 B. 40

 C. 50

 D. 80

6-10 Which of the following disk configurations would you choose for your NT Workstation if performance were your primary criteria?

    A. Volume set

    B. Disk mirroring

    C. Disk striping

    D. Disk striping with parity

6-11 You run Performance Monitor and see that the Memory object, Pages/Sec counter is averaging 12. What bottleneck is indicated?

    A. You need to upgrade the processor.

    B. You need to increase the size of the paging file.

    C. You need to add more memory.

    D. There is no bottleneck indicated.

6-12 Which of the following steps would you take if you were trying to optimize the NT page file? Choose all that apply:

    A. Place the paging file on the hard drive that contains the system and boot partition.

    B. Place the paging file on a stripe set for best performance.

    C. If possible, create multiple page files, spread over multiple physical disks.

    D. If possible, create multiple page files, spread over multiple logical disks.

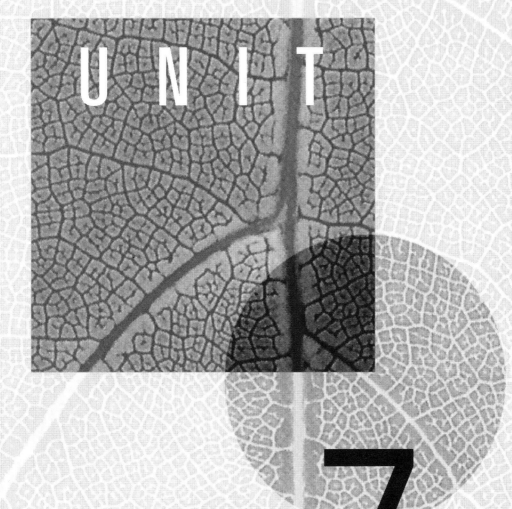

UNIT

7

Troubleshooting

Test Objectives: Troubleshooting

- Choose the appropriate course of action to take when the boot process fails.

- Choose the appropriate course of action to take when a print job fails.

- Choose the appropriate course of action to take when the installation process fails.

- Choose the appropriate course of action to take when an application fails.

- Choose the appropriate course of action to take when a user cannot access a resource.

- Modify the Registry using the appropriate tool in a given situation.

- Implement advanced techniques to resolve various problems.

Exam objectives are subject to change at any time without prior notice and at Microsoft's sole discretion. Please visit Microsoft's Training & Certification website (www.microsoft.com/Train_Cert) for the most current exam objectives listing.

roubleshooting is a daily occurrence for most NT MCSEs. This unit will not prepare you for every problem you may encounter, but does cover some of the more common problems you may see, as well as possible solutions to those problems.

Troubleshooting a Failed Boot Process

The NT boot process could fail for many reasons, but in most cases it fails due to BOOT.INI file errors, missing or corrupted boot files, and hardware configuration errors. This section provides an overview of the problems that may occur in the boot process on Intel platforms through:

- An overview of the boot process
- The NT boot files
- Using the Emergency Repair Disk (ERD)
- The Last Known Good Option in the boot sequence

Overview of the NT Boot Process

When NT boots, the following steps occur:

1. The Power On Self Test (POST) runs on the computer.

2. The master boot record (MBR) is located and loaded. The MBR is scanned for the active partition and the boot sector from the active partition is loaded.

3. The boot sector specifies that the NTLDR be loaded and initialized. The NTLDR file specifies that the processor use a 32-bit memory model.

4. NTLDR starts the mini file system that will be used to boot NT from the system partition. Mini file systems include FAT and NTFS.

5. NTLDR accesses the BOOT.INI file. The BOOT.INI file is used to specify the choices that are seen in the boot loader menu that is displayed during the NT boot sequence. This includes the option to boot NT Workstation, NT Workstation VGA mode, or any operating systems previously installed.

6. When booting to NT, NTLDR then calls NTDECTECT.COM, which scans for hardware installed on the computer. The information that is collected is passed on to the Registry.

7. NTLDR then loads NTOSKERNEL.EXE. At this point the Hardware Abstraction Layer (HAL) is loaded and the Registry is scanned for any drivers or services that should be loaded. During this stage of the NT boot process, you see a blue screen across the top of the screen with the operating system build number, last service pack installed, processor type and number, and physical RAM identified.

8. The kernel initialization phase begins and drivers are initialized.

9. The services load phase begins and the session manager is loaded. AUTOCHK.EXE is run, which checks each disk partition. The page file is set up and any subsystems are loaded.

10. When the WIN32 subsystem is installed, the WINLOGON process starts and the user sees the press Ctrl+Alt+Del message to start the logon process.

11. Any services that are still waiting to start are initialized at this point. The NT boot process is complete as the configuration is then copied to the Clone control set to update the Last Known Good option for subsequent system boots.

NT Boot Files

Corrupt or missing boot files can cause boot errors. In troubleshooting boot failures, you must first identify which file is causing the boot error, then correct the problem.

Boot File Descriptions

The primary files that are used to boot NT on an Intel platform are:

- NTLDR
- BOOT.INI
- BOOTSECT.DOS

- NTDETECT.COM
- NTOSKRNL.EXE

These files are described in the following subsections.

NTLDR   This file is used to control the NT boot process.

BOOT.INI   This configuration file is responsible for building the menu choices that are displayed upon boot up. It is the only file that the end user can modify to directly control the boot process. If you select an NT option, it also provides the location on the boot partition that NT is installed on. The BOOT.INI file has two main sections. The boot loader and the operating systems sections.

The boot loader section is used to specify which operating system is selected by default and how long the boot process waits before the default selection will be chosen.

The operating system section lists the operating systems you select during the boot process. Each line in the operating system selection contains a description of the operating system and the Advanced RISC Computing (ARC) path to the location of the operating systems boot partition.

You can configure the boot loader section through the BOOT.INI file or through the Control Panel ➢ System ➢ Startup/Shutdown configuration tab. Remember that it is stored as a read-only file.

BOOTSECT.DOS   This file is used to load any DOS-compliant operating system that was installed prior to NT. This file is loaded if you choose an alternate operating system that would expect to see a DOS environment during the boot process.

NTDETECT.COM   This file is used to detect installed hardware and add the hardware it detects to the Registry.

NTOSKRNL.EXE   This is the NT kernel.

If you are using a SCSI controller with the BIOS disabled, you also need the NTBOOTDD.SYS file.

Boot File Error Messages

If the any of the boot files are missing or corrupt, you will see the following error messages:

NTLDR
```
    Boot: Couldn't find NTLDR.
    Please insert another disk.
```

BOOT.INI
```
    Windows NT could not start because the following file is
    missing or corrupt:
    \winnt root\system32\ntoskrnl.exe
    Please re-install a copy of the above file.
```

BOOTSECT.DOS
```
    I\O Error accessing boot sector file multi(0)disk(0)rdisk(0)
    partition(1):\bootsect.dos
```

NTDETECT.COM
```
    NTDETECT v1.0 Checking Hardware…
    NTDETECT v1.0 Checking Hardware…
```

NTOSKRNL.EXE
```
    Windows NT could not start because the following file is
    missing or corrupt:
    winnt root\system32\ntoskrnl.exe
    Please re-install a copy of the above file.
```

If you use Disk Administrator and your system fails to boot, suspect the BOOT.INI file first. By adding logical partitions, you can cause the ARC name to change. When using Disk Administrator, pay careful attention to the exit messages, because you will be warned if the BOOT.INI needs to be edited, and if so, what the edits should be. Many times users ignore this message. If the BOOT.INI has the wrong ARC path name, then you will get the following message:

```
    Windows NT could not start because of a computer disk hardware
    configuration problem. Could not read from the selected boot
    disk. Check boot path and disk hardware.
```

If the NT boot files are missing or corrupt, you can restore them through the emergency repair disk.

Emergency Repair Disk (ERD)

The ERD is used to create a snapshot of your system's configuration. To create an ERD, you use the RDISK command. The ERD is not bootable, and is used in conjunction with the NT Startup disks. When you use the Startup disks, you choose the repair option, and insert the ERD when prompted.

You can then use the emergency repair disk to perform the following operations:

- Inspect the Registry files

- Inspect the startup environment

- Verify the NT system files

- Inspect the boot sector

Whenever you make changes to your computer's configuration—for example, adding or deleting disk partitions through Disk Administrator—you should always update your ERD.

Recovery of NT Boot Files

If any of your boot files are missing or corrupt, you can repair the failure through the emergency repair disk (ERD). To repair your boot files, you need the three NT setup disks and the ERD.

- If you do not already have the setup disks you can create them from the Windows NT Workstation CD by typing **WINNT /ox**.

- To create the ERD, you type **RDISK** from a command prompt on the computer the ERD is being created for.

The steps to recover your boot files are as follows:

1. Boot with the NT Setup Boot disks. Insert Disk 1 and Disk 2 when prompted.

2. When prompted, choose R for Repair.

3. Insert Setup Disk 3 when prompted.

4. As requested, insert the ERD.

5. Select the Verify Windows NT system files option.

6. Select the components you wish to restore.

At this point, your NT boot files should be properly restored.

Contents of the ERD

The ERD contains the following:

- An information file that can be used to verify and re-create the NT boot files

- The SAM

- Portions of the Registry that relate to the computers configuration

- The CONFIG.NT and AUTOEXEC.NT configuration files

The files on the ERD are compressed and can be expanded through the EXPAND command line utility.

To force the entire Registry to be saved to the ERD, you should use RDISK /s. This assumes that the Registry is not so large that it is able to be compressed and still fit on the ERD disk.

The Last Known Good Option

Each time a user successfully logs on, the system boot information is stored in the Registry. The purpose of Last Known Good is that it allows you to recover from system failures caused by incorrect system configuration change or an incompatible driver.

To access the Last Known Good option, a user hits the space bar when prompted during the boot process. The system can also access the Last Known Good option if a serious or critical error keeps the computer from successfully booting.

Troubleshooting Failed Print Jobs

Print errors have many causes. To troubleshoot a printer error, you should first try and isolate where the problem is occurring within the print process. The print process is composed of the following areas:

1. A shared printer is created on a print server by the administrator.

2. A client makes a connection to the shared printer.

3. The client generates a print job and sends it to the shared printer.

4. The print server receives the job spools, and possibly renders (processes) the job.

5. The print server directs the job to the print device.

6. The print device prints the job.

NT installs printer drivers for NT 3.x and 4.0 for all CPU types and Windows 95 only. Additional operating system printer drivers must be added separately. Some common print errors that you might encounter are listed in Table 6.1 along with possible solutions.

T A B L E 7.1 Common Print Problems and Solutions	Error	Possible Solution
	The print job is printed as garbage, or prints with strange characters or fonts.	Make sure the correct print driver is installed on the print server for the operating system on the client workstation.
	Win16 applications report that they are out of memory or you are unable to select any fonts.	A default printer has not been selected.
	Hard disk is thrashing and print jobs are not being sent to the print device.	Make sure that the disk has sufficient space to allow for spool file expansion; if not, move the spool file to another location.
	Jobs are reaching the server and not printing, or are not reaching the print server.	Stop and restart the spooler service.

You can also manage print jobs from the printer dialog screen. Each printer lists the jobs that are waiting to be serviced by the printer. Users can remotely manage jobs from other Windows NT or 95 operating systems, but are limited to only those jobs that they have created or have access to. Through the Document configuration, you can control print jobs through:

- **Pause:** Pause allows you to temporarily stop a print job from printing.

- **Resume:** Resume starts the print job at the point where it left off.

- **Restart:** Restart causes a print job to be resubmitted from the beginning.

- **Properties:** Allows you to configure properties of the print job such as notification, priority, and scheduling.

Troubleshooting Failed Installations

Installation errors can have many causes. Some of the common causes are:

- **Media errors:** You could have a bad floppy or the NT Server CD may be corrupt. If you suspect that you have media errors, try a different set of setup disks or another NT Workstation CD. To recreate the NT Setup disks, use the NT Workstation CD and the command WINNT /ox.

- **Hardware that is not on the HCL (Hardware Compatibility List):** NT is picky about the hardware it uses. You should verify that all of the hardware you are using is on the HCL.

- **CD is not supported by Windows NT:** If your CD is supported under another operating system such as DOS or Windows 95, you can boot that operating system and copy the contents of the NT CD (on an Intel platform this would be the I386 folder) to the hard drive or to a shared network drive. The installation is then run from the local or network drive. The CD is still unavailable from the NT operating system until an NT driver can be installed.

- **Incorrect hardware configuration:** Check hardware components such as network card, video adapter, sound card, modems, etc. for configuration settings. There must be no overlap in IRQ, base memory, base i/o addresses, or DMA. In addition, the software configurations must match the hardware configurations.

- **Blue screen or stop messages:** Blue screen or stop messages during installation can be caused by incorrect or outdated drivers being initialized.
One common problem is that NT cannot detect the mass storage (disk)
driver correctly. If this is a problem, don't let NT auto-detect your mass
storage device. Instead, manually identify the mass storage you are using,
and provide the correct driver. You should be able to get the correct
driver from the manufacturers web site.

 NT 4.0 does not support plug-and-play. If your installation depends on plug-
and-play hardware, you may have problems in this area.

Troubleshooting Failed Applications

NT ships with a utility called Dr. Watson, which is used to diagnose and
log application errors. To access the Dr. Watson utility, you type **DRWTSN32**
from Run or through a command prompt. You then see the dialog box shown
in Figure 7.1.

FIGURE 7.1

Dr. Watson dialog
screen

Through this utility you can specify whether a crash dump file will be created upon an application failure and what the location of the crash file will be.

Troubleshooting Resource Access Problems

If you are having trouble accessing a resource, the most common problem is that the user account does not have the appropriate access permissions. The following subsections provide suggestions to help you troubleshoot access of local and network resources.

File and Directory Access

If you're accessing a resource locally, you should determine if the resource is on a FAT or NTFS partition.

- If the partition is FAT, then you know the problem does not relate to access permissions.

- If the partition is NTFS, the problem may be related to access permissions.

Figure 7.2 is used to illustrate some common access problems.

- Brenda is a member of Sales and Sales Temps. Because Sales Temps has been assigned No Access, Brenda will have No Access regardless of permissions she has been assigned through her membership in Sales.

- Dana is a member of Sales. She tries to access E:\DATA\SUBDIR. When she tries to access the folder she is denied. When the administrator set up the permissions, the Replace Permissions on Subdirectories box was not checked. This is the default NTFS directory setting.

- Ron has been a member of the Sales group. He was recently promoted to a manager and added to the Sales Managers group. However, when he accesses the E:\DATA folder, he can only Read data. Ron needs to log out and logon again to have his access token updated with his new membership.

FIGURE 7.2

NTFS Permissions
example

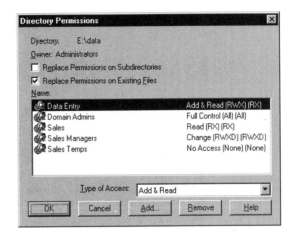

Editing the Registry

The Registry is a hierarchical database used to store NT configuration information. It is made up of five main subtrees which include:

- HKEY_USERS
- HKEY_CURRENT_CONFIG
- HKEY_CLASSES_ROOT
- HKEY_CURRENT_USER
- HKEY_LOCAL_MACHINE

You can view and modify the information that is stored within the Registry through the Registry Editor. NT 4.0 ships with two utilities that can be used to edit the Registry, REGEDT32 and REGEDIT.

REGEDT32

The REGEDT32 application is a 32-bit Registry Editor and is designed for NT. This utility provides better support for NT and has more safeguards to prevent accidental or inadvertent changes. Unless you are using the search capabilities of REGEDIT, this is the preferred utility to use when editing the registry.

REGEDIT

The REGEDIT Registry editor is from the Windows 95 operating system and is included with NT. REGEDIT has better search capabilities than REGEDT32. REGEDIT can search for keys and text. REGEDT32 can only search based on keys.

You should always use the Registry Editors with caution. Incorrect settings can cause serious system malfunctions and can even cause NT to hang. Before editing the Registry, you should always back it up with the NT Backup program. If the system won't boot after editing the Registry, you should first try the Last Known Good option. If this does not correct the problem, you can then use the backup you previously created to restore a known good Registry.

Advanced Problem Resolution

Through advanced problem resolution, you will learn how to create a memory dump, use the Event Viewer, restore the Administrator password, troubleshoot RAS errors, and troubleshoot display errors.

Creating a Memory Dump

You can configure NT to create a memory dump if a blue screen is generated. To create a memory dump, access Control Panel ➤ System ➤ Startup/Shut-down property tab, as shown in Figure 7.3.

To configure NT to create the dump file, you check the Write debugging information to: box. By default the dump file is created in %SystemRoot%\ Memory.dmp.

To create a dump file, you must have a paging file on the boot partition that is at least 2MB larger than the amount of RAM installed on the NT Server.

FIGURE 7.3

Control Panel ➤
System ➤ Startup/
Shutdown property
tab dialog box

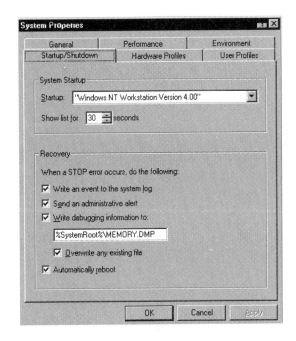

The Event Viewer

The Event Viewer is used in NT to provide informational logs regarding your computer. Three different logs are kept which include:

- **System:** This log is used to provide information about the NT operating system. You can see information such as hardware failures, software configuration errors, and the general well-being of your computer.

- **Security:** Contains information related to auditing. If you choose to enable auditing, you will see success or failure events related to auditing.

- **Application:** The application log contains errors from applications that are running on your server. For example, SQL errors would be logged here.

Within each log, events are recorded into one of five event categories. These include:

- Error
- Information

- Warning

- Success Audit

- Failure Audit

To access Event Viewer, select Start ➤ Programs ➤ Administrative Tools (Common) ➤ Event Viewer. Figure 7.4 shows an example of this screen.

FIGURE 7.4

Event Viewer
System Log

Date	Time	Source	Category	Event	User	Computer
12/5/96	7:12:58 PM	Print	None	10	Administrator	INSTRU
12/5/96	7:11:39 PM	Print	None	10	Administrator	INSTRU
12/4/96	6:55:12 PM	Print	None	10	Administrator	INSTRU
12/4/96	6:12:16 PM	Print	None	10	Administrator	INSTRU
12/4/96	6:07:44 PM	Wins	None	4097	N/A	INSTRU
12/4/96	6:07:03 PM	BROWSER	None	8015	N/A	INSTRU
12/4/96	6:07:00 PM	BROWSER	None	8015	N/A	INSTRU
12/4/96	6:06:58 PM	BROWSER	None	8015	N/A	INSTRU
12/4/96	6:06:38 PM	DhcpServer	None	1024	N/A	INSTRU
12/4/96	6:05:22 PM	EventLog	None	6005	N/A	INSTRU
12/4/96	2:24:39 PM	Service Control Mar	None	7023	N/A	INSTRU
12/4/96	2:24:13 PM	DhcpServer	None	1008	N/A	INSTRU
12/4/96	2:24:13 PM	DhcpServer	None	1006	N/A	INSTRU
12/4/96	2:24:11 PM	Wins	None	4165	N/A	INSTRU
12/4/96	2:24:11 PM	Service Control Mar	None	7023	N/A	INSTRU
12/4/96	2:24:11 PM	Wins	None	4193	N/A	INSTRU
12/4/96	2:23:38 PM	EventLog	None	6005	N/A	INSTRU
12/4/96	2:23:40 PM	Service Control Mar	None	7000	N/A	INSTRU
12/4/96	2:23:40 PM	NE2000	None	5003	N/A	INSTRU
12/4/96	2:21:39 PM	BROWSER	None	8033	N/A	INSTRU

By default, the oldest events are at the bottom of the list and the newest events are recorded at the top of the list. In the case of Figure 7.4, the bottom Stop message is related to NE2000. If you click on this entry, you will see more detailed information, as shown in Figure 7.5.

In this case, the reported error specifies that the NE2000 adapter could not be found. It is important to identify the first error, because subsequent errors are often dependencies that are corrected when you correct the initial problem.

In this example, the NE2000 card has been configured incorrectly. To correct the problem, you would verify the NT settings though Control Panel ➤ Network ➤ Adapters ➤ Properties with the actual configuration on your network card.

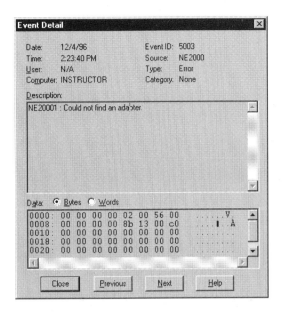

F I G U R E 7.5

Event Detail within
Event Viewer

Restoring the Administrator Password

The best way to restore a forgotten Administrator's password is to have a backup administrative account that you can logon with and change the Administrators password.

If this is not an option, you can restore the password by using the ERD or restoring a backup of the Registry. This assumes that you know the Administrator's password for when the ERD or backup was made.

If you restore the Administrator password through the ERD or backup, then any changes that have been made to the SAM since the backup was made will be lost.

Troubleshooting RAS Problems

You can use the following options to troubleshoot RAS problems:

Remote Access Monitor

You can use the Remote Access Monitor to view the status of your RAS ports, as well as the monitoring of incoming data, outgoing data, and any errors that have occurred.

DEVICE.LOG

The DEVICE.LOG file provides verbose information that you can use to diagnose RAS communication problems.

This file is enabled by editing the Registry so that the HKEY_LOCAL_MACHINE\SYSTEM\CurrentControlSet\Services\RasMan\Parameters\Logging value is set to 1.

You can then view this file through the \winnt root\system32\RAS folder in a file called DEVICE.LOG.

Troubleshooting Display Errors

Display errors should be minimized because NT forces you to test the driver you select. When the driver is tested, you can verify the color palette, the desktop area, and the refresh frequency. If any of these settings are incorrect, it could cause the display to be unreadable.

If this happens, you can select VGA mode from the NT boot screen. This will cause a standard VGA driver to be loaded.

This concludes the troubleshooting unit.

Troubleshooting a Failed Boot Process

1. The _____ file is used to load any alternate operating systems during the NT boot process.

2. The _____ file is used to build the menu that displays the operating systems you can select during the NT boot process.

3. The _____ file is used to detect any hardware that has been installed on your computer during the NT boot process.

4. The _____ file controls the NT boot process.

5. The _____ file is the NT kernel.

6. The following boot error message could be generated if either of these files were missing or corrupt:

```
Windows NT could not start because the following file is missing or corrupt:
\winnt root\system32\ntoskrnl.exe
Please re-install a copy of the above file.
```

_____

_____

7. What is the easiest way to recover missing or corrupt NT boot files?

_____

8. What command do you use to create or update an emergency repair disk?

_____

9. True/False: The ERD is a bootable disk.

10. What would cause the following error message to be displayed during the NT boot process?

```
I\0 Error accessing boot sector file
multi(0)disk(0)rdisk(0) partition(1):\bootsect.dos
```

_____

11. What additional boot file is required if you use a SCSI controller that has the BIOS disabled?

_____

12. What command can you use to create the NT Setup boot disks from a computer running the NT operating system?

_____

13. What is the main use of the Last Known Good option?

_____

14. True/False: The ERD files are stored in a compressed format by default.

15. What file would you most likely need to edit if you recently made changes to your disk configuration, and NT would not successfully reboot?

_____

16. List the four operations that can be completed through the use of the ERD.

_____

_____

_____

_____

17. True/False: The ERD contains a copy of the Workstation SAM.

Troubleshooting Failed Print Jobs

18. What would you do if you wanted to pause a print job, then finish the job from where it had left off?

_____

19. What is the most likely problem if your Win16 applications can't select any fonts when trying to submit a print job?

_____

20. What do you need to do to restart a print job that has already started printing, but that you want to start over again, without the user having to resubmit a new print job?

_____

21. What is the most likely problem if an NT printer prints a job as garbage or is printing with odd characters and fonts?

_____

22. What is the most likely problem if the hard disk is thrashing when you attempt to submit print jobs or the jobs are not being correctly sent to the print device?

_____

23. What is the most likely solution if jobs reach the print server, but are not printing correctly?

_____

Troubleshooting Failed Installations

24. What two options can you use to install NT Workstation if the CD you are using is accessible under another operating system, but is not accessible through NT?

_____

_____

25. To verify that your hardware will work with NT, you should make sure that all of your hardware components are on the _____ prior to NT installation.

26. True/False: NT 4.0 supports plug-and-play hardware.

27. When installing hardware, you should verify that the following four hardware settings are unique:

_____

_____

_____

_____

28. True/False: If the NT Workstation CD does not have the driver to support your hardware, you should select hardware that does have a driver on the Windows NT Workstation CD.

Troubleshooting Failed Applications

29. What utility do you use to diagnose application problems?

30. What command line utility is used to access the Dr. Watson utility?

Troubleshooting Resource Access Problems

31. True/False: If a resource has share and NTFS permissions applied, the NTFS permissions will be applied preferentially.

32. Terry is a member of the TECH WRITERS, EDITORS, and TEMPS groups. The D:\DATA folder has the following permissions applied:

TECH WRITERS	Full Control
EDITORS	Change
TEMPS	No Access

What are Terry's effective permissions for this folder?

33. Terry is a member of the TECH WRITERS, EDITORS, and TEMPS groups. The D:\DATA folder has the following permissions applied:

TECH WRITERS	Full Control
EDITORS	Change
TEMPS	Read

What are Terry's effective permissions for this folder?

_____

34. Terry is a member of the TECH WRITERS, EDITORS, and TEMPS groups. The D:\DATA folder has the following permissions applied. In addition the folder is shared as \\NTWS\DATA and has had share permissions applied.

	NTFS	Share
TECH WRITERS	Full Control	Read
EDITORS	Change	Read
TEMPS	Read	Read

What access does Terry have when she accesses this folder locally?

_____

35. Terry is a member of the TECH WRITERS, EDITORS, and TEMPS groups. The D:\DATA folder has the following permissions applied. In addition the folder is shared as \\NTWS\DATA and has had share permissions applied.

	NTFS	Share
TECH WRITERS	Full Control	Read
EDITORS	Change	Read
TEMPS	Read	Read

What access does Terry have when she accesses this folder over the network?

_____

36. If a user is added to a new group, what must happen so that the user can access resources to which the new group membership has permissions?

_____

37. True/False: If you assign permissions to an NTFS folder, the permissions will also apply to the subfolders below the folder where the permissions were assigned.

38. True/False: If you assign permissions to an NTFS folder, the permissions will also apply to the files within the NTFS folder.

Editing the Registry

39. What utility is the native NT Registry Editor?

_____

40. What utility ships with NT that allows you to search the Registry for keys, values, or data within the Registry?

_____

41. What is the most reliable form of Registry backup?

_____

42. If you make changes to the Registry and your computer will not reboot, what is the quickest way to attempt to get up and running again?

_____

Advanced Problem Resolution

43. You can use the _____ utility to view the status of RAS ports. It can also be used to monitor incoming data, outgoing data, and any errors that have occurred.

44. You can enable the _____ file through the Registry. This file provides verbose information that can be used to troubleshoot RAS connection problems.

45. How do you configure NT to create a dump file any time the operating system encounters a fatal error which causes NT to hang?

_____

46. List the three logs tracked through Event Viewer.

_____

_____

_____

47. List the five types of events that are recorded through Event Viewer.

_____

_____

_____

_____

_____

48. What happens if you restore a lost administrator password using the ERD?

_____

49. List three items that are tested when you install a display driver.

_____

_____

_____

┌───┐
│   **S A M P L E   T E S T**   │
└───┘

7-1   What course of action would you take if your NT system partition was corrupt and you needed to restore the NT boot files?

  A. Copy the boot files from the ERD.

  B. Edit the `BOOT.INI` file so that you use the `/ERD` option. When NT boots, supply the ERD when prompted.

  C. Boot the workstation to DOS. Copy the files from the \WINNT\System32 folder.

  D. Boot the workstation using the NT Setup disks. Select the Repair option when prompted and use the ERD to restore the missing or corrupt boot files.

7-2   You recently joined a company and have been allocated a computer that NT reports as being registered to John Smith. Since you are now using the computer, you want the registration to reflect your name. You know that you can change this through the Registry, but are not sure what key to change. What utility lets you search the Registry for the data string "John Smith"?

  A. `REGEDIT`

  B. `REGEDT32`

  C. NT Diagnostics ➤ Tools ➤ Registry Editor

  D. Server Manager ➤ Tools ➤ Registry Editor

7-3   You have just installed an updated driver for your network adapter card. When you restart your NT Workstation, you see a blue screen and the boot process will not successfully complete. What should your first course of action be?

  A. Boot the workstation using the NT Setup disks. Select the Repair option when prompted and use the ERD to restore the previous version of the network adapter driver.

  B. Edit the `BOOT.INI` file so that you use the `/ERD` option. When NT boots, supply the ERD when prompted. This lets you restore the previous version of the network adapter driver.

  C. Boot the workstation to DOS. Copy the correct driver to the \WINNT\System32 folder. Delete the driver that is causing the boot process to fail.

  D. When prompted during the boot process, use the Last Known Good option.

7-4 You are an applications developer who writes applications for the NT platform. One of your applications keeps failing and you need to create a crash dump file that will be used to trouble-shoot the problem. What should you configure in NT to create the dump file?

  A. Through Dr. Watson, activate the Create Crash Dump File option.

  B. Specify that you want to create a dump file through Control Panel ≻ System ≻ Startup/Shutdown tab by activating the Write debugging information to: option.

  C. Through Windows NT Diagnostics, activate the Create Crash Dump File option.

  D. Through the Event Viewer ≻ Tools, activate the Create Crash Dump File option.

7-5 Your NT Workstation keeps crashing and displaying blue screens on an intermittent basis. You suspect that the problem is caused by something in the NT operating system. You call Microsoft Technical Support and are asked to send in a memory dump file from a crash. How do you configure your computer to create this crash file?

  A. Through Dr. Watson, activate the Create Crash Dump File option.

  B. Specify that you want to create a dump file through Control Panel ≻ System ≻ Startup/Shutdown tab by activating the Write debugging information to: option.

  C. Through Windows NT Diagnostics, activate the Create Crash Dump File option.

  D. Through the Event Viewer ≻ Tools, activate the Create Crash Dump File option.

7-6 Your RAS connection is not being properly established with the RAS server. What file can you enable that will provide you with more verbose error messages?

  A. RASDEBUG.LOG

  B. DEBUG.LOG

  C. DEVICE.LOG

  D. RAS.LOG

7-7 You have an NT workgroup with a member server. The administrator of your company leaves without any notice. There is no other user who has been added to the Administrators group on the member server. You need to access the computer, so you restore the SAM with the ERD that was created when the server was installed. What will happen?

    A. The Administrator password will be set to the original password. All other accounts will be unaffected. The data will not be affected.

    B. The SAM will return to whatever was configured when the ERD was created. Any accounts that were created since the ERD was created will be lost. The data will not be affected.

    C. The Administrator password will be set to the original password. All other accounts will be unaffected. The data that has been created since the ERD was created will not be accessible.

    D. The SAM will return to whatever was configured when the ERD was created. Any accounts that were created since the ERD was created will be lost. The data that has been created since the ERD was created will not be accessible.

7-8 You created an NT boot disk that contains all the files needed to boot NT. This disk works on your computer. When you try and boot another computer using the boot diskette, you get the following error message:

```
Windows NT could not start because the following file is missing or corrupt:
\winnt root\system32\ntoskrnl.exe
Please re-install a copy of the above file.
```

What file is most likely causing the boot failure?

    A. NTLDR

    B. BOOT.INI

    C. NTOSKRNL.EXE

    D. WIN32.INI

7-9   Rick is a member of TEMPS, SALES, and SALES DATA. The \\SALES\DB share has the following permissions assigned:

TEMPS	No Access
SALES	Read
SALES DATA	Change
ADMINISTRATORS	Full Control

When Rick tries to access \\SALES\DB, he is denied access. He requires Change permission to be able to do his work. What is the most likely problem?

   A. Rick needs to log out and log back on to have his access token updated.

   B. Rick needs to be added to the ADMINISTRATORS group.

   C. Rick needs to be removed from the TEMPS group.

   D. Rick needs to be removed from the TEMPS and SALES groups.

7-10   When loading NT Workstation, your computer reports a STOP error because one or more services have failed to load. What utility will provide more information on the error?

   A. Windows NT Diagnostics

   B. Event Viewer

   C. Service Manager

   D. Server Manager

7-11   You are printing a report that requires a special continuous feed form. In the middle of the print job, the printer jams, and the form is torn. What do you need to do so that the job is resent from the beginning?

   A. From the Printers menu, choose Document ➤ Restart.

   B. From the Printers menu, choose Document ➤ Resume.

   C. From the Printer Management menu, choose Document ➤ Restart.

   D. From the Printer Management menu, choose Document ➤ Resume.

7-12 Your computer is configured to dual-boot between Windows 95 and NT Workstation. When you select the Windows 95 operating system during the NT boot process, you see the following error message:

```
I\O Error accessing boot sector file multi(0)disk(0)rdisk(0) partition(1):
\bootsect.dos
```

What file is most likely corrupt or missing?

   A. NTLDR

   B. BOOT.INI

   C. BOOTSECT.DOS

   D. WIN95.LDR

7-13 You have just used the REGEDT32 command to make some changes to your NT Workstations Registry. Now when you attempt to reboot your computer, NT will not properly start. What should be your first course of action?

   A. Boot the workstation using the NT Setup disks. Select the Repair option when prompted and use the ERD to restore the previous version of the Registry.

   B. Edit the BOOT.INI file so that you use the /ERD option. When NT boots, supply the ERD when prompted. This will allow you to restore the previous version of the Registry.

   C. Use the NT Backup program and restore the last Registry you backed up.

   D. When prompted during the boot process, use the Last Known Good option.

7-14   You are attempting to install NT Workstation on your home computer. The installation starts, but after NT reboots, the installation hangs. After some initial troubleshooting you determine that your CD player is recognized through DOS, but does not have an NT driver. You call the manufacturer of the CD drive and they tell you that a driver will be available within two weeks. What can you do to install NT Workstation in the meantime? Choose two answers.

    A. Boot your computer to DOS and copy the NT Workstation CD's \I386 folder to the hard drive. Run the WINNT command from the hard drive.

    B. Boot your computer to DOS and copy the NT Workstation CD's \I386 folder to a shared network drive. Run the WINNT command from the shared network drive.

    C. When running WINNT, use the /c switch. This will force the NT installation program to copy all the files the installation process will need before the computer is rebooted.

    D. When running WINNT, use the /x switch. This will force the NT installation program to copy all the files the installation process will need before the computer is rebooted.

7-15   You are about to make several changes to your NT Workstation's Registry. What step should you take?

    A. Use the ERD command to update your emergency repair disk.

    B. Use the RDISK command to update your emergency repair disk.

    C. Create a backup copy of the Registry through the NT Backup program.

    D. Use the NTBACKUP /r command line utility to create a backup of the Registry.

7-16   You have just made several changes to your computer's configuration and want to save them to the ERD. What command or utility do you use?

    A. Use the NT Diagnostics ➤ Tools ➤ Update Emergency Repair Disk option.

    B. Use the Event Viewer ➤ Tools ➤ Update Emergency Repair Disk option.

    C. Use the ERD command line utility.

    D. Use the RDISK command line utility.

7-17 You are attempting to use the ERD, but are unable to locate the NT Setup disks. How can you re-create these disks from a Windows 95 computer using the NT Workstation CD?

    A. Use the `WINNT /ox` command.

    B. Use the `WINNT32 /ox` command.

    C. Use the `SETUP /ox` command.

    D. Use the `SETUP32 /ox` command.

7-18 Your users are complaining that their print jobs are not printing. You check the Printer and see that the print jobs are there. This printer was working previously. What should you do?

    A. Reinstall the print driver. It is probably corrupt.

    B. Make sure that the spool file has enough disk space.

    C. Stop and restart the spooler service.

    D. Make sure that the users have a default printer selected.

7-19 Which of the following actions can you perform when using the ERD repair process? Choose all that apply.

    A. Inspect the Registry files

    B. Inspect and replace the MBR

    C. Verify the system files

    D. Inspect the boot sector

7-20 What file is required to boot NT Workstation if you are using a SCSI controller with the BIOS disabled?

    A. `SCSI.SYS`

    B. `NTBOOTDD.SYS`

    C. `SCSIBIOS.SYS`

    D. `SCSIBOOT.SYS`

SAMPLE TEST

7-21   You have just created a new printer. When you test the printer, the print job does not print correctly and appears to contain strange symbols and other errors. What should you do?

A. Reinstall the print driver. It is probably corrupt.

B. Make sure that the spool file has enough disk space.

C. Stop and restart the spooler service.

D. Make sure that you chose the correct print driver. The driver you selected is most likely not compatible with the print device.

7-22   Your users are complaining that their print jobs are not being sent to the printer. What is the most likely problem?

A. Reinstall the print driver. It is probably corrupt.

B. Make sure that the spool file has enough disk space.

C. Stop and restart the spooler service.

D. Make sure that you chose the correct print driver. The driver you selected is most likely not compatible with the print device.

7-23   You are trying to configure Dr. Watson to create a dump file in the event that you encounter application errors. What utility do you use to access the Dr. Watson utility?

A. DRWTSN.EXE

B. DRWTSN32.EXE

C. WATSON.EXE

D. WATSON32.EXE

7-24 Which log in the Event Viewer is used to view the status of auditing that has been enabled?

    A. System

    B. Auditing

    C. Security

    D. Application

7-25 Which items are tested and verified when you install a video driver? Choose all that apply.

    A. Color palette

    B. Desktop area

    C. Refresh frequency

    D. Font size

UNIT

8

Final Review

FINAL REVIEW

T hink you're ready for the exam yet? Here's a good way to find out. Grab your watch and take note of the time. The real exam will have about 50-55 questions with a 90 minute time limit. Currently you have to score about 70.5 percent or better to pass (705 on a scale of 1,000). These 55 questions are representative of what you'll see. Good Luck!

1 You installed your NT Workstation into a workgroup called WORKGROUP. You now want to join a domain called CORP. What step do you need to complete at the NT Workstation?

   A. From Control Panel ➤ Network ➤ Identification tab, specify that you want to join the CORP domain.

   B. Use Server Manager to specify that the workstation is now a part of the domain.

   C. From the Control Panel ➤ System ➤ Identification tab, specify that you want to join the CORP domain.

   D. Use the NT Diagnostics ➤ Identification tab to specify that the workstation is now a part of the domain.

2 You have a single print device that services jobs from the entire accounting department. Most of the documents are very short, but near month end, reports must be printed that are several hundred pages long. How should you configure this print environment?

   A. Create a printer called ACCT. Specify that users who send long print jobs should configure the print job to only be submitted after working hours.

   B. Create two logical printers, one called ACCT and one called REPORTS. Give the REPORTS printer a priority of 1 and the ACCT printer a priority of 99. Specify that normal jobs be sent to ACCT printer and long jobs be submitted to the REPORTS printer.

   C. Create two logical printers, one called ACCT and one called REPORTS. Give the REPORTS printer a priority of 99 and the ACCT printer a priority of 1. Specify that normal jobs be sent to ACCT printer and long jobs be submitted to the REPORTS printer.

   D. Create two logical printers, one called ACCT and one called REPORTS. Use the Schedule tab to specify that the REPORTS printer is only available during off-peak hours. Use the Scheduling tab to specify that the ACCT printer is available 24 hours a day. Specify that normal jobs be sent to ACCT printer and long jobs be submitted to the REPORTS printer.

3   You have noticed that your server seems to be running very slowly. You want to see what the processor and memory usage is. Which two utilities can you use?

    A. Performance Monitor

    B. Event Viewer

    C. Windows NT Diagnostics

    D. Task Manager

4   When you joined the company, you inherited a computer that had been used by a former employee named Kevin. Every time you press Control + Alt + Delete, you see a message that states:

`"Welcome to Kevin's computer"`

You want to delete this message. You know that it is a Registry entry, but you don't know the Registry location or key. What utility can you use to search the Registry for this string of text?

    A. REGEDT32

    B. REGEDIT32

    C. REGEDIT

    D. You cannot search for text strings through the Registry editor.

5   You want to configure your NT Workstation to act as an FTP server so that Internet clients can download files you provide. What two things should you install?

    A. SNMP

    B. TCP/IP

    C. IIS

    D. Microsoft Peer Web Services

    E. Internet Explorer

6 Your network consists of an NT Server configured as a PDC and 100 NT Workstations. You use TCP/IP as your main transport protocol. You want to automate your NT Workstations IP configuration as much as possible. What service or protocol should you install on your NT Server?

    A. DNS

    B. DHCP

    C. WINS

    D. IPCONFIG

7 You need to install NT Workstation on three computers and add them to the existing network. Each of the computers has a CD-ROM drive that connects through a sound card that is not on the HCL and does not have an NT driver. How should you install these computers?

    A. Boot from DOS, use `WINNT /c`. This copies all the NT installation files to the hard drive before the system reboots to NT.

    B. Boot from DOS, use `WINNT32 /c`. This copies all the NT installation files to the hard drive before the system reboots to NT.

    C. Boot from DOS, use `WINNT /v`. This copies all the NT installation files to the hard drive before the system reboots to NT.

    D. Copy the NT Workstation distribution files to a network share. Access the network share from the computers that need to have NT Workstation installed, and type `WINNT /S:<share path>` from the shared network drive.

8 Kate uses the NT Workstation called NTW1. She is a member of the USERS group. Kate wants to share a folder called C:\DATA. The C:\ partition is NTFS and Kate has Full Control to the entire C:\ partition. Which of the following statements is true? Choose all that apply:

    A. Because Kate has Full Control on the NTFS partition, she can create the share.

    B. Members of the Administrators group on the NT Workstation can create a share.

    C. Members of the Server Operators group on the NT Workstation can create a share.

    D. Members of the Power Users group on the NT Workstation can create a share.

FINAL   REVIEW

9   You have two 16-bit applications that are integrated with each other. In addition, you also use two other 16-bit applications that are independent applications. Sometimes, one of the integrated applications fails, causing all of the 16-bit applications to fail. How should you configure this computer for more fault tolerance?

   A. Configure each 16-bit application to run in its own memory space.

   B. Configure the integrated applications to use the default, shared memory space, and configure all other 16-bit applications to run in separate memory spaces.

   C. Configure the integrated applications to run in separate memory spaces, and configure all other 16-bit applications so they use the default, shared memory space.

   D. Allow all stable applications to run in the default shared memory space. Configure the application that fails to run in its own separate memory space.

10   Your NT Workstation connects to a NetWare printer through the CSNW redirector. Each time one of your jobs is sent, a banner is printed with your name and the name of your print job. Being an environmentalist, you consider this a waste of paper. How do you disable this feature?

   A. Through CSNW, disable the Print Banner option.

   B. On the NetWare print server, disable the Print Banner option.

   C. On the NetWare print queue, disable the Print Banner option.

   D. On the NetWare printer, disable the Print Banner option.

11   You have a computer at home running NT Workstation that has two modems attached to it. Your RAS server has several modems that you can dial into. You want to utilize both modems through multilink. The RAS server is configured so that it uses the Preset to: dialback option. How should you configure your NT Workstation?

   A. Create a phonebook entry for each phone line that you will dial into. Callback security will then call back both entries.

   B. Create one phonebook entry for both phone lines. When dialing into the RAS server, it will detect that you are using multilink and call back both of the phone numbers you have specified.

C. Create one phonebook entry for both phone lines. When dialing into the RAS server, it will detect that you are using multilink and call back only the first number that was specified.

D. You cannot use multilink if the callback feature has been set on the RAS server.

---

12 You have a folder called `D:\PAYROLL` that contains sensitive corporate data. You enable auditing on this folder so you can see any changes that are made within the folder. After editing several of the files, you check the audit log and notice that it is empty. What do you need to set to enable auditing in User Manager ➤ Policies ➤ Auditing?

A. File and object access

B. NTFS access

C. File and printer access

D. File and object tracking

---

13 You run a computer lab that tests application performance under different operating system platforms. You currently have a computer that is configured with NT Workstation 4.0. The system files are stored in `C:\WINNT`. The computer only contains a single drive that has a single partition. You want to install NT Server 4.0 on the same computer and be able to dual-boot between each operating system depending on the test that you are running. How should you install NT Server?

A. Delete the existing partition, and create two partitions, C:\ and D:\. Install NT Workstation on C:\ and NT Server on D:\.

B. Install both operating systems in the `C:\WINNT` directory. This allows both operating systems to use applications without installing them under each operating system. Edit the `BOOT.INI` file so you can choose which operating system you will boot to.

C. Install the NT Server on the existing partition, but make sure that you install it into another directory besides `C:\WINNT`, such as `C:\WINNTSRV`.

D. You need to add a second hard drive to the computer to support this configuration.

```
  ┌──────────────────────────┐
──┤    F I N A L   R E V I E W    ├──
  └──────────────────────────┘
```

14   Your NT Workstation is currently configured with a single NTFS partition on the C:\ drive. You want the computer to dual-boot between NT Workstation and Windows 95. To support the dual-boot environment, you need a FAT partition. What utility should you use?

    A. CONVERT C: /fs:FAT

    B. Use the Disk Administrator utility.

    C. UNCONVERT C: /fs:FAT

    D. Use the DOS FDISK utility to delete the partition, then use FORMAT with the /s option to make the drive bootable.

15   Your network consists of a mixture of NT Workstations and Macintosh computers. One of the Macintosh computers has a color printer attached to it that is shared. You want to connect to this printer. What protocol would you use to connect to this printer?

    A. DLC

    B. AppleTalk

    C. NetBEUI

    D. TCP/IP

16   Guy is the head of the accounting department. He recently decided to leave the company, and has given his two weeks notice. You have hired a replacement, Melissa, who will take over for Guy. You want Melissa to have all the permissions that Guy had, as well as ownership to any folders or files that Guy owns. What is the easiest way to accomplish this task?

    A. In User Manager, select Guy, then select Copy and create Melissa's account by copying Guy's user properties.

    B. Rename Guy's account to Melissa when Guy leaves.

    C. Create an account named Melissa that is a member of all of the groups that Guy belonged to. While logged in as Melissa, take ownership of any folders and files that Guy owned.

    D. In User Manager, select Guy, then select Clone and create Melissa's account by cloning Guy's user account.

FINAL REVIEW

17   Karen is a member of the ACCOUNTING, ACCOUNTING MANAGERS, and USERS groups. The following permissions have been applied to the D:\DATA folder which is on an NTFS partition.

ACCOUNTING	Change
ACCOUNTING MANAGERS	Full Control
USERS	No Access
EVERYONE	Read

What access does Karen have to this folder?

A. No Access

B. Read

C. Change

D. Full Control

18   Your user account is a member of the ADMINISTRATORS group. Sometimes you forget to lock your workstation when leaving your desk. How should you configure the computer so that if no activity is detected for five minutes, the workstation is protected?

A. Configure the Idle service to lock the computer if there is no activity within a five minute period.

B. Create a user profile that locks the computer if it is idle for more than five minutes.

C. Create a system policy that locks the computer if it is idle for more than five minutes.

D. Configure the screen saver so that it is password protected if there is no user activity after a five minute period.

19   You have just installed an updated driver for your SCSI adapter. At the end of the day, you shut down your computer. The next day, your computer will not successfully boot and only displays a blue screen. What is your first course of action?

A. Boot with the NT Workstation Setup disk and use the Repair option. Insert the ERD when prompted.

B. While booting, select the Last Known Good option.

C. Boot the computer to DOS, copy the correct driver to \WINNT\SYSTEM32\DRIVERS folder.

D. Use you last tape backup to restore the Registry from when the computer was still working.

20 What is the smallest unit of work that is processed by the NT operating system?

A. Thread

B. Process

C. Byte

D. Bit

21 Which of the following statements are true of DOS and Win16 applications?

A. By default, DOS applications run in separate VDM memory spaces.

B. By default, Win16 applications run in separate VDM memory spaces.

C. By default, DOS applications run in a shared VDM memory space.

D. By default, Win16 applications run in a shared VDM memory space.

22 You are running Performance Monitor on your NT Workstation and notice that excessive paging is occurring. What is the best solution to this problem?

A. Increase the page file.

B. Upgrade the processor to a faster processor.

C. Add more memory to the computer.

D. Spread the page file over multiple physical disks.

FINAL REVIEW

23   You're installing NT Workstation on a new computer. You do not yet have the network card, but are planning on buying an NE2000 compatible Ethernet card. You want to install networking support for the computer. How should you install NT on the computer?

  A. Choose the NE2000 driver, but do not bind any protocols to the driver until the network card is installed.

  B. Choose the NE2000 driver. Choose the protocols you will use and bind them to the driver. When the network card is installed, you will be ready to go.

  C. Choose the Loopback driver. This lets you install any protocols you wish to use. When the network card is installed, you can then configure the correct driver and bindings.

  D. Don't install any networking components. When you get the network card installed, then you can install all of the components you need to support networking.

24   Your computer is configured as follows:

Drive 0
C:\
System partition

Drive 1
D:\
Boot partition
Data drive

Due to a virus, all files on the C:\ drive have become corrupt. In the process of cleaning the files, several of the boot files were deleted. What is the easiest way to recover these files?

  A. Copy the files from the ERD.

  B. Boot the workstation and use the Last Known Good option.

  C. Boot the workstation with the Setup disk and use the Repair option.

  D. Boot the workstation to DOS and use the WINNT /r with the workstation CD to replace the missing files.

25   You have four SCSI drives on your NT Workstation that are each 4GB. You want to configure the computer for optimal speed. Which of the following configurations do you use?

    A. Configure the first drive to be the system and boot partition, and configure the other three drives as a volume set.

    B. Configure the first drive to be the system and boot partition, and configure the other three drives as a stripe set.

    C. Configure all four drives to be a volume set.

    D. Configure all four drives to be a stripe set.

26   You are configuring your NT Workstation using the TCP/IP protocol. The workstation will communicate with computers on the local subnet and on remote subnets. What IP configuration is required? Choose all that apply:

    A. IP address

    B. Fully Qualified Domain Name (FQDN)

    C. Subnet mask

    D. Default gateway

    E. Frame type

    F. IP domain name

27   Your NT Workstation keeps blue screening whenever you are running a specific accounting application. You are working with the application vendor to try and resolve the problem. The application vendor has asked you to send a memory dump the next time the failure occurs. How do you configure this?

    A. Configure the memory dump from Control Panel ➤ System.

    B. Configure the memory dump from Control Panel ➤ Server.

    C. Configure the Dr. Watson utility to create the memory dump.

    D. Configure the Windows NT Diagnostics utility to create a memory dump.

28 Your network uses the NetBEUI and the NWLink IPX/SPX protocols. You have just received a HP Network printer. What protocol will the print server and the printer use?

    A. NetBEUI

    B. NWLink IPX/SPX

    C. TCP/IP

    D. DLC

29 You are upgrading a computer that has been running OS/2 to NT Workstation. The computer currently uses a HPFS partition. How should you install this computer?

    A. Install NT using the HPFS partition.

    B. Change the partition to FAT before installing the NT Workstation.

    C. Change the partition to NTFS before installing the NT Workstation.

    D. Upgrade the partition to NTFS during the NT Workstation installation.

30 You are printing a document that requires a multi-part continuous form. As the job is printing, the print device becomes jammed. You insert a new form, and want to start the job from the beginning. What do you do from the Print Monitor?

    A. Click on Document ➤ Resume printing.

    B. Click on Document ➤ Restart print job.

    C. Click on Printer ➤ Resubmit print job.

    D. Click on Print Spooler ➤ Restart print job.

31 You suspect that someone is attempting to logon at your NT Workstation when you are not there. You enable auditing for logon success and failure and see that there are many unsuccessful logon attempts. What should you configure to help prevent unauthorized access?

   A. Configure Account Lockout in the Account Policies through User Manager.

   B. Specify that all user accounts use 12 character passwords through the Account Policies in User Manager.

   C. Specify that all user accounts must change their passwords every 30 days through the Account Policies in User Manager.

   D. Configure Intruder Detection in the Account Policies through User Manager.

32 What command do you use to start a 16-bit application called `APP.EXE` in its own memory space in a maximized window?

   A. `START /max /separate APP.EXE`

   B. `CMD /max /separate APP.EXE`

   C. `NET START /max /separate APP.EXE`

   D. `RUN /max /separate APP.EXE`

33 You need to install 50 NT Workstations. Each workstation should have the NT operating system installed and all of the applications that your company has chosen as the corporate standard. Each of the computers is using the same hardware configuration. What utility can you use to automate the installation of the applications?

   A. `sysdiff.exe`

   B. `windiff.exe`

   C. `setup.inf`

   D. `sysdiff.udf`

34 Your network consists of a domain with a PDC and 50 NT Workstations. You have created a system policy file for the Domain Users group and checked the Remove Run command from Start menu option. The system policy file is stored in the Netlogon share. Most of the users are restricted by this policy, but some users are not being restricted by this option. You do not have any BDCs in your domain. What is the most likely cause?

    A. The users have computer policies that conflict with this setting.

    B. The users have a user profile that conflicts with this setting.

    C. The users have a user policy defined, so the group policy is not being used.

    D. The users are not configured to use the system policy file through the user properties in User Manager for Domains.

35 You have just installed a RAS client on your NT Workstation that is dialing into a RAS server. You cannot get the RAS client to connect properly and are trying to see diagnostic information about the connection. What do you use on the RAS server?

    A. The Remote Access Admin utility

    B. Windows NT Diagnostics

    C. RAS Diagnostics utility

    D. Control Panel ➤ Network ➤ RAS ➤ Properties ➤ Status button

36 You suspect that there may be security breaches on your NT Workstation. The possibility exists that unauthorized users are accessing your computer and accessing sensitive data. You enable auditing on your computer. You want John to monitor your audit logs. What do you need to do so that John will have access?

    A. Put the audit log on an NTFS partition and grant John access to the file with Full Control permission.

    B. Put the audit log on an NTFS partition and grant John access to the file with Read permission.

    C. Give John permission to view the audit log through Event Viewer.

    D. Add John to the Administrators group on your computer.

37   You have a folder called C:\DATA that exists on your NT Workstation. This folder is shared as \\NTWS\DATA. The following permissions have been applied:

> **To C:\DATA:**
> Everyone   Full Control
>
> **To \\NTWS\DATA**
> Everyone   Read

Based on these assignments, which two statements are true?

  A. When accessing the folder locally, the users will have Full Control access.

  B. When accessing the folder remotely, the users will have Full Control access.

  C. When accessing the folder locally, the users will have Read Control access.

  D. When accessing the folder remotely, the users will have Read Control access.

38   You have just installed an application that requires that you set environment variables so that the application will run properly. These environment variables should be set for all of the users who access the computer. Where do you configure the environment variables?

  A. AUTOEXEC.BAT

  B. AUTOEXEC.NT

  C. CONFIG.NT

  D. Control Panel ➤ System

39   You have just received a UPS that needs to be installed and configured on your NT Workstation. Which of the following steps must you take?

  A. Attach the UPS through the mouse port.

  B. Install the UPS through the serial port.

  C. Install the UPS through the parallel port.

  D. Configure the UPS through Control Panel ➤ Devices.

  E. Configure the UPS through Control Panel ➤ UPS.

40   Your network consists of a PDC and 50 NT Workstations. You have decided to implement a system policy that will disable the Registry editing tools for the Domain Users group. Which two statements pertain to the system policy configuration?

    A. The system policy file should be called `NTCONFIG.POL`.

    B. The system policy file should be called `NTCONFIG.DAT`.

    C. The system policy file should be stored in the \WINNT\SYSTEM32\POLICIES folder on the PDC.

    D. The system policy file should be stored in the NETLOGON share on the PDC.

41   You are installing a printer that will be used by Windows NT 4.0, Windows NT 3.51 clients, and Windows 95 clients. What is the minimum configuration required to support this configuration?

    A. When configuring the printer, install the NT 4.0 driver and the Windows 95 driver. The Windows 3.51 clients can use the NT 4.0 drivers. Nothing else is required.

    B. When configuring the printer, the NT 4.0 and NT 3.51 print drivers are installed by default. Install the Windows 95 driver on each Windows 95 client that will access the printer.

    C. When configuring the printer, install the NT 3.51 driver and the Windows 95 driver. The NT 4.0 clients can use the NT 3.51 drivers. Nothing else is required.

    D. When configuring the printer, the NT 4.0 driver, the NT 3.51 driver, and the Windows 95 driver are installed by default. Nothing else is required.

42   You have a computer that has Windows 95 installed, and want to upgrade to NT Workstation. You want all of the applications that were used under Windows 95 to be available in NT Workstation. What do you do?

    A. When installing NT Workstation, use `WINNT /u` to specify that you are upgrading from Windows 95.

    B. Install NT Workstation into the same directory that Windows 95 was installed in.

    C. Install NT Workstation using the `WINNT /95` switch to specify that you are upgrading from Windows 95.

    D. There is no upgrade path. You will have to reinstall and reconfigure all of your applications after the upgrade is complete.

43   Your NT Workstation has Internet access. You are trying to map a drive to a computer called NTSCORP in the CORP.COM domain. The shared folder is called DATA. What syntax do you use to map this drive?

    A. `NET USE \\NTSCORP.CORP.COM\DATA`

    B. `NET USE .NTSCORP.CORP.COM\DATA`

    C. `WWW.CORP.COM\NTSCORP\DATA`

    D. `WWW.NTSCORP\CORP.COM\DATA`

44   You have a share called `\\ACCT\DATA` that has the following permissions assigned:

ACCT TEMPS	No Access
ACCT USERS	Read
ACCT MANAGERS	Change
DOMAIN ADMINS	Full Control

This share points to a folder called C:\DATA that is on an NTFS partition. The NTFS permissions have been left at the default value, so EVERYONE has Full Control. Dustin is a member of ACCT USERS and ACCT MANAGERS. When accessing this drive locally, what are Dustin's effective permissions?

A. No Access

B. Read

C. Change

D. Full Control

45   You have CSNW installed so that you can access a NetWare 3.1x server called NWSERVER. On your NT Workstation, you have an account called Ryan. Your NetWare account is also called Ryan. While accessing the NetWare server, you decide to change your password. Which two methods can you use?

A. Use the NetWare SETPASS command line utility.

B. Use the NetWare PASSWORD utility.

C. Use the NT NET PASS utility.

D. Press Control + Alt + Delete to access the Windows NT security dialog box, and select the Change Password button.

46   You want to automate the installation of 50 NT Workstations. Which configuration file is used to specify user information to prompts that a user sees during a normal installation?

A. SYSDIFF.EXE

B. UNATTEND.TXT

C. SETUP.INF

D. Uniqueness Database File (UDF)

47 You want to move an NTFS file from a local drive to a network drive. What happens to the files permissions?

   A. The file retains the permissions from the source folder.

   B. The file has the permissions that the destination folder has assigned.

   C. The file has the default NTFS permission of Full Control.

   D. The file has the Read permission assigned to it for group Everyone.

48 You have NT Workstation installed on your home computer and telecommute one to two days a week. You access large data files and are trying to improve your throughput. You have access to two phone lines, so decide to add a second modem and use the multilink capabilities of RAS. How do you configure the RAS client?

   A. Create a single phonebook entry that is configured to dial-out using both modems. Specify a separate phone number for each modem to dial.

   B. Create a separate phonebook entry for each modem. Specify a separate phone number for each modem to dial.

   C. Create a single dialout configuration entry that is configured to dial-out using both modems. Specify a separate phone number for each modem to dial.

   D. Create a separate dialout configuration entry for each modem. Specify a separate phone number for each modem to dial.

49 You are in charge of installing 100 new computers into your domain called CORP. Seventy-five of the computers are desktop machines, and 25 of the computers are laptops. Each platform uses identical hardware. The following requirements have been specified:

Required: You must automate the installation process.

Optional: You want the computers to have the standard application your company uses to be installed automatically.

You want the computers to join the C+ORP domain during installation.

Proposed Solution: Install a sample workstation with all of the applications installed on it. Create an image of this computer on a shared network drive. Connect each computer to this drive and copy the image down. Rename each computer so that it has a unique name.

What does the proposed solution accomplish?

A. It meets the required element and both optional elements.

B. It meets the required element and one optional element.

C. It meets the required element, but not the optional elements.

D. It does not meet the required or the optional elements.

50   You are in charge of installing 100 new computers into your domain called CORP. Seventy-five of the computers are desktop machines, and 25 of the computers are laptops. Each platform uses identical hardware. The following requirements have been specified:

Required: You must automate the installation process.

Optional: You want the computers to have the standard applications your company uses to be installed automatically.

You want the computers to join the CORP domain during installation.

Proposed Solution: Use the unattended installation process. Create two different answer files for each platform. Create a UDF file that will be used to answer prompts during the installation. Create a reference computer with the applications you will use and use the SYSDIFF utility to create a snapshot of the reference computer. When installing each computer, use the appropriate WINNT switches to point to the unattended installation configuration files.

What does the proposed solution accomplish?

A. It meets the required element and both optional elements.

B. It meets the required element and one optional element.

C. It meets the required element, but not the optional elements.

D. It does not meet the required or the optional elements.

51   What service is used to resolve fully qualified domain names to IP addresses?

    A. DNS

    B. ARP

    C. WINS

    D. DHCP

52   You have just purchased a new computer that will be shared by two users. The following requirements have been specified:

Required: Each user should be able to customize the desktop however they want.

Optional: Each user should have the ability to set security on their private files.

Each user should be able to create shares on their private data folders.

Proposed Solution: Install NT onto the computer using a single partition formatted with NTFS. Create a user account for each user. Create a home directory for each user. Only assign the directory's owner Full Control permission to their personal home directory. Instruct each user to log on with their unique logon name.

What does the proposed solution accomplish?

    A. It meets the required element and both optional elements.

    B. It meets the required element and one optional element.

    C. It meets the required element, but not the optional elements.

    D. It does not meet the required or the optional elements.

53 Lynne has an account on her NT Workstation called Lynne, and an account on a NetWare 3.1x server called Lynne. She uses the CSNW redirector to access a NetWare 3.1x server called NWSERVER. How should Lynne configure her computer so that she can attach to the NetWare server transparently?

    A. She should configure Preferred Server in the CSNW properties.

    B. She should configure Preferred Tree in the CSNW properties.

    C. She should configure Preferred Context in the CSNW properties.

    D. She should configure Preferred Server in the NWLink IPX/SPX Compatible transport properties.

54 Your NT Workstation is configured to use the NetBEUI, NWLink IPX/SPX Compatible Transport protocol, and TCP/IP. You use NetBEUI to access your local network. You use the NWLink IPX/SPX Compatible Transport protocol when accessing NetWare servers. TCP/IP is used to access network resources on remote subnets. Currently 75 percent of your access is on the local subnet, 10 percent is to NetWare resources, and 15 percent is to remote subnets. How should you configure the binding order on your computer?

    A. NetBEUI, TCP/IP, NWLink

    B. NWLink, TCP/IP, NetBEUI

    C. The system will automatically configure the binding order so that it is optimized.

    D. Binding order does not affect system performance.

55 One of the NT Servers has been configured with a network monitoring tool. What service must be running on your NT Workstation if you want to forward trap messages to the monitoring computer?

    A. Network Monitor Agent

    B. SNMP

    C. You must start the Alerter service.

    D. Configure the computer to forward messages through Performance Monitor.

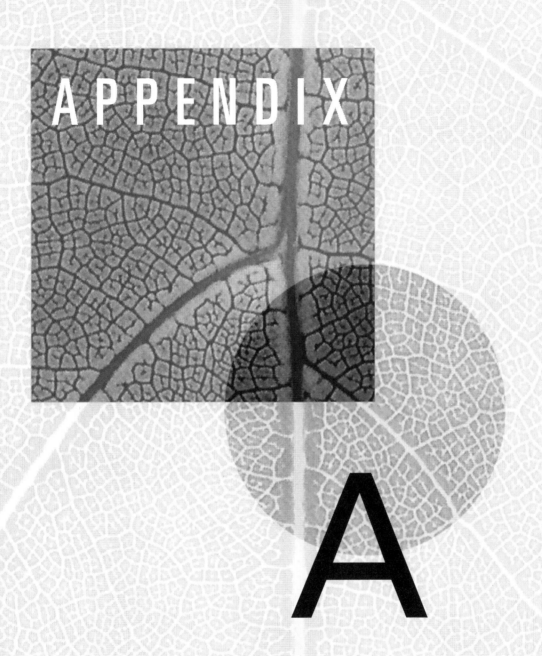

APPENDIX

A

Study Question and
Sample Test Answers

Unit 1 Answers

Study Questions

Create Unattended Installation Files

1. True

2. UDF file

3. This file is located on the NT Workstation CD-ROM, or in the NT Resource Kit CD-ROM.

4. It allows you to configure the General Setup, Networking Setup, and Advanced Setup portion of the unattended installation text file.

5. True

6. User Information

7. In the Computer Role tab

8. The display setting information

9. False

    Explanation: The License Mode information is for servers only.

10. It lets you specify whether you're installing networking during the installation process or from the Setup Manager program.

11. The Protocols tab

12. True

13. The advanced screen, in the File Systems tab

14. False

Explanation: You need an answer file for each different hardware platform and NT operating system configuration.

15. The /U option in WINNT and WINNT32 allows you to specify an unattended answer file for a Windows NT installation.

16. False

Explanation: The /S switch may be selected, specifying the source directory.

17. False

Explanation: The answer file provides the answers the user usually *would* need to respond to during setup.

18. When using different setup configurations, and specific items like computer name and domain that vary from installation to installation are to be automatically applied.

19. Unattended answer files can be created by editing a copy of the Unattend.TXT file that is included with the Workstation 4.0 resource kit, or by using the Setup Manager utility.

20. False

Explanation: The UDF identifies the differences between installations.

21. When you need to provide replacements for sections of the answer file, or supply additional sections unique to an individual installation.

22. Computer name

23. Answer: WINNT /U; answer_filename /UDF; ID[,database_filename]

24. False

Explanation: You can use either WINNT or WINNT32.

25. To record the difference between a normal Windows NT installation and an installation to which you have added application or other data files

26. True

27. Sysdiff records the differences between the state of a previous snapshot of a Windows NT installation and the state of the installation at the time Sysdiff is run again.

28. False

    Explanation: Sysdiff /Snap takes a snapshot of the state of the Windows NT operating system Registry *and* the state of the file system and files and directories.

29. When you want to see the details of the difference file in a readable text file format

30. By using the command Sysdiff /Diff

Plan Strategies for Sharing and Securing Resources

31. A hand underneath the directory identifies that the directory is being shared over a network.

32. The Server Service must be started on your computer.

33. True

    Explanation: If you installed the networking components of Windows NT, this service should start automatically when Windows NT starts.

34. Administrators and Power Users

35. Access permissions

    Explanation: There is no special access, beyond simply being able to access the directory, required.

36. List

37. False

Explanation: You can only share directories. The files are then accessible through the shared directory. Files cannot be shared individually.

38. NT Explorer, and My Computer on the desktop

39. False

40. Up to 255 characters

41. False

Explanation: Some DOS-based systems may not be able to see the share name if it is longer than eight characters.

42. 10

43. False

Explanation: You can set the maximum number of connections from one to 10, with 10 being the maximum.

44. The User Limit field

45. False

Explanation: You can create many shares with the same directory; however, they must have different names.

46. The New Share field

47. False

Explanation: Share permissions are not part of the NTFS partition permissions, rather they're in addition to the NTFS permissions.

48. False

Explanation: The most restrictive permissions prevail.

49.

Permission	Function
No Access	User can connect to the resources but can't access the directory or list its comments.
Read	Users can display the files and subdirectories contained by the shared directory, run program files from the shared directory, access subdirectories of the shared directory, and read and copy files from the shared directory.
Change	User can create subdirectories and files, delete files and subdirectories, read and write to files in the directory, and change file attributes.
Full Control	User can change file permissions, and take ownership of files on an NTFS volume.

Choose the Appropriate File System to Use in a Given Situation

50. True

51. False

Explanation: The New Technology File System was created by Microsoft specifically to work with Windows NT.

52. It's a log-based file system that allows recovery of files if corrupted or emergency shutdown

53. False

Explanation: Share permissions are in addition to NTFS permissions.

54. 16 exabytes

55. 50MBs

56. True

57. False

Explanation: NTFS can compress or expand an individual file or all the files in a directory.

58. Two directory entries that point to the same file

59. Supports files and partitions as large as 4GB; Accessible by many operating systems, including MS-DOS, NT, Windows 95, OS/2, MacOS, and many variants of the UNIX family of operating systems; The least file system overhead of any file system, which makes it good for small partitions (smaller then 50MBs) or the only one usable with most removable disk media; The only PC-compatible file system that can be used on a floppy; Many removable hard disks are too small to take advantage of NTFS.

60. VFAT is used in MS-DOS version 7, Windows 95 and Windows NT version 3.51 and 4.0.

61. True

62. True

63. True

64. Eight characters with a three-letter extension

65. True

66. False

Explanation: Windows NT supported read and write access to OS/2 High Performance File System (HPFS) partitions through version 3.51. This support has been removed in Windows NT version 4.0.

67. To denote which users have access to certain files and directories, providing different levels of access for different users

68. Event Viewer

69. It records changes to files and directories as they happen, and records how to undo the changes in case of a system failure.

70. False

Explanation: Only NT can read from an NTFS volume, so if you're using Windows 95 or OS/2, they must have their own partition. You can use any partition type you want in any combination.

71. Boot.INI

72. False

Explanation: Windows 95 can't read an NTFS partition, regardless if it is on Workstation or Server.

Sample Test

1-1   B, D, and F

Explanation: NT uses WINNT or WINNT32 to launch its setup routine. An unattended installation uses the UNATTEND.TXT answer file to provide setup parameter answers. The UDF file provides machine specific information, such as a computer name. SYSDIFF.EXE takes a snapshot of a configuration before and after application software has been installed, so the difference files can be applied to an automated installation including application software.

1-2   C

Explanation: CONVERT.EXE is a one-way conversion only to NTFS. NTFS supports long filenames. NT 4.0 does not support HPFS.

1-3   A

Explanation: Julie's account is a member of the Users group. User's group has No Access, which is an overriding permission. Julie cannot read the files in the directory.

1-4   A, B, and C

Explanation: Change permissions allow read, write, delete and change attributes. Take Ownership requires Full Control permissions, or membership in the Administrators group.

1-5   B

Explanation: This solution does not provide a UDF to specify individual computer names and user names.

1-6   D

Explanation: WINNT32 is the command that is run from an existing NT installation. These machines were booted with a DOS diskette and WINNT needs to be used.

1-7   A

Explanation: This solution produces the required result and both optional results.

1-8   D

Explanation: Disks can be formatted as FAT only. You can't use NTFS with disks.

1-9   D

Explanation: NT 4.0 is incompatible with the FAT32 file system used by Windows 95 OSR2. Deleting existing partitions allows normal NT installation to proceed.

1-10   C

Explanation: Administrators can always take ownership, even when explicitly granted NO ACCESS. Once you've taken ownership, you have Creator-Owner permissions, which are FULL CONTROL by default.

1-11   A

Explanation: An UDF is similar to an answer file, except an UDF file can map unique IDs to individual user or computer names.

1-12   B

Explanation: You need an answer file for each type of hardware platform. You only need one UDF, but must specify each user name and computer name in this file.

1-13   C

Explanation: An answer file answers all or some of the user prompts during setup. For example, joining a domain or specifying keyboard layouts.

1-14   D

Explanation: The Sysdiff.EXE is used to automate the installation of software applications.

1-15 A, B, and C

Explanation: An answer file provides answers to user prompts. The UDF supplies additional sections with information unique to each user and the Sysdiff.EXE automates application installations.

1-16 B

Explanation: Windows NT automatically recognizes other operating systems (such as DOS and Windows) and allows you to boot them. You should not install Windows 95 after you install Windows NT because that may damage the Windows NT boot process. You should not use NTFS because you can't access files on NTFS from Windows 95.

1-17 C

Explanation: Each hardware platform is different, and therefore requires a different answer file. Differences for all computers on the network regardless of hardware configuration are stored in one Uniqueness Database File.

1-18 B

Explanation: The Sysdiff utility can place files on the hard drive and make changes in the registry when it adds software packages to a Windows NT Workstation installation. Placing the software installation files on network shares makes the installation process easier, but it does not automate it (you still must run the software setup programs and respond to the prompts for each computer).

1-19 C

Explanation: The Setup Manger (SETUPMGR.EXE) provides you with a graphical interface for creating an unattended answer file.

1-20 A

Explanation: A user's level of access to a shared NTFS directory from a remote computer is determined by the most restrictive level of access, share or NTFS. Thus, the user's effective level of access to a folder from a remote location must be either the same or more restrictive than his level of access to the folder had he been logged on locally.

Unit 2 Answers

Study Questions

Installing Windows NT Workstation

1. They initiate the Setup program by booting a minimal version of Windows NT, which accesses the CD-ROM for installation.

2. Access WINNT.EXE on the CD-ROM

3. **Microprocessor:** 486/33 or higher

   Disc Storage: 120 MB

   Memory: 12MB (16MB recommended)

   Display: VGA or higher

   Required Additional Drive: CD-ROM, or access to files from a networked CD-ROM drive

4. False

   Explanation: You can connect to a network drive by loading a minimal operating system.

5. You can copy the distribution files to your hard drive and run the setup program from there.

6. The HCL is used to check to make sure your hardware is compatible with Windows NT.

7. False

   Explanation: By booting with the three boot floppies, you can install NT on a PC with no existing operating system.

8. False

   Explanation: You can only do a straight installation. For example, you cannot choose the installation directory.

9. C:\WINNT

10. True

11. NTLDR; BOOT.INI; BOOTSECT.DOS; NTDETECT.COM

    Explanation: If the system is SCSI-based, NTBOOTDD.SYS must also be located in the root of the startup disk.

12. True

13. Boot partition (default is C:\WINNT\SYSTEM32)

14. Installs without making the three boot disks

15. False

    Explanation: NT is not available on floppies. It would take over 100 floppies to hold all the files.

16. False

    Explanation: NT can detect some hardware but is not plug and play like Windows 95.

17. False

18. False

    Explanation: Neither Windows 95 or NT can do a system transfer to load the operating system on a PC. You must do an installation.

19. False

    Explanation: WINNT32 is designed to be used on a computer already running a true 32-bit OS, such as NT. This is used to upgrade or install NT into a different folder.

20. False

    Explanation: The HCL contains hardware certified to run on Windows NT.

21. True

22. 1. Creates three setup disks for installation. 2. Creates the WIN_NT.~LS temporary folder and copies the installation files to this directory. 3. Prompts the user to reboot.

Dual Boot Systems

23. BOOT.INI

24. NTFS

25. Windows 3.1, Windows for Workgroups, Windows 95, DOS, NT and OS/2

26. Load NT in its own directory.

27. You must install your applications in both operating systems.

28. Go to Disk Administrator and make active the OS/2 boot partition.

29. Windows 95B uses the FAT32 file systems and Windows NT does not support it.

30. Install Windows 95 first, then Windows NT Workstation. If you install Windows NT first then windows 95, the NT boot loader will be disabled.

Removing Windows NT Workstation

31. Boot the NT installation boot floppies and use delete partition option.

32. The Windows NT and Program Files\Windows NT directories

33. True

34. False

Explanation: FDISK cannot delete an NTFS volume if it has a logical drive.

35. False

36. True

37. Run the SYS.COM command (sys c:\).

38. This is the swap file that allows NT to use more memory than is physically installed in the system.

Installing, Configuring, and Removing Hardware Components

39. False

40. True

   Explanation: There are some exceptions to this. If you are installing NT Server and want to make it a BDC to an already existing domain, then you must have a NIC card installed. The setup program will not continue until the NIC card is working properly and communicating with the domain.

41. One

   Explanation: Additional NICs can be added at any later time.

42. D, B, A, C

43. B, A, E, D, C

44. A, B, D, C, E

45. Check that the drives are set to primary and secondary.

46. Hard drives

   CD-ROM players

   Scanners

47. True

48. False

49. www.microsoft.com\kb

50. Termination is the number one problem with SCSI devices.

51. True

52. True

53. False

    Explanation: They use serial cables.

54. In the UPS applet in the Control Panels

55. Sound and MIDI

56. Through the Display Type button on the Settings tab of the Display Control Panel

57. False

58. VGA

59. The General tab of the Keyboard Control Panel

60. Keyboard repeat rate and repeat delay
    Keyboard layout

61. This is where you select and set the mouse driver.

Use Control Panel Applications to Configure a Windows NT Workstation Computer

62. True

63. The color depth, desktop size, and display driver of the video display

64. True

65. True

66. Language

    Number currency

    Time representations

    Input locales for the current user

67. Sounds

68. The User Profile tab, located in the System applet

69. The Network applet, under the adapter tab

70. False

    Explanation: NT does not have an Add New Hardware applet, only Windows 95 does.

Upgrade to Windows NT Workstation 4.0

71. The main difference between installing and upgrading is that when you upgrade, the new operating system will replace the existing one. Many of the new settings for the existing version of Windows are transferred into the new Windows NT Workstation 4.0 configuration. Installing an operating system is done to put a second OS on the machine for a specific role.

72. True

73. False

74. False

    Explanation: NT version upgrades preserve all the existing system settings since the NT registry is used in it's entirety.

Configure Server-Based Installation for Wide-Scale Deployment

75. True

76. I386

77. An Answer file (unattend.txt)

78. UDF (Uniqueness Database File)

Sample Test

2-1 B

Explanation: The Modems applet is specifically used to add and configure modems, and the Telephony applet configures telephony drivers and dialing properties, not modem hardware. NT is not a Plug-and-Play operating system, and the Add New Hardware applet is a feature of Windows 95, not NT Workstation.

2-2 D

Explanation: NT Workstation 4.0 requires an Intel 80486 or better CPU, so the Intel 80386 NT Workstation 3.51 machine cannot be upgraded.

2-3 C

Explanation: WINNT with the /OX parameter builds a set of NT installation disks on any Intel based computer.

2-4 B

Explanation: The Add New Hardware applet exists in Windows 95, not NT. The Devices applet lets you disable a device and configure NT startup device handling, and there is no Devices tab in the Sound applet.

2-5 C

Explanation: Use the Tape Devices applet in the Control Panel

2-6 B, C, and D

Explanation: You must specify upgrade to retain user preferences, and convert from HPFS to NTFS. You don't need to boot from the installation disk—it's faster to load from the existing NT installation.

2-7 C, F

Explanation: Uninterruptable Power Supplies communicate with the computer using a serial data cable, and you configure them using the UPS applet. Remember, the UPS works only if you plug it in.

2-8 A, B, C, D

Explanation: All of these four operating systems can coexist easily with Windows NT Workstation.

2-9 D, E, and G

Explanation: SYS C: causes the system to boot to Windows 95 on system startup. You need to remove the NT startup files. The default installation directory for NT files is C:\WINNT.

2-10 C, B

Explanation: Run the NTHQ and check the output against the HCL.

2-11 C

Explanation: The multimedia applet in the control panel lets you change drivers for MIDI devices.

2-12 B

Explanation: You need at least 12MBs to load and run NT Workstation. However, 128MBs would make it run a lot smoother.

2-13 A

Explanation: WINNT32.EXE /b runs the installation but doesn't make the boot floppies, and /o creates the floppies.

2-14 B

Explanation: If you install NT into the same directory in which Windows is running, it upgrades the existing installation. You must install Windows NT into a new directory if you want to dual boot with an existing installation.

2-15 A, C

Explanation: Deleting the NT partition is good, since that removes the NT directories, but the system will still try to load NT even without the partition. You must "sys" the drive to reset the Master Boot Record. Several files will still remain in the system partition that can be removed later.

2-16 B

Explanation: To upgrade from Windows 3.1 to NT you can only use the WINNT.EXE program. WINNT32.EXE is used only to upgrade from another version of NT.

2-17 C

Explanation: If you have a UPS on your NT system, it may be necessary to add the line /NoSerialMouse into the Boot.INI. This prevents NT's check for a serial mouse which shuts the UPS down.

2-18 C

Explanation: The Multimedia applet in the Control Panel is where you can load and unload sound card drivers.

2-19 C

Explanation: The Input Local tab in the Keyboard applet lets you change the international settings for your keyboard.

2-20 C

Explanation: Use the Startup/Shutdown tab in the System applet of the Control Panel to change the default startup operating system.

Unit 3 Answers

Study Questions

1. Administrator and Guest

2. False

   Explanation: The two default use accounts can be renamed, but not deleted.

3. By creating new user accounts or by making copies of existing user accounts.

4. User Manager

5. Dial in access for User Accounts that need Remote Access. The Users must be given individual rights, or they won't be able to log on remotely.

6. True

7. True (if default Account Options are retained which permit blank passwords)

8. 20

9. False

   Explanation: The administrator can only uncheck the account if the account has been locked out. No user, including the administrator can check the Locked-out box.

10. False

    Explanation: You create a template by creating a user account, then using the copy operation in the User menu to duplicate the selected user account so it retains the security information.

11. True

12. **Copied**   **Left Blank**
    Group Account memberships   Full Name
    Description   User Must Change Password at Next Logon
    Profile Settings   Account Disabled
    User Cannot Change Password   User Name
    Password Never Expires   Password

13. If you give local group permissions to a printer, file, or directory, you only have to add users to the group to give them the permissions to the resource.

14. False

    Explanation: Users that belong to groups have all of the permissions assigned to that group.

15. Local and Global

16. Global groups. These groups can become members of local groups, but local groups cannot be members of global groups.

17.
A.	4
B.	1
C.	5
D.	3
E.	6
F.	2

18. Select New Local Group from the User menu in the User Manager window. Enter the Group Name, Description and Members in the New Local Group dialog box.

Explanation: The Group Name field identifies the local group. The criteria for group names is the same as it is for a user name.

Set Up and Modify User Profiles

19. False

Explanation: Profiles do not store user data, they store user preferences.

20. True

21. Ntuser.dat and Ntuser.dat.log

22. %systemroot%/profiles

23. On a Windows NT Server acting as a Domain Controller

24. If you need to use the profile on more than one machine

Explanation: By storing the user's roaming profile on the server, instead of storing a local profile on each of the Windows NT workstations that you use, profile changes will be in effect for all workstations you use, rather than just the one on which you make the change.

25. Specify a path to the profile in User Manager for Domains. The existing profile must then be moved from the Workstation to the Domain Controller.

26. Create a roaming profile subdirectory. Specify the path to that directory in User Manager for Domains on an NT Server acting as a Domain Controller. Copy the user profile to the roaming profile subdirectory using the User Properties tab of the System Control Panel. Rename the file ntuser.dat to ntuser.man.

27. A collection of hardware information about a certain workstation. These were specifically designed for laptops, since the hardware could change each time the user goes to the office or home.

Set Up Shared Folders and Permissions

28. Server

29. Administrators and Power Users

30. True

31. False

    Explanation: You can share both permissions and directories on an NTFS partition. You can only share directories on a FAT partition.

32. Up to 255 characters, but some DOS-based systems may not be able to read it if it's longer than eight characters.

33. True

34. 10

35. True

36. False

37. No Access, Read, Change, and Full Control

38. False

Explanation: The most restrictive permission always prevails.

39. False

Explanation: Hidden shares are created by placing a $ sign at the end of a share.

40. Net share Sales=C:\Business

41. Net share sales /DELETE

42. C$: This shares the root of the computer's C drive.

ADMIN$: Shares the root of the system drive, regardless of where it is located.

Set Permissions on NTFS Partitions, Folders, and Files

43. Users can view and read existing files and also save new files in the directory, but cannot modify existing files.

44. Users can view and read existing files in the directory and also save new files in the directory. Users can also modify and delete existing files and change attributes.

45. Read (R)

Write (W)

Execute (X)

Delete (D)

Change Permissions (P)

Take Ownership (O)

46. Users can read the file, or execute it, but cannot modify it.

47. RXWD

48. Through the Explorer or through My Computer

    Explanation: Chose File ➤ Properties on the file you want to change permissions, and then click on the permission button on the Security tab of the File properties dialog box (NTFS only).

Install and Configure Printers in a Given Environment

49. A printing device

50. Pool

51. Windows NT downloads a new version of the printer driver to the client machine.

52. To the client spooler

    Explanation: The client spooler spools the data to a file, then makes a RPC (remote procedure call) to the server spooler.

53. Printer Graphics Driver DDL, Printer Interface Driver DDL, Characterization Data File or Minidriver

54. By using the Service Manager applet found in the Control Panel

55. Any current jobs that have already been spooled are deleted

56. %systemroot%\system32\spool\printers

57. True

58. False

    Explanation: The print spooler tracks print job location.

59. True

60. True

61. Go to the printers property page and select the Sharing tab.

Sample Test

3-1   D

Explanation: You can't delete the default user accounts, only rename them.

3-2   C

Explanation: Disabling the account leaves all permissions and group rights intact. Deleting and recreating deletes the SID, in which you would then have to re-create all permissions and group rights for the user.

3-3   B

Explanation: The user name is required information. Password, description and full name are all optional if default Account options are retained.

3-4   D

Explanation: The default minimum password length is 0 characters. It can be up to 14 characters.

3-5   B

Explanation: the user's local profile folder structure is created from the default profile when a user first logs on to the workstation.

3-6   B

Explanation: A user's profile is placed in %systemroot%\profiles directory by default.

3-7   A

Explanation: The User Manager utility is used specify the path to the profile. However, you still must go through Control Panel ➤ Network ➤ Service to specify the profile as roaming.

3-8   D

Explanation: You can't set NTFS permissions on a FAT partition. However, you can set Share permissions on a NTFS partition.

3-9   B

Explanation: All network shares are assigned the permission Everyone: Full Control by default.

3-10   A, C

Explanation: There is only Read, No Access, change, and Full Control.

3-11   E

Explanation: File permissions can't be applied to a FAT partition.

3-12   C

Explanation: The printing devices are the physical parts of the printing system. Typically you would call these printers, but Microsoft calls them printing devices.

3-13   A

Explanation: Windows NT Workstation can support up to 10 network connections.

3-14   D

Explanation: The Everyone group, by default, has Full Control permissions on a network share.

3-15   B, D

Explanation: A roaming user profile can be created from a Windows NT Workstation computer by using either the System option in Control Panel or User Manager in Administrative Tools. The Copy To button on the User Profiles tab of the System option can be used to copy a user's local workstation profile to a shared folder on a server. The User Environment Profile window in User Manager can be used to create a roaming user profile on a share or to point to a user profile previously created on a share

3-16   B

Explanation: Fifteen characters is the maximum amount of characters allowed for a NetBIOS name.

3-17 B

> **Explanation:** If jobs do not print and can't be deleted, it's likely that the print spooler is stalled. To fix the problem, select Services in Control Panel, stop the spooler service, then restart it.

3-18 C

> **Explanation:** Mandatory user profiles are roaming user profiles that can't be modified and saved by a user. Mandatory user profiles are created by establishing a roaming user profile for a user, copying that profile to a shared directory, assigning the appropriate users to the profile, changing the name of the `Ntuser.Dat` file in the directory to Ntuser.Man, and entering the profile UNC path into the User Profile Path located in the User Environment Profile dialog box for each user.

3-19 B

> **Explanation:** By updating the print driver on the print server, all users that attach to the print server will have the new print driver copied automatically to the client.

3-20 A

> **Explanation:** The General tab of the printer's property sheet will let you specify the separator page.

Unit 4 Answers

Study Questions

1. An interface used in Windows networks to communicate between applications and the network

2. TCP/IP and NetBEUI.

3. Create shares on the network.

4. Workstation service

   Explanation: The Workstation service allows you to browse and connect as a client to a network share. The Server service allows you to create and mange shares on the network.

5. TCP/IP, NWLink, and NetBEUI

6. True

7. Network

8. Protocols

9. Identification

10. True

11. False

    Explanation: You can load the MSLoopback adapter, which lets you load protocols.

12. False

    Explanation: The protocol that is bound first should be the protocol that is used the most.

13. 255

14. 15

15. Net Use F: \\acme\sales

16. By placing a $ sign at the end of the name; for example Sales$.

17. Net View

18. Net Share sharename /DELETE

Implement Windows NT Workstation as a Client in a NetWare Environment

19. Control Panel ➤ Network ➤ Services and add CNSW

20. GSNW

21. NWLink and CSNW

22. GSNW

    Explanation: GSNW also includes a CSNW client for the NT Server.

23. NWLink

24. True

25. 802.2

26. 802.3

27. The frame type

28. Only install NWLink. To run a client/server application, you do not have to install the CSNW.

29. False

    Explanation: It will load the NWLink protocol in the background.

30. 3.1x

31. True

32. True

33. Setpass

34. True

35. False

36. Net Logon

37. The Print Banner option should be set if a user wants a banner page with their user account information printed at the start of every print job.

Use Various Configurations to Install Windows NT Workstation as a TCP/IP Client

38. False

Explanation: IP addresses can only go up to 255 per octet.

39. Subnet mask

40. 32

41. If you have more then one network segment connected together with a router the you must set the default gateway address on each workstation if they need to communicate on each side of the router.

42. DHCP

43. WINS

44. DNS

45. Unique IP Address, Subnet mask, and default gateway

46. Displays the current IP configuration of a NT workstation or server

47. PING

48. Telnet

49. LMHOSTS

Configuring and installing Dial-Up Networking

50. PPTP

51. TCP/IP, NWLink, and NetBEUI

52. One of these: Only supports TCP/IP; Requires static IP address information; Does not support password encryption; Uses a script file.

53. False

54. True

55. One

56. PPP

Configuring Microsoft Peer Web Services

57. WWW and FTP

58. FTP

59. HTTP

60. Internet Service Manager

Sample Test

4-1   A, C

Explanation: When installing TCP/IP on a routed network, the IP address, the subnet mask and the default gateway parameters must be specified. However, if there are not routers in a small network, then the default gateway would not have to be defined.

4-2   C

Explanation: You can install the MS Loopback Adapter driver using the Network option in Control Panel. This driver allows you to install other network components, then load your actual NIC card driver later.

4-3   B

Explanation: Check the Print Banner option in Client Services for NetWare. This prints out a banner page between all print jobs specifying the user name and file name of the job that was printed.

4-4   C

Explanation: A DNS server is responsible for resolving IP addresses to fully qualified domain names (FQDNs).

4-5   B

Explanation: Since it is a NetWare 3.1x server, you must use bindery based utilities. Set-pass can be run from a command prompt to change your Novell password.

4-6   D

Explanation: You can run the Syscon utility from Windows NT Workstation or Server.

4-7   A, B, D

Explanation: A Dynamic Host Configuration Protocol (DHCP) server is responsible for dynamically assigning and maintaining IP addresses for DHCP clients. In addition, a DHCP server can also automatically configure the DNS server address, the WINS server address, the default gateway address and a variety of other TCP/IP settings for client machines.

4-8   A

Explanation: To access a client/server application on a NetWare server, you do not have to have CSNW running on your workstation, only NWLink.

4-9   B

Explanation: Your ISP will assign you an IP addresses dynamically.

4-10   C

Explanation: Domain Name System (DNS) servers contain host name to IP address mappings for servers on the Internet. If you are planning to develop a corporate intranet and further divide your corporation into zones, you need to install a DNS server to provide name resolution for clients accessing the various departmental servers on your intranet.

4-11   A

Explanation: If a NetWare 4.x server is using bindery emulation, then the Preferred Server option in Client Service for NetWare should be set, and the server name should be selected in the Preferred Server combo box. If the NetWare 4.x server is part of an NDS tree, then the Default Tree and Context option should be set, and the NDS tree name should be entered in the Tree field and the default context should be entered in the Context field.

4-12   B

Explanation: You need to execute the script file (SLIP.SCP) after a connection has been established and then a terminal window can also be used after a connection has been established.

4-13   A, B, C, D

Explanation: You can do all of the above. Use Setpass to change your password on a bindery based Novell server, or use the Windows NT Security window to change your password on NetWare NDS based server. You can use the Map Network Drive option in Windows NT Explorer to connect to NetWare 3.x and 4.x volumes. You can connect to a NetWare print queue by using the Add Printer icon in the Printers window of Windows NT.

4-14   D

Explanation: When mapping a network drive to an Internet path, the proper syntax to use is two backslashes, the server name, a single backslash, and a share name.

4-15   D

Explanation: The easiest way to change a password when attaching to a NDS server is to use the security box in NT Workstation.

4-16   A

Explanation: The Client Service for NetWare main window allows a user to set three printing options: Add Form Feed, Notify When Printed, and Print Banner.

4-17   B, D

Explanation: In able to resolve UNIX host names, you must either run a DNS server or configure an LMHOSTS file on your computer.

4-18   B

Explanation: The LMHOSTS requires a manual configuration on all hosts. This would not be recommended on n a network this size. Use DNS and WINS instead.

4-19   A, D

Explanation: The user must know the IP address of the print server and the printer name as it is defined on the LPD print server.

4-20 D

Explanation: By double-clicking on the Telephony applet in Control Panel, you can get to the Dialing properties.

4-21 D

Explanation: Two ways to troubleshoot connection problems with RAS are the Device.Log file and Dial-Up Networking Monitor.

4-22 B

Explanation: A single phone book entry should be created, along with unique phone numbers for your RAS server. Unique phone numbers need to be entered so that three simultaneous connections can be established.

4-23 D

Explanation: The Device.log file is stored in the %SYSTEMROOT%\System32\RAS directory and records dialog between the RAS server and the modem. It is created and enabled by setting a flag in the system registry. It contains initialization strings sent to the modem as well as modem response strings.

4-24 D

Explanation: You cannot use Multilink when using enforced callback. The exception to this rule is certain circumstance when using ISDN, way beyond the exam objectives. Just remember for the NT workstation exam, always answer "you cannot do this."

Unit 5 Answers

Study Questions

Starting Applications on Intel and RISC Platforms

1. True

2. False

   Explanation: By default, Win16 applications use a shared WOW and VDM.

3. WOW

4. VDM (Virtual DOS Machine)

5. WOW, VDM

6. MS-DOS applications and Win16 applications

7. False

   Explanation: The only things that are read from AUTOEXEC.BAT are environment variables and the PATH statement. CONFIG.SYS is not used. Instead, NT uses AUTOEXEC.NT and CONFIG.NT to provide configuration information to MS-DOS and Win16 applications.

8. START /separate /min ABC.EXE

9. False

   Explanation: MS-DOS applications always run in separate VDMs.

10. False

    Explanation: NT only supports OS/2 1.x applications.

11. False

    Explanation: MS-DOS applications always run in separate VDM's, so one failing DOS application will not affect other DOS applications.

12. One

    Explanation: By using the shared WOW and VDM, you only use one thread for program execution.

13. Three

    Explanation: MS-DOS applications always run in separate VDMs. Each VDM uses a single thread for program execution; in this case, three VDMs, three threads.

14. The applications should all be run in the default shared VDM.

    Explanation: If you were to run each Win16 application in its own memory space, you would increase memory usage.

15. The Registry

16. From the Run command

    From the command prompt using the Start command

    Creating an association for the application through NT Explorer

    Starting the task through Task Manager

Setting Application Priority

17. Control Panel ➤ System ➤ Performance tab

18. START /high ABC.EXE

19. START /low /max ABC.EXE

20. False

    Explanation: By default foreground applications run at a higher priority than background applications.

Sample Test

5-1   A

5-2   C

5-3   A, B

5-4   D

5-5 B

5-6 C

5-7 B

Explanation: If you set the priority through Control Panel ➤ System ➤ Performance tab, all background applications are effected. You must start the application with the Start command using the /high switch.

5-8 B, D

Explanation: NT does not use AUTOEXEC.BAT and CONFIG.SYS to provide DOS application configuration information.

5-9 B

5-10 A

5-11 B

5-12 A

Explanation: NT provides very minimal support for OS/2 applications.

Unit 6 Answers

Study Questions

Monitoring System Performance

1. Task Manager

   Performance Monitor

2. True

3. False

   Explanation: You can monitor application usage through Performance Monitor, but you cannot start or stop processes or applications through Performance Monitor.

4. DISKPERF -y

5. 80

6. Process

7. Thread

8. 20

9. Upgrade the processor. If possible, add additional processors.

10. Network Monitor Agent

11. SNMP

   Explanation: To manage the SNMP trap messages, you must have an SNMP console installed somewhere on your network.

12. True

13. 50

14. Add more physical RAM.

   Explanation: You can try and maximize your paging file, but the best solution to improve performance is to add more physical RAM, which reduces the activity on the paging file.

15. False

   Explanation: A volume set writes data to the disks sequentially and does not improve performance.

Optimizing System Performance

16. Disk striping

17. False

> **Explanation:** A volume stripe set writes data to the disks in 64K blocks sequentially (meaning data is not striped over multiple I/O channels) and does not improve performance.

18. False

> **Explanation:** Stripe sets with parity can only be implemented on the NT Server operating system.

19. False

20. Through Control Panel ➤ System ➤ Performance ➤ Virtual Memory ➤ Change button

21. False

> **Explanation:** For best performance, you want the page file on less frequently used disk channels.

22. True

> **Explanation:** A stripe set (without parity) offers no fault tolerance.

Sample Test

6-1   B

6-2   A

6-3   C

6-4   A

6-5   C, D

6-6   D

6-7   A

6-8   A

6-9   D

6-10 C

6-11 D

> **Explanation:** A memory bottleneck would be indicated if the Pages/Sec counter were above 20.

6-12 C

> **Explanation:** For best performance, you should not place the page file on the system or boot partition. You cannot place a page file on a stripe set. Page files should be created on separate physical drives, not logical drives since you are trying to take advantage of multiple I/O channels.

Unit 7 Answers

Study Questions

Troubleshooting a Failed Boot Process

1. BOOTSECT.DOS

2. BOOT.INI

3. NTDETECT.COM

4. NTLDR

5. NTOSKRNL.EXE

6. NTOSKRNL.EXE

   BOOT.INI

7. Use the Emergency Repair Disk (ERD).

   Explanation: To use the ERD, you must first use the three NT Setup disks, when prompted, choose *R* for repair, and choose the "Verify Windows NT system files" option.

8. `RDISK`

9. False

    Explanation: To use the ERD you must use the three NT Setup disks to boot, then choose the *R* for repair option, then you can supply the ERD. The ERD is not bootable, and all files stored on the ERD are in compressed format.

10. Trying to load an alternate file system. This message would be stored if there was a problem with the `BOOTSECT.DOS` file.

11. `NTBOOTDD.SYS`

12. `WINNT32 /OX`

13. To recover from misconfiguration or other serious errors by restoring the configuration that was used in your last successful boot.

14. True

    Explanation: If you don't use the NT Setup disks to restore files from the ERD, you can use `EXPAND` command to uncompress the files.

15. `BOOT.INI`

    Explanation: The `BOOT.INI` contains the ARC path to your boot partition. When you add or delete logical partitions through Disk Administrator, this may cause your ARC path to change. If you do not edit `BOOT.INI`, then NT will not boot successfully.

16. Inspect the Registry files

    Inspect the startup environment

    Verify the system files

    Inspect the boot sector

17. True

Troubleshooting Failed Print Jobs

18. Choose Document ➤ Resume from the Print Monitor.

19. You probably have not selected a default printer.

20. Choose Document ➤ Restart from the Print Monitor.

21. The print server or client is not using the correct driver.

22. Your print spooler file is full and you need more disk space.

23. You need to stop and restart the spooler service.

Troubleshooting Failed Applications

24. 1. Copy the contents of the CD to your hard drive and run the installation from hard drive. 2. Copy the contents of the CD to a network drive and run the installation from a the network drive.

25. Hardware Compatibility List (HCL)

26. False

Explanation: This feature is supported by Windows 95, but not NT 4.0. This feature should be available in NT 5.0.

27. IRQ

Base memory

Base I/O address

DMA

28. False

Explanation: Through the NT installation process, you can specify alternate locations from which to provide drivers.

Troubleshooting Failed Applications

29. Dr. Watson

30. DRWTSN32.EXE

Troubleshooting Resource Access Problems

31. False

Explanation: The most restrictive of the share or NTFS permissions will be applied.

32. No Access

Explanation: Normally, access permissions are cumulative, but if a user has No Access through user or group membership, then that user will have No Access.

33. Full Control

Explanation: Normally access permissions are cumulative, so in this case Terry would have Full Control.

34. Full Control

Explanation: Terry has Full Control since share permissions are not applied when a user accesses a resource locally.

35. Read

Explanation: In this case Terry is bound by the more restrictive of either the share or NTFS permissions since she is accessing this resource over the network.

36. They must log off and log on again to update their access token.

37. False

Explanation: By default NTFS permissions only apply to files within the folder, not sub-folders.

38. True

Editing the Registry

39. REGEDT32

40. REGEDIT

41. Use the NT Backup program.

42. Use the Last Known Good option during the boot process.

Advanced Problem Resolution

43. Remote Access Monitor

44. DEVICE.LOG

45. Control Panel ➤ System ➤ Startup/Shutdown tab ➤ check the Write debugging information to: box.

46. System

Security

Application

47. Error

Information

Warning

Success audit

Failure audit

48. You will restore the SAM to however it was configured when the ERD was saved. Any changes that have been made since the ERD was saved will be lost

49. Color palette

Desktop area

Refresh frequency

Sample Test

7-1 D

7-2 A

7-3 D

7-4 A

7-5 B

7-6 C

7-7 B

Explanation: The ERD can restore a SAM, but has nothing to do with the data stored on the computer.

7-8 B

Explanation: You need to edit the BOOT.INI to reflect the ARC location on the computer in which it will be booting.

7-9 C

Explanation: Rick needs to be removed from any groups that have No Access assigned if he will require access to the resource.

7-10 B

7-11 A

7-12 C

7-13 D

7-14 A, B

7-15 D

Explanation: To get the most reliable backup of your Registry, you should use the NT Backup program. The ERD does not back up the entire Registry by default.

7-16 D

7-17   A

7-18   C

Explanation: Print problems can usually be resolved by stopping and restarting the spooler service.

7-19   A, C, D

7-20   B

7-21   D

Explanation: If the driver has just been installed, reinstalling it probably won't help. If it has never worked before, then you probably installed an incompatible print driver.

7-22   B

Explanation: Make sure the print server has enough disk space to accommodate all waiting print jobs. If the spool file is full, users cannot submit jobs to the printer.

7-23   B

7-24   C

7-25   A, B, C

Unit 8 Answers

Final Review

8-1   A

Explanation: To join a domain, you configure the NT Workstation through the Control Panel ➤ Network ➤ Identification tab. You can create a computer account through this screen by specifying an administrative name and password, or the account can already be created through the Server Manager utility. By default Server Manager only exists on NT domain controllers.

8-2   D

Explanation: If you have long print jobs that should only be printed during low volume hours, the best solution is to create a printer with limited hours and specify that users send their long jobs to the specified printer. If you tried to manage the printers through priority, as soon as the high priority jobs finished printing, the print device would take jobs from the low priority printer which would then tie up the print device until the long job completed printing.

8-3   A, D

8-4   C

Explanation: You can use the REGEDT32 command to search for keys, but not for data strings. The REGEDIT command provides full search capabilities.

8-5   B, D

Explanation: To act as an FTP server, you must install TCP/IP and Microsoft Peer Web Services. IIS is only available on NT Server and Internet Explorer is an Internet client.

8-6   B

8-7   D

Explanation: Once NT reboots during the installation process, it tries to access the distribution files again. If the CD drive has no NT support, the installation can't be completed. By copying the files to a network share point, you can reconnect and access the distribution files from the network share point.

8-8   B, D

Explanation: Only Administrators and Power Users can create shares on NT Workstations. Server Operators is a special group that only exists on NT domain controllers.

8-9   B

Explanation: If the 16-bit applications are integrated, they must run in a shared memory space. For fault tolerance, you can run all other 16-bit applications in their own separate memory space.

8-10 A

8-11 D

Explanation: RAS dialback can only be configured to call back a single number.

8-12 A

8-13 C

8-14 D

Explanation: There are no NT utilities that allow you to convert an NTFS partition to FAT.

8-15 B

Explanation: Macintosh computers use the AppleTalk protocol. To connect to the printer, you must use a common protocol.

8-16 B

8-17 A

Explanation: If Karen is a member of any group that has No Access permission, it does not matter if other access permissions have been assigned, she will still have No Access.

8-18 D

8-19 B

Explanation: The Last Known Good option restores the Registry that was used in your last successful boot.

8-20 A

8-21 A, D

8-22 C

Explanation: While increasing the paging file or spreading the paging file over multiple physical disks might help a little, the best solution to excessive paging is to add more physical RAM.

8-23 C

Explanation: The Loopback option is used to configure network services when no physical network card has been installed.

8-24 C

8-25 B

Explanation: A volume set does not provide any performance enhancements. It is only used to expand the volume with more space. A stripe set provides better performance. The system and boot partition cannot be a part of a stripe set.

8-26 A, C, D

8-27 C

Explanation: Dr. Watson is an application debugger. You can use Dr. Watson to create a memory dump by configuring it to Create Crash Dump File. The memory dump created through Control Panel ➤ System is used to diagnose problems with the NT OS.

8-28 D

Explanation: The HP direct connect printers either use the TCP/IP or DLC protocols.

8-29 B

Explanation: This is a tricky question. NT 4.0 does not support or recognize HPFS. You can't change a partition to NTFS before NT is installed, since NT is the only operating system that recognizes NTFS and it has not yet been installed. You must back up the HPFS data, and reformat the drive as FAT. After installation, you can restore the data and convert the partition to NTFS.

8-30 B

8-31 A

Explanation: To protect against intruder access to your computer, you can set Account Lockout in the Account Policy for the computer. This allows you to specify that if there are x number of bad logon attempts within the time period you specify, that the account should be locked for whatever time period you specify, or until the Administrator unlocks the account. This also causes an event to be written the Event Log.

8-32 A

8-33 A

8-34 C

Explanation: If the users have a user policy defined, they will not use the group policy. Computer policies specify different settings that user or group policies. System policies take precedence over user profiles.

8-35 A

8-36 D

8-37 A, D

Explanation: If a user access a resource locally, only NTFS permissions apply. If a users accesses a resource over a network share, then the more restrictive of the NTFS or share permissions apply.

8-38 D

8-39 B, E

Explanation: NT only provides UPS support through serial ports. To configure the UPS, use Control Panel ➢ UPS.

8-40 A, D

8-41 D

8-42 D

8-43 A

8-44 D

Explanation: The share permissions are not applied since Dustin is accessing the resource locally.

8-45 A, D

8-46 B

8-47   B

Explanation: When moving files, you must determine if the destination directory is on the same or on a different NTFS partition. If you move to the same NTFS partition, the file keeps its original permissions. A move to a different NTFS partition is treated as a copy and the file inherits the permissions from the destination directory.

8-48   A

Explanation: You can only dial-out from one phonebook entry at a time.

8-49   D

8-50   A

8-51   A

8-52   B

Explanation: To create network shares, you have to make the users members of the Administrators or Power Users groups.

8-53   A

8-54   A

Explanation: You should place the most commonly used protocols at the top of the bindings list.

8-55   B

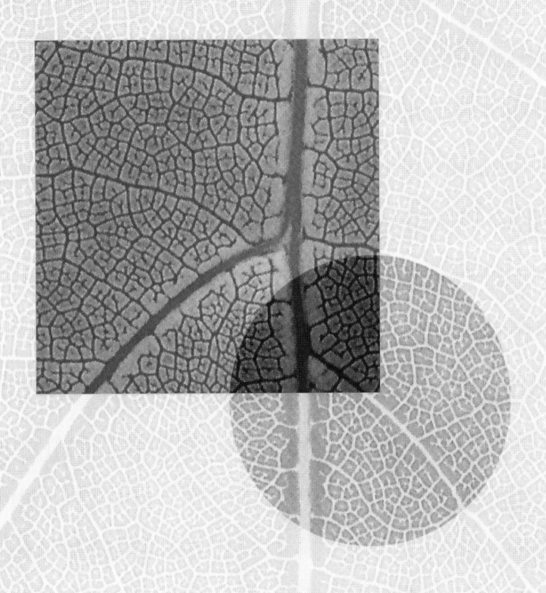

Glossary

80386   The Intel microprocessor that introduced the power of 32-bit computing to the IBM PC-compatible computer. The 80386 also introduced memory management, which allowed the use of virtual memory and hardware level multitasking, and protected mode, which increased the stability of operating systems by allowing them to restrict the activities of user-level programs. See *i486, Pentium.*

Access Control List (ACL)   A list of security identifiers contained by an object. Only the processes identified on the ACL with appropriate permissions can activate the services of that object. See *Object, Security Identifiers, Permissions.*

Access Tokens   Objects containing the security identifier of a running process. A process started by another process inherits the starting process's access token. The access token is checked against each object's ACL to determine whether appropriate permissions are granted to perform any requested service. See *Access Control List, Permissions, Object, Security Identifiers, Process.*

Accounts   Containers for security identifiers, passwords, permissions, group associations, and preferences for each user of a system. The User Manager administers accounts. See *Security Identifiers, Preferences, Permissions, Password, Groups.*

ACL   See *Access Control List.*

Adapter   Any hardware device that allows communications to occur through physically dissimilar systems. This term usually refers to peripheral cards permanently mounted inside computers that provide an interface from the computer's bus to another media such as a hard disk or a network. See *Network Interface Card, Small Computer Systems Interface.*

Address Resolution Protocol (ARP)   An Internet protocol for resolving an IP address into a Physical layer address (such as an Ethernet media access controller address). See *Physical Layer, Internet Protocol.*

Administrator Account   A special account in Windows NT that has the ultimate set of security permissions and can assign any permission to any user or group. The Administrator account is used to correct security problems. See *Permissions.*

Administrators   Users who are part of the Administrators group. This group has the ultimate set of security permissions. See *Administrator Account, Permissions, Groups.*

AltaVista   A World Wide Web indexing service operated by Digital Equipment Corporation. This service allows you to query nearly the entire set of World Wide Web pages by key word and returns a best-match-first result. This site is located at `www.altavista.digital.com`.

AppleTalk   The built-in (to firmware) suite of network protocols used by Macintosh computers. Windows NT Server uses AppleTalk to service Macintosh clients by simulating an Apple server. See *Macintosh*.

Application   Large software packages that perform specific functions, such as word processing, Web browsing, or database management. Applications typically consist of more than one program. See *Programs*.

Application Layer   The layer of the OSI model that interfaces with User mode applications by providing high-level network services based upon lower-level network layers. Network file systems like named pipes are an example of Application layer software. See *Named Pipes, Open Systems Interconnect Model, Application*.

ARP   See *Address Resolution Protocol*.

Asymmetrical Multiprocessing   A multiple processor architecture in which certain processors are designated to run certain threads or in which scheduling is not done on a fair-share basis. Asymmetrical multiprocessing is easier to implement than symmetrical multiprocessing, but does not scale well as processors are added. See *Microprocessor, Symmetrical Multiprocessing*.

Asynchronous Transfer Mode (ATM)   A wide area transport protocol that runs at many different speeds and supports real-time, guaranteed packet delivery in hardware, as well as lower-quality levels of service on a bandwidth-available basis. ATM will eventually replace all other wide area protocols, as most worldwide PTSN providers have declared their support for the international standard. See *Public Switched Telephone Network, Wide Area Network*.

Audit Policy   Audit policy determines which user events you want to track for security reasons. Audit policy can track the success or failure of specified security events; it is set in the User Manager. See *Security*.

Back Up   The process of writing all the data contained in online mass storage devices to offline mass storage devices for the purpose of safe keeping. Backups are usually performed from hard disk drives to tape drives. Also referred to as archiving. See *Hard Disk Drive*.

Backup Browser   A computer on a Microsoft network that maintains a list of computers and services available on the network. The Master Browser supplies this list. The backup browser distributes the Browsing service load to a workgroup or domain. See *Master Browser*.

Backup Domain Controllers   Servers that contain accurate replications of the security and user databases; servers can authenticate workstations in the absence of a primary domain controller. See *Primary Domain Controller*.

Basic Input/Output System (BIOS)   A set of routines in firmware that provides the most basic software interface drivers for hardware attached to the computer. The BIOS contains the bootstrap routine. See *Boot, Driver, Firmware*.

Bindery   A NetWare structure that contains user accounts and permissions. It is analogous to the Registry in Windows NT. See *Registry*.

Binding   The process of linking network services to network service providers. The binding facility allows users to define exactly how network services operate in order to optimize the performance of the system. By default, Windows enables all possible bindings. The Network control panel is used to change bindings. See *Network Layer, Data Link Layer*.

BIOS   See *Basic Input/Output System*.

Bit   A binary digit. A numeral having only two possible values, 0 or 1. Computers represent these two values as high (voltage present) or low (no voltage present) state on a control line. Bits are accumulated in sets of certain sizes to represent higher values. See *Byte*.

Boot   The process of loading a computer's operating system. Booting usually occurs in multiple phases, each successively more complex until the entire operating system and all its services are running. Also called bootstrap. The computer's BIOS must contain the first level of booting. See *Basic Input/Output System*.

Bottlenecks   Components operating at their peak capacity that restrict the flow of information through a system. Used singularly, the term indicates the single, most restrictive component in a system.

Bridge   A device that connects two networks of the same data link protocol by forwarding those packets destined for computers on the other side of the bridge. See *Router, Data Link Layer.*

Browser   A computer on a Microsoft network that maintains a list of computers and services available on the network.

Browsing   The process of requesting the list of computers and services on a network from a browser.

Byte   A set of 8 bits taken as a unit that represent up to 2^8, or 256, possible values. Because bytes are convenient for storing characters such as letters or numbers, they are the baseline used to measure memory sizes. See *Bit.*

Caching   A speed optimization technique that keeps a copy of the most recently used data in a fast, high-cost, low-capacity storage device rather than in the device upon which the actual data resides. Caching assumes that recently used data is likely to be used again. Fetching data from the cache is faster than fetching data from the slower, larger storage device. Most caching algorithms also copy the data most likely to be used next and perform write caching to further increase speed gains. See *Write-back Caching, Write-through Caching.*

CD-ROM   See *Compact Disk-Read Only Memory.*

Central Processing Unit (CPU)   The central processing unit of a computer. In microcomputers such as IBM PC- compatible machines, the CPU is the microprocessor. See *Microprocessor.*

Client   A computer on a network that subscribes to the services provided by a server. See *Server.*

Client/Server   A network architecture that dedicates certain computers called servers to act as service providers to computers called clients, which users operate to perform work. Servers can be dedicated to providing one or more network services such as file storage, shared printing, communications, e-mail service, and Web response. See *Share, Peer.*

Client/Server Applications   Applications that split large applications into two components: computer-intensive processes that run on application servers and user interfaces that run on clients. Client/server applications communicate over the network through interprocess communication mechanisms. See *Client, Server, Interprocess Communications.*

Client Services for NetWare (CSNW)   A service provided with Windows NT that connects a workstation to NetWare file servers. See *NetWare*.

Code   Synonymous with software but used when the software itself, rather than the utility it provides, is the object of discussion. See *Software*.

COM Port   Communications port. A serial hardware interface conforming to the RS-232 standard for low-speed serial communications. See *Modem, Serial*.

Compact Disk-Read Only Memory (CD-ROM)   A media for storing extremely large software packages on optical read-only discs. CD-ROM is an adaptation of the CD medium used for distributing digitized music. CD-ROM discs can hold up to 650MB of information and cost very little to produce in quantity. See *Hard Disk Drive*.

Components   Interchangeable elements of a complex software or hardware system. See *Module*.

Compression   A space optimization scheme that reduces the size (length) of a data set by exploiting the fact that most useful data contains a great deal of redundancy. Compression reduces redundancy by creating symbols smaller than the data they represent and an index that defines the value of the symbols for each compressed set of data.

Computer   A device capable of performing automatic calculations based upon lists of instructions called programs. The computer feeds the results of these calculations (output) to peripheral devices that can represent them in useful ways, such as graphics on a screen or ink on paper. See *Microprocessor*.

Control Panel   A software utility that controls the function of specific operating system services by allowing users to change default settings for the service to match their preferences. The Registry contains the Control Panel settings on a system and/or per-user basis. See *Registry, Accounts*.

Cooperative Multitasking   A multitasking scheme in which each process must voluntarily return time to a central scheduling route. If any single process fails to return to the central scheduler, the computer will lock up. Both Windows and the Macintosh operating system use this scheme. See *Preemptive Multitasking, Windows 3.11 for Workgroups*.

CPU   See *Microprocessor*.

CSNW   See *Client Services for NetWare.*

Data Link Control (DLC)   An obsolete network transport protocol that allows PCs to connect to older IBM mainframes and HP printers. See *Transmission Control Protocol/Internet Protocol.*

Data Link Layer   In the OSI model, the layer that provides the digital interconnection of network devices and the software that directly operates these devices, such as network interface adapters. See *Physical Layer, Network Layer, Open Systems Interconnect Model.*

Database   A related set of data organized by type and purpose. The term also can include the application software that manipulates the data. The Windows NT Registry (a database itself) contains a number of utility databases such as user account and security information. See *Registry.*

DDE   See *Dynamic Data Exchange.*

Default Shares   Resources shared by default when Windows NT is installed. See *Share, Resource.*

Desktop   A directory that the background of the Windows Explorer shell represents. By default objects on the Desktop contain the local storage devices and available network shares. See *Explorer, Shell.*

DHCP   See *Dynamic Host Configuration Protocol.*

Dial-up Connections   Data Link layer digital connections made via modems over regular telephone lines. The term *dial-up* refers to temporary digital connections, as opposed to leased telephone lines, which provide permanent connections. See *Data Link Layer, Public Switched Telephone Network, Modem.*

Directories   In a file system, directories are containers that store files or other directories. Mass storage devices have a root directory that contains all other directories, thus creating a hierarchy of directories sometimes referred to as a *directory tree.* See *File, File System.*

DLC   See *Data Link Control.*

DNS   See *Domain Name Service.*

Domain   In Microsoft networks a domain is an arrangement of client and server computers referenced by a specific name that share a single security permissions database. On the Internet a domain is a named collection of hosts and subdomains registered with a unique name by the InterNIC. See *Workgroup*.

Domain Controllers   Servers that authenticate workstation network logon requests by comparing a username and password against account information stored in the user accounts database. A user cannot access a domain without authentication from a domain controller. See *Primary Domain Controller, Backup Domain Controllers, Domain*.

Domain Name Service (DNS)   The TCP/IP network service that translates textual Internet network addresses into numerical Internet network addresses. See *Transmission Control Protocol/Internet Protocol, Internet*.

Drive   See *Hard Disk Drive*.

Drive Letters   Single letters assigned as abbreviations to the mass storage volumes available to a computer. See *Volume*.

Driver   A program that provides a software interface to a hardware device. Drivers are written for the specific device they control, but they present a common software interface to the computer's operating system, allowing all devices (of a similar type) to be controlled as if they were the same. See *Data Link Layer, Operating System*.

Dynamic Data Exchange (DDE)   A method of interprocess communication within the Microsoft Windows operating systems.

Dynamic Host Configuration Protocol (DHCP)   DHCP is a method of automatically assigning IP addresses to client computers on a network.

Electronic Mail (E-Mail)   A type of client/server application that provides a routed, stored-message service between any two user e-mail accounts. E-mail accounts are not the same as user accounts, but a one-to-one relationship usually exists between them. Because all modern computers can attach to the Internet, users can send e-mail over the Internet to any location that has telephone or wireless digital service. See *Internet*.

Encryption   The process of obscuring information by modifying it according to a mathematical function known only to the intended recipient. Encryption secures information being transmitted over nonsecure or untrusted media. See *Security*.

Environment Variables   Variables, such as the search path, that contain information available to programs and batch files about the current operating system environment.

Ethernet   The most popular Data Link layer standard for local area networking. Ethernet implements the carrier sense multiple access with collision detection (CSMA/CD) method of arbitrating multiple computer access to the same network. This standard supports the use of Ethernet over any type of media including wireless broadcast. Standard Ethernet operates as 10 megabits per second. Fast Ethernet operates at 100 megabits per second. See *Data Link Layer*.

Exchange   Microsoft's messaging application. Exchange implements Microsoft's mail application programming interface (MAPI) as well as other messaging protocols such as POP, SNMP, and faxing to provide a flexible message composition and reception service. See *Electronic Mail, Fax Modems*.

Explorer   The default shell for Windows 95 and Windows NT 4.0. Explorer implements the more flexible Desktop objects paradigm rather than the Program Manager paradigm used in earlier versions of Windows. See *Desktop*.

FAT   See *File Allocation Table*.

Fault Tolerance   Any method that prevents system failure by tolerating single faults, usually through hardware redundancy.

Fax Modems   Special modems that include hardware to allow the transmission and reception of facsimiles. See *Modem, Exchange*.

Fiber Distributed Data Interface (FDDI)   A Data Link layer that implements two counter-rotating token rings at 100 megabits per second. FDDI was a popular standard for interconnecting campus and metropolitan area networks because it allows distant digital connections at high speed, but ATM is replacing FDDI in many sites. See *Asynchronous Transfer Mode, Data Link Layer*.

File   A set of data stored on a mass storage device identified by a directory entry containing a name, file attributes, and the physical location of the file in the volume. See *Volume, Mass Storage Device, Directories, File Attributes*.

File Allocation Table (FAT)   The file system used by MS-DOS and available to other operating systems such as Windows (all variations), OS/2, and the Macintosh. FAT has become something of a mass storage compatibility standard because of its simplicity and wide availability. FAT has few fault tolerance features and can become corrupted through normal use over time. See *File System*.

File Attributes   Bits are stored along with the name and location of a file in a directory entry to show the status of the file, such as archived, hidden, read-only, etc. Different operating systems use different file attributes to implement such services as sharing, compression, and security.

File System   A software component that manages the storage of files on a mass storage device by providing services that can create, read, write, and delete files. File systems impose an ordered database of files on the mass storage device, called volumes, that use hierarchies of directories to organize files. See *Mass Storage Device, File, Database, Volume, Directories.*

File Transfer Protocol (FTP)   A simple Internet protocol that transfers complete files from an FTP server to a client running the FTP client. FTP provides a simple no-overhead method of transferring files between computers but cannot perform browsing functions. You must know the URL of the FTP server to which you want to attach. See *Internet, Uniform Resource Locator.*

Firmware   Software stored permanently in nonvolatile memory and built into a computer to provide its BIOS and a bootstrap routine. The entire operating system of simple computers may be built into firmware. See *Basic Input/Output System, Boot, Software.*

Floppy Disk   The first convenient removable media mass storage device. Floppy disks typically store 1.4MB of data magnetically on a thin mylar film coated with ferric particles encased in a protective plastic shell. Because floppy disks have been around longer than hard disk drives, most computers are capable of booting operating systems from a floppy disk. See *Mass Storage Device.*

Format   The process of preparing a mass storage device for use with a file system. There are actually two levels of formatting. Low-level formatting writes a structure of sectors and tracks to the disk with bits used by the mass storage controller hardware. The controller hardware requires this format, and it is independent of the file system. High-level formatting creates file system structures such as an allocation table and a root directory in a partition, thus creating a volume. See *Mass Storage Device, Volume.*

Frame   A data structure that network hardware devices use to transmit data between computers. Frames consist of the addresses of the sending and receiving computers, size information, and a checksum. Frames are envelopes around packets of data that allow them to be addressed to specific computers on a shared media network. See *Ethernet, Fiber Distributed Data Interface, Token Ring.*

FTP   See *File Transfer Protocol.*

Gateway   A computer that serves as a router, a format translator, or a security filter for an entire network.

Graphical Device Interface (GDI)   The programming interface and graphical services provided to Win32 for programs to interact with graphical devices such as the screen and printer. See *Programming Interfaces, Win32.*

Graphical User Interface (GUI)   A computer shell program that represents mass storage devices, directories, and files as graphical objects on a screen. A cursor driven by a pointing device, such as a mouse, manipulates the objects. Typically, icons that can be opened into windows that show the data contained by the object represent the objects. See *Shell, Explorer.*

Group Identifiers   Security identifiers that contain the set of permissions allowed to a group. When a user account is part of a group, the group identifier is appended to that user's security identifier, thus granting the individual user all the permissions assigned to that group. See *Security Identifiers, Accounts, Permissions.*

Groups   Security entities to which users can be assigned membership for the purpose of applying the broad set of group permissions to the user. By managing permissions for groups and assigning users to groups, rather than assigning permissions to users, security administrators can maintain control of very large security environments. See *Permissions, Accounts, Security.*

GUI   See *Graphical User Interface.*

HAL   See *Hardware Abstraction Layer.*

Hard Disk Drive   Hard disk drives are mass storage devices that read and write digital information that is stored on spinning disks. The spinning disks must be precisely aligned and cannot normally be removed. Hard disk drives are an inexpensive way to store gigabytes of computer data permanently. See *Mass Storage Device.*

Hardware Abstraction Layer (HAL)   A Windows NT service that provides basic input/output services such as timers, interrupts, and multiprocessor management for computer hardware. The HAL is a device driver for the motherboard circuitry that allows the Windows NT operating system to treat different families of computers the same way. See *Driver, Service, Interrupt Request.*

High Performance File System (HPFS)   The file system native to OS/2 that performs many of the same functions of NTFS when run under OS/2. See *File System, New Technology File System.*

Host   In remote access the computer providing data to the RAS client and hosting its connection to the remote network. See *Remote Access Service.*

HPFS   See *High Performance File System.*

HTML   See *Hypertext Markup Language.*

HTTP   See *Hypertext Transfer Protocol.*

Hub   An Ethernet Data Link layer device that connects point-to-point Physical layer links, such as twisted pair or fiber optic cables, into a single shared media network. See *Data Link Layer, Ethernet.*

Hypertext Markup Language (HTML)   A textual data format that identifies sections of a document as headers, lists, hypertext links, and so on. HTML is the data format used on the World Wide Web for the publication of Web pages. See *Hypertext Transfer Protocol, World Wide Web.*

Hypertext Transfer Protocol (HTTP)   Hypertext transfer protocol is an Internet protocol that transfers HTML documents over the Internet and responds to context changes that happen when a user clicks on a hypertext link. See *Hypertext Markup Language, World Wide Web.*

I/O   Input/Output.

i486   An Intel 80386-compatible microprocessor that includes an onboard floating point unit for increased mathematical speed and operates at higher clock speeds than the 80386. See *80386, Pentium, Microprocessor.*

Icon   A graphical representation of a resource in a graphical user interface that usually takes the form of a small (32 × 32) bitmap. See *Graphical User Interface.*

IDE   A simple mass storage device interconnection bus that operates at 5Mbps and can handle no more than two attached devices. IDE devices are similar to but less expensive than SCSI devices. See *Small Computer Systems Interface, Mass Storage Device.*

Industry Standard Architecture (ISA)   The design standard for 16-bit Intel-compatible motherboards and peripheral buses. The 32/64-bit PCI bus standard is replacing the ISA standard. Adapters and interface cards must conform to the bus standard(s) used by the motherboard in order to be used with a computer.

Ink-Jet Printers   Output devices that create paper copies of computer data by squirting microscopic ink dots onto paper from a rapidly moving ink-jet nozzle. Ink-jet printers create very high quality, inexpensive documents and have replaced most forms of mechanical impact printers. See *Laser Printers, Printers.*

Integrated Services Digital Network (ISDN)   A direct, digital dial-up PSTN Data Link layer connection that operates at 64KB per channel over regular twisted pair cable between a subscriber site and a PSTN central office. ISDN provides twice the data rate of the fastest modems per channel. Up to 24 channels can be multiplexed over two twisted pairs. See *Public Switched Telephone Network, Data Link Layer, Modem.*

Intel Architecture   A family of microprocessors descended directly from the Intel 8086, itself descended from the first microprocessor, the Intel 4004. The Intel architecture is the dominant microprocessor family. It was used in the original IBM PC microcomputer adopted by the business market and later adapted for home use.

Internet   An interconnected global network of computers based upon the TCP/IP protocol suite. TCP/IP was originally developed by the U.S. Department of Defense's Advanced Research Projects Agency to facilitate the interconnection of military networks and was provided free to universities. The obvious utility of worldwide digital network connectivity and the availability of free complex networking software developed at universities doing military research attracted other universities, research institutions, private organizations, businesses, and finally the individual home user. The Internet is now available to all current commercial computing platforms. See *File Transfer Protocol, Telnet, UseNet, World Wide Web, Transmission Control Protocol/Internet Protocol.*

Internet Explorer   A World Wide Web browser produced by Microsoft and included free with Windows 95 and Windows NT 4.0. See *World Wide Web, Internet.*

Internet Protocol (IP)   The Network layer protocol upon which the Internet is based. IP provides a simple connectionless packet exchange. Other protocols such as UDP or TCP use IP to perform their connection-oriented or guaranteed delivery services. See *Transmission Control Protocol/Internet Protocol, Internet.*

Internet Service Provider (ISP)   A company that provides dial-up connections to the Internet. See *Internet*.

Internetwork Packet eXchange (IPX)   The Network and Transport layer protocol developed by Novell for its NetWare product. IPX is a routable, connection-oriented protocol similar to TCP/IP but much easier to manage and with lower communication overhead. See *Internet Protocol, NetWare, NetWare Link*.

Interprocess Communications (IPC)   A generic term describing any manner of client/server communication protocols, specifically those operating in the Application layer. Interprocess communications mechanisms provide a method for the client and server to trade information. See *Named Pipes, Remote Procedure Calls, Network Basic Input/Output System, Mailslots, Network Dynamic Data Exchange, Local Procedure Call*.

Interrupt Request (IRQ)   A hardware signal from a peripheral device to the microcomputer indicating that it has I/O traffic to send. If the microprocessor is not running a more important service, it will interrupt its current activity and handle the interrupt request. IBM PCs have 16 levels of interrupt request lines. Under Windows NT each device must have a unique interrupt request line. See *Microprocessor, Driver, Peripheral*.

IP   See *Internet Protocol*.

IP Address   A four-byte number that uniquely identifies a computer on an IP internetwork. InterNIC assigns the first bytes of Internet IP addresses and administers them in hierarchies. Huge organizations like the government or top-level ISPs have class A addresses, large organizations and most ISPs have class B addresses, and small companies have class C addresses. In a class A address, InterNIC assigns the first byte, and the owning organization assigns the remaining three bytes. In a class B address, InterNIC or the higher level ISP assigns the first two bytes, and the organization assigns the remaining two bytes. In a class C address, InterNIC or the higher level ISP assigns the first three bytes, and the organization assigns the remaining byte. Organizations not attached to the Internet can assign IP addresses as they please. See *Internet Protocol, Internet*.

IPC   See *Interprocess Communications*.

IPX   See *Internetwork Packet eXchange*.

IRQ   See *Interrupt Request*.

ISA   See *Industry Standard Architecture.*

ISDN   See *Integrated Services Digital Network.*

ISP   See *Internet Service Provider.*

Kernel   The core process of a preemptive operating system, consisting of a multitasking scheduler and the basic services that provide security. Depending upon the operating system, other services such as virtual memory drivers may be built into the Kernel. The Kernel is responsible for managing the scheduling of *threads* and processes. See *Operating System, Driver.*

LAN   See *Local Area Network.*

LAN Manager   The Microsoft brand of a network product jointly developed by IBM and Microsoft that provided an early client/server environment. LAN Manager/Server was eclipsed by NetWare but was the genesis of many important protocols and IPC mechanisms used today, such as NetBIOS, named pipes, and NetBEUI. Portions of this product exist today in OS/2 Warp Server. See *Operating System 2, Interprocess Communications.*

LAN Server   The IBM brand of a network product jointly developed by IBM and Microsoft. See *LAN Manager.*

Laser Printers   Output devices that produce paper copies of computer data by creating an electrostatic charge on a metallic cylinder using a laser, which is then passed through a toner reservoir. Toner (ink) sticks to the charged areas of the drum. The toner is pressed into paper and then heat cured. Because of the fine resolution that the extremely narrow laser beam achieves, laser printers create very high quality paper documents. Laser printers are faster than many other printers but are generally more expensive.

LaserJet   The most popular brand of laser printer in the world, manufactured by Hewlett Packard. See *Laser Printers, Ink-Jet Printers.*

Local Area Network (LAN)   A network of computers operating on the same high-speed, shared media network Data Link layer. The size of a local area network is defined by the limitations of high speed shared media networks to generally less than 1 kilometer in overall span. Some LAN backbone data link protocols such as FDDI can create larger LANs called metropolitan or medium area networks (MANs). See *Wide Area Network, Data Link Layer.*

Local Procedure Call (LPC) A mechanism that loops remote procedure calls without the presence of a network so that the client and server portion of an application can reside on the same machine. Local procedure calls look like remote procedure calls (RPCs) to the client and server sides of a distributed application. See *Remote Procedure Calls.*

Logging The process of recording information about activities and errors in the operating system.

Login The term used by Novell NetWare to indicate opening a session with a server by providing a valid user account name and password. See *NetWare, Logon.*

Logoff The process of closing an open session with a server. See *Logon.*

Logon The process of opening a network session by providing a valid authentication consisting of a user account name and a password to a domain controller. After logon, network resources are available to the user according to the user's assigned permissions. See *Domain Controllers.*

Logon Scripts Command files that automate the logon process by performing utility functions such as attaching to additional server resources or automatically running different programs based upon the user account that established the logon. See *Logon.*

Long Filename (LFN) A filename longer than the eight characters plus three-character extension allowed by MS-DOS. In Windows NT and Windows 95, long filenames may be up to 255 characters.

LPC See *Local Procedure Call.*

Macintosh A brand of computer manufactured by Apple. Macintosh is the only successful line of computers neither based upon the original IBM PC nor running the UNIX operating system. Windows NT Server supports Apple computers despite their use of proprietary network protocols.

MacOS The operating system that runs on an Apple Macintosh computer. See *Macintosh.*

Mailslots A connectionless messaging IPC mechanism that Windows NT uses for browse request and logon authentication. See *Interprocess Communications.*

Mainframes   A generic term for large powerful computers not based upon single-chip microprocessor technology. Mainframes usually used terminals with no computing ability for user interfaces and shared a central CPU throughout an organization. The central processing paradigm of the mainframe/terminal architecture is the antithesis of the distributed processing architecture implemented by local area networks and the client/server paradigm. Distributed processing has won the market, and mainframes are now being used as superservers. See *Client/Server, Server.*

Mass Storage Device   Any device capable of storing many megabytes of information permanently, but especially those capable of random access to any portion of the information, such as hard disk drives and CD-ROM drives. See *Small Computer Systems Interface, IDE, Hard Disk Drive.*

Master Browser   The computer on a network that maintains a list of computers and services available on the network and distributes the list to other browsers. The Master Browser may also promote potential browsers to be browsers. See *Browser, Browsing, Potential Browser, Backup Browser.*

Memory   Any device capable of storing information. This term is usually used to indicate volatile random access semiconductor memory (RAM) capable of high-speed access to any portion of the memory space, but incapable of storing information without power. See *Random Access Memory, Mass Storage Device.*

Microprocessor   An integrated semiconductor circuit designed to automatically perform lists of logical and arithmetic operations. Modern microprocessors independently manage memory pools and support multiple instruction lists called threads. Microprocessors are also capable of responding to interrupt requests from peripherals and include onboard support for complex floating point arithmetic. Microprocessors must have instructions when they are first powered on. These instructions are contained in nonvolatile firmware called a BIOS. See *Basic Input/Output System, Operating System.*

Microsoft Disk Operating System (MS-DOS)   A 16-bit operating system designed for the 8086 chip that was used in the original IBM PC. Because IBM was unable to ship a better operating system, MS-DOS became the standard operating system used in microcomputers and is still the most widely used. MS-DOS is a simple program loader and file system that turns over complete control of the computer to the running program and provides very little service beyond file system support and that provided by the BIOS.

Modem   Modulator/demodulator. A Data Link layer device used to create an analog signal suitable for transmission over telephone lines from a digital data stream. Modern modems also include a command set for negotiating connections and data rates with remote modems and for setting their default behavior. The fastest modems run at about 33Kbps and will probably not get much faster due to the inherent physical bandwidth limitations of telephone cables. See *Data Link Layer.*

Module   A software component of a modular operating system that provides a certain defined service. Modules can be installed or removed depending upon the service requirements of the software running on the computer. Modules allow operating systems and applications to be customized to fit the needs of the user.

MS-DOS   See *Microsoft Disk Operating System.*

Multilink   A capability of RAS to combine multiple data streams into one network connection for the purpose of using more than one modem or ISDN channel in a single connection. This feature is new to Windows NT 4.0. See *Remote Access Service.*

Multiple Universal Naming Convention Provider (MUP)   A software component of Windows NT that allows two or more UNC providers, for example, for Microsoft networks and NetWare networks to exist simultaneously. The MUP determines which UNC provider will handle a particular UNC request and forwards the request to that provider. See *Universal Naming Convention, Multiprovider Router.*

Multiprocessing   Using two or more processors simultaneously to perform a computing task. Depending upon the operating system, processing may be done asymmetrically, wherein certain processors are assigned certain threads independent of the load they create, or symmetrically, wherein threads are dynamically assigned to processors according to an equitable scheduling scheme. The term usually describes a multiprocessing capacity built into the computer at a hardware level in that the computer itself supports more than one processor. However, *multiprocessing* can also be applied to network computing applications achieved through interprocess communication mechanisms. Client/server applications are, in fact, examples of multiprocessing. See *Asymmetrical Multiprocessing, Symmetrical Multiprocessing, Interprocess Communications.*

Multiprovider Router   A software component of Windows NT that allows two or more Win32 network API providers to exist simultaneously. The MUP determines which Win32 network provider handles a particular API request and forwards the request to that provider. See *Multitasking*.

Multitasking   The capacity of an operating system to rapidly switch among threads of execution. Multitasking allows processor time to be divided among threads as if each thread ran on its own slower processor. Multitasking operating systems allow two or more applications to run at the same time and can provide a greater degree of service to applications than single-tasking operating systems like MS-DOS. See *Multiprocessing*.

MUP   See *Multiple Universal Naming Connection Provider*.

Named Pipes   An interprocess communication mechanism that is implemented as a file system service, allowing programs to be modified to run on it without using a proprietary application programming interface. Named pipes were developed to support more robust client/ server communications than those allowed by the simpler NetBIOS. See *Operating System 2, File System, Interprocess Communications*.

NDIS   See *Network Driver Interface Specification*.

NDS   See *NetWare Directory Services*.

NetBEUI   See *NetBIOS Extended User Interface*.

NetBIOS   See *Network Basic Input/Output System*.

NetBIOS Extended User Interface (NetBEUI)   A simple Network layer transport developed to support NetBIOS installations. NetBEUI is not routable, and so it is not appropriate for larger networks. NetBEUI is the fastest transport protocol available for Windows NT.

NetBIOS Gateway   A service provided by RAS that allows NetBIOS requests to be forwarded independent of transport protocol. For example, NetBIOS requests from a remote computer connected via NetBEUI can be sent over the network via NWLink. See *Network Basic Input/Output System, NetWare Link, NetBIOS over TCP/IP, NetBEUI*.

NetBIOS over TCP/IP (NetBT)   A network service that implements the NetBIOS IPC over the TCP/IP protocol stack. See *Network Basic Input/Output System, Interprocess Communications, Transmission Control Protocol/Internet Protocol*.

NetDDE   See *Network Dynamic Data Exchange.*

NetWare   A popular network operating system developed by Novell in the early 1980s. NetWare is a cooperative, multitasking, highly optimized, dedicated-server network operating system that has client support for most major operating systems. Recent versions of NetWare include graphical client tools for management from client stations. At one time, NetWare accounted for more than 60 percent of the network operating system market. See *Windows NT, Client Services for NetWare, NetWare Link.*

NetWare Directory Services (NDS)   In NetWare, a distributed hierarchy of network services such as servers, shared volumes, and printers. NetWare implements NDS as a directory structure having elaborate security and administration mechanisms. The CSNW provided in Windows NT 4.0 supports the NDS tree. See *NetWare, Client Services for NetWare.*

NetWare Link (NWLink)   A Windows NT transport protocol that implements Novell's IPX. NWLink is useful as a general purpose transport for Windows NT and for connecting to NetWare file servers through CSNW. See *Internetwork Packet eXchange, Client Services for NetWare.*

NetWare NetBIOS Link (NWNBLink)   NetBIOS implemented over NWLink. See *Network Basic Input/Output System, NetWare Link, NetBIOS over TCP/IP.*

Network   A group of computers connected via some digital medium for the purpose of exchanging information. Networks can be based upon many types of media, such as twisted pair telephone-style cable, optical fiber, coaxial cable, radio, or infrared light. Certain computers are usually configured as service providers called *servers.* Computers that perform user tasks directly and that utilize the services of servers are called *clients.* See *Client/Server, Server, Network Operating System.*

Network Basic Input/Output System (NetBIOS)   A client/server interprocess communication service developed by IBM in the early 1980s. NetBIOS presents a relatively primitive mechanism for communication in client server/ applications, but its widespread acceptance and availability across most operating systems makes it a logical choice for simple network applications. Many Windows NT network IPC mechanisms are implemented over NetBIOS. See *Interprocess Communications, Client/Server.*

Network Driver Interface Specification (NDIS) A Microsoft specification to which network adapter drivers must conform in order to work with Microsoft network operating systems. NDIS provides a many-to-many binding between network adapter drivers and transport protocols. See *Transport Protocol*.

Network Dynamic Data Exchange (NetDDE) An interprocess communication mechanism developed by Microsoft to support the distribution of DDE applications over a network. See *Interprocess Communications, Dynamic Data Exchange*.

Network Interface Card (NIC) A Physical layer adapter device that allows a computer to connect to and communicate over a local area network. See *Ethernet, Token Ring, Adapter*.

Network Layer The layer of the OSI model that creates a communication path between two computers via routed packets. Transport protocols implement both the Network layer and the Transport layer of the OSI stack. IP is a Network layer service. See *Internet Protocol, Transport Protocol, Open Systems Interconnect Model*.

Network Operating System A computer operating system specifically designed to optimize a computer's ability to respond to service requests. Servers run network operating systems. Windows NT Server and NetWare are both network operating systems. See *Windows NT, Server, NetWare*.

New Technology File System (NTFS) A secure, transaction-oriented file system developed for Windows NT that incorporates the Windows NT security model for assigning permissions and shares. NTFS is optimized for hard drives larger than 500MB and requires too much overhead to be used on hard disk drives smaller than 50MB.

Nonbrowser A computer on a network that will not maintain a list of other computers and services on the network. See *Browser, Browsing*.

NTFS See *New Technology File System*.

NWLink See *NetWare Link, Internetwork Packet eXchange*.

NWNBLink See *NetWare NetBIOS Link*.

Object A software service provider that encapsulates both the algorithm and the data structures necessary to provide a service. Usually, objects can inherit data and functionality from their parent objects, thus allowing complex services to be constructed from simpler objects. The term *object oriented* implies a tight relationship between algorithms and data structures. See *Module*.

Object Counters Containers built into each service object in Windows NT that store a count of the number of times an object performs its service or to what degree. You can use performance monitors to access object counters and measure how the different objects in Windows NT are operating. See *Object*.

Open Graphics Language (OpenGL) A standard interface for the presentation of two- and three-dimensional visual data.

Open Systems Interconnect Model (OSI Model) A model for network component interoperability developed by the International Standards Organization to promote cross-vendor compatibility of hardware and software network systems. The OSI model splits the process of networking into seven distinct services. Each layer uses the services of the layer below to provide its service to the layer above. See *Physical Layer, Data Link Layer, Network Layer, Transport Layer, Session Layer, Presentation Layer, Application Layer*.

OpenGL See *Open Graphics Language*.

Operating System A collection of services that form a foundation upon which applications run. Operating systems may be simple I/O service providers with a command shell, such as MS-DOS, or they may be sophisticated, preemptive, multitasking, multiprocessing applications platforms like Windows NT. See *Network Operating System, Preemptive Multitasking, Kernel*.

Operating System 2 (OS/2) A 16-bit (and later, 32-bit) operating system developed jointly by Microsoft and IBM as a successor to MS-DOS. Microsoft bowed out of the 32-bit development effort and produced its own product, Windows NT, as a competitor to OS/2. OS/2 is now a preemptive, multitasking 32-bit operating system with strong support for networking and the ability to run MS-DOS and Win16 applications, but IBM has been unable to entice a large number of developers to produce software that runs native under OS/2. See *Operating System, Preemptive Multitasking*.

Optimization Any effort to reduce the workload on a hardware component by eliminating, obviating, or reducing the amount of work required of the hardware component through any means. For instance, file caching is an optimization that reduces the workload of a hard disk drive.

OS/2 See *Operating System 2*.

OSI Model See *Open Systems Interconnect Model*.

Page File   See *Swap File.*

Partition   A section of a hard disk that can contain an independent file system volume. Partitions can be used to keep multiple operating systems and file systems on the same hard disk. See *Volume, Hard Disk Drive.*

Password   A secret code used to validate the identity of a user of a secure system. Passwords are used in tandem with account names to log on to most computer systems.

Pathworks   A version of LAN Manager for DEC computer systems running the VMS operating system and DEC Unix. See *Network Operating System.*

PC   See *Personal Computer.*

PCI   See *Peripheral Connection Interface.*

PDC   See *Primary Domain Controller.*

Peer   A networked computer that both shares resources with other computers and accesses the shared resources of other computers. A nondedicated server. See *Server, Client.*

Pentium   The fifth generation of the Intel family of microprocessors upon which PC-compatible computers are based. The Pentium includes advanced microprocessor features like parallel pipeline, out-of-order execution, large on-chip caches, built-in support for multiprocessing, and extremely fast floating point math performance.

Pentium Pro   The sixth generation of the Intel family of microprocessors, the Pentium Pro is actually a RISC microprocessor that translates Pentium op codes into multiple RISC instructions for execution. This architecture allows the Pentium Pro to take advantage of advancements in microprocessor design more efficiently than complex instruction set computers (CISC) like the Pentium can. See *Reduced Instruction Set Computer.*

Peripheral   An input/output device attached to a computer. Peripherals can be printers, hard disk drives, monitors, and so on.

Peripheral Connection Interface (PCI)   A high speed 32/64-bit bus interface developed by Intel and widely accepted as the successor to the 16-bit ISA interface. PCI devices support I/O throughput about 40 times faster than the ISA bus.

Permissions   Security constructs used to regulate access to resources by user name or group affiliation. Permissions can be assigned by administrators to allow any level of access, such as read only, read/write, delete, by controlling the ability of users to initiate object services. Security is implemented by checking the user's security identifier against each object's access control list. See *Security Identifiers, Access Control List.*

Personal Computer (PC)   A microcomputer used by one person at a time (i.e., not a multiuser computer). PCs are generally clients or peers in an networked environment. High-speed PCs are called *workstations.* Networks of PCs are called LANs. The term PC is often used to refer to computers compatible with the IBM PC.

Physical Layer   The cables, connectors, and connection ports of a network. The passive physical components required to create a network. See *Open Systems Interconnect Model.*

Plotters   Print devices that use a numeric-control stylus to draw on paper rather than the raster print processes employed by laser and ink-jet printers. Plotters are typically used to produce large, high-resolution line art such as blueprints.

Point-to-Point Protocol (PPP)   A Network layer transport that performs over point-to-point network connections such as serial or modem lines. PPP can negotiate any transport protocol used by both systems involved in the link and can automatically assign IP, DNS, and gateway addresses when used with TCP/IP.

Policies   General controls that enhance the security of an operating environment. In Windows NT, policies affect restrictions on password use and rights assignment and determine which events will be recorded in the Security log.

POP   See *Post Office Protocol.*

Portable Open Systems Interconnect (POSIX)   A set of standards used to ensure cross-platform compatibility of client/server applications.

Post Office Protocol (POP)   An Internet protocol that manages the routing and delivery of e-mail.

Potential Browser A computer on a network that may maintain a list of other computers and services on the network if requested to do so by a Master Browser. See *Browser, Master Browser.*

PowerPC A microprocessor family developed by IBM to compete with the Intel family of microprocessors. The PowerPC is a RISC-architecture microprocessor with many advanced features that emulate other microprocessors. PowerPCs are currently used in a line of IBM computers and in the Apple Power Macintosh. Windows NT is available for the PowerPC.

PPP See *Point-to-Point Protocol.*

Preemptive Multitasking A multitasking implementation in which an interrupt routine in the Kernel manages the scheduling of processor time among running threads. The threads themselves do not need to support multitasking in any way because the microprocessor will preempt the thread with an interrupt, save its state, update all thread priorities according to its scheduling algorithm, and pass control to the highest priority thread awaiting execution. Because of the preemptive nature, a thread that crashes will not affect the operation of other executing threads. See *Kernel, Thread, Operating System, Process.*

Preferences Characteristics of user accounts, such as password, profile location, home directory, and logon script.

Presentation Layer That layer of the OSI model that converts and translates (if necessary) information between the Session and Application layers. See *Open Systems Interconnect Model.*

Primary Domain Controller (PDC) The domain server that contains the master copy of the security, computer, and user accounts databases and that can authenticate workstations. The primary domain controller can replicate its databases to one or more backup domain controllers and is usually also the Master Browser for the domain. See *Domain, Master Browser.*

Printers Peripheral devices that produce paper copy of computer data. See *Laser Printers, Ink-Jet Printers, Plotters, Peripheral.*

Priority A level of execution importance assigned to a thread. In combination with other factors, the priority level determines how often that thread will get computer time according to a scheduling algorithm. See *Preemptive Multitasking.*

Process   A running program containing one or more threads. A process encapsulates the protected memory and environment for its threads.

Processor   A circuit designed to automatically perform lists of logical and arithmetic operations. Unlike microprocessors, processors may be designed from discrete components rather than be a monolithic integrated circuit. See *Microprocessor*.

Program   A list of processor instructions designed to perform a certain function. A running program is called a process. A package of one or more programs and attendant data designed to meet a certain application is called software. See *Software, Application, Process, Microprocessor*.

Programming Interfaces   Interprocess communications mechanisms that provide certain high-level services to running processes. Programming interfaces may provide network communication, graphical presentation, or any other type of software service. See *Interprocess Communications*.

Protocol   An established communication method that the parties involved understand. Protocols provide a context in which to interpret communicated information. Computer protocols are rules used by communicating devices and software services to format data in a way that all participants understand. See *Transport Protocol*.

Public Switched Telephone Network (PSTN)   A global network of interconnected digital and analog communication links originally designed to support voice communication between any two points in the world but quickly adapted to handle digital data traffic when the computer revolution occurred. In addition to its traditional voice support role, the PSTN now functions as the Physical layer of the Internet by providing dial-up and leased lines for the interconnections. See *Internet, Modem, Physical Layer*.

RAID   See *Redundant Array of Inexpensive Disks*.

RAID Controllers   Hard disk drive controllers that implement RAID in hardware. See *Redundant Array of Inexpensive Disks*.

Random Access Memory (RAM)   Integrated circuits that store digital bits in massive arrays of logical gates or capacitors. RAM is the primary memory store for modern computers, storing all running software processes and contextual data. See *Microprocessor*.

RARP   See *Reverse Address Resolution Protocol.*

RAS   See *Remote Access Service.*

Real-Time Application   A process that must respond to external events at least as fast as those events can occur. Real-time threads must run at very high priorities to ensure their ability to respond in real time. See *Process.*

Redirector   A software service that redirects user file I/O requests over the network. Novell implements the Workstation and Client services for NetWare as redirectors. Redirectors allow servers to be used as mass storage devices that appear local to the user. See *Client Services for NetWare, File System.*

Reduced Instruction Set Computer (RISC)   A microprocessor technology that implements fewer and more primitive instructions than typical microprocessors and can therefore be implemented quickly with the most modern semiconductor technology and speeds. Programs written for RISC microprocessors require more instructions (longer programs) to perform the same task as a normal microprocessor but are capable of a greater degree of optimization and therefore usually run faster. See *Microprocessor.*

Redundant Array of Inexpensive Disks (RAID)   A collection of hard disk drives, coordinated by a special controller, that appears as one physical disk to a computer but stores its data across all the disks to take advantage of the speed and/or fault tolerance afforded by using more than one disk. RAID disk storage has several levels, including 0 (striping), 1 (mirroring), and 5 (striping with parity). RAID systems are typically used for very large storage volumes or to provide fault-tolerance features such as hot swapping of failed disks or automatically backing up data onto replacement disks.

Registry   A database of settings required and maintained by Windows NT and its components. The Registry stores Control Panel settings. You can use the Registry Editor to change these settings.

Remote Access Service (RAS)   A service that allows network connections to be established over PSTN lines with modems. The computer initiating the connection is called the RAS client; the answering computer is called the RAS host. See *Modem.*

Remote Procedure Calls (RPC)   A network interprocess communication mechanism that allows an application to be distributed among many computers on the same network. See *Local Procedure Call, Interprocess Communications.*

Requests for Comments (RFCs)   The set of standards defining the Internet protocols as determined by the Internet Engineering Task Force and available in the public domain on the Internet. RFCs define the functions and services provided by each of the many Internet protocols. Compliance with the RFCs guarantees cross-vendor compatibility. See *Internet*.

Resource   Any useful service, such as a shared network directory or a printer. See *Share*.

Reverse Address Resolution Protocol (RARP)   The TCP/IP protocol that allows a computer that has a Physical layer address (such as an Ethernet address) but does not have an IP address to request a numeric IP address from another computer on the network. See *Transfer Control Protocol/Internet Protocol*.

RFCs   See *Requests for Comments*.

RISC   See *Reduced Instruction Set Computer*.

Router   A Network layer device that moves packets between networks. Routers provide internetwork connectivity. See *Network Layer*.

RPC   See *Remote Procedure Calls*.

SAM   See *Security Accounts Manager*.

Scheduling   The process of determining which threads should be executed according to their priority and other factors. See *Preemptive Multitasking*.

SCSI   See *Small Computer Systems Interface*.

Security   Measures taken to secure a system against accidental or intentional loss, usually in the form of accountability procedures and use restriction. See *Security Identifiers, Security Accounts Manager*.

Security Accounts Manager (SAM)   The module of the Windows NT executive that authenticates a username and password against a database of accounts, generating an access token that includes the user's permissions. See *Security, Security Identifiers, Access Tokens*.

Security Identifiers   Unique codes that identify a specific user to the Windows NT security system. Security identifiers contain a complete set of permissions for that user.

Serial   A method of communication that transfers data across a medium one bit at a time, usually adding stop, start, and check bits to ensure quality transfer. See *COM Port, Modem.*

Serial Line Internet Protocol (SLIP)   An implementation of the IP protocol over serial lines. SLIP has been obviated by PPP. See *Point-to-Point Protocol, Internet Protocol.*

Server   A computer dedicated to servicing requests for resources from other computers on a network. Servers typically run network operating systems such as Windows NT Server or NetWare. See *Windows NT, NetWare, Client/Server.*

Service   A process dedicated to implementing a specific function for other processes. Most Windows NT components are services used by User-level applications.

Session Layer   The layer of the OSI model dedicated to maintaining a bidirectional communication connection between two computers. The Session layer uses the services of the Transport layer to provide this service. See *Open Systems Interconnect Model, Transport Layer.*

Share   A resource (e.g., a directory or a printer) shared by a server or a peer on a network. See *Resource, Server, Peer.*

Shell   The user interface of an operating system; the shell launches applications and manages file systems.

Simple Network Management Protocol (SNMP)   An Internet protocol that manages network hardware such as routers, switches, servers, and clients from a single client on the network. See *Internet Protocol.*

SLIP   See *Serial Line Internet Protocol.*

Small Computer Systems Interface (SCSI)   A high-speed, parallel-bus interface that connects hard disk drives, CD-ROM drives, tape drives, and many other peripherals to a computer. SCSI is the mass storage connection standard among all computers except IBM compatibles, which use either SCSI or IDE.

SNMP   See *Simple Network Management Protocol.*

Software   A suite of programs sold as a unit and dedicated to a specific application. See *Program, Application, Process.*

Spooler   A service that buffers output to a low-speed device such as a printer so the software outputting to the device is not tied up.

Stripe Set   A single volume created across multiple hard disk drives and accessed in parallel for the purpose of optimizing disk access time. NTFS can create stripe sets. See *New Technology File System, Volume, File System.*

Subdirectory   A directory contained in another directory. See *Directories.*

Subnet Mask   A number mathematically applied to Internet protocol addresses to determine which IP addresses are a part of the same subnetwork as the computer applying the subnet mask.

Swap File   The virtual memory file on a hard disk containing the memory pages that have been moved out to disk to increase available RAM. See *Virtual Memory.*

Symmetrical Multiprocessing   A multiprocessing methodology that assigns processes to processors on a fair-share basis. This method balances the processing load among processors and ensures that no processor will become a bottleneck. Symmetrical multiprocessing is more difficult to implement than asymmetrical multiprocessing, as processors must share certain hardware functions. See *Asymmetrical Multiprocessing, Multiprocessing.*

Task Manager   An application that manually views and closes running processes. Press Ctrl+Alt+Del to launch the Task Manager.

TCP   See *Transmission Control Protocol.*

TCP/IP   See *Transmission Control Protocol/Internet Protocol.*

TDI   See *Transport Driver Interface.*

Telnet   A terminal application that allows a user to log into a multiuser UNIX computer from any computer connected to the Internet. See *Internet.*

Thread   A list of instructions running in a computer to perform a certain task. Each thread runs in the context of a process, which embodies the protected memory space and the environment of the threads. Multithreaded processes can perform more than one task at the same time. See *Process, Preemptive Multitasking, Program.*

Throughput   The measure of information flow through a system in a specific time frame, usually one second. For instance, 28.8Kbps is the throughput of a modem: 28.8 kilobits per second can be transmitted.

Token Ring   The second most popular Data Link layer standard for local area networking. Token ring implements the token passing method of arbitrating multiple-computer access to the same network. Token ring operates at either 4 or 16Mbps. FDDI is similar to token ring and operates at 100Mbps. See *Data Link Layer*.

Transmission Control Protocol (TCP)   A transport layer protocol that implements guaranteed packet delivery using the Internet Protocol (IP). See *Transmission Control Protocol/Internet Protocol, Internet Protocol*.

Transmission Control Protocol/Internet Protocol (TCP/IP)   A suite of Internet protocols upon which the global Internet is based. TCP/IP is a general term that can refer either to the TCP and IP protocols used together or to the complete set of Internet protocols. TCP/IP is the default protocol for Windows NT.

Transport Driver Interface (TDI)   A specification to which all Window NT transport protocols must be written in order to be used by higher level services such as programming interfaces, file systems, and interprocess communications mechanisms. See *Transport Protocol*.

Transport Layer   The OSI model layer responsible for the guaranteed serial delivery of packets between two computers over an internetwork. TCP is the Transport layer protocol for the TCP/IP transport protocol.

Transport Protocol   A service that delivers discrete packets of information between any two computers in a network. Higher level connection-oriented services are built upon transport protocols. See *TCP/IP, NetWare Link, NetBIOS Extended User Interface, Transport Layer, Internet Protocol, Internet*.

UDP   See *User Datagram Protocol*.

UNC   See *Universal Naming Convention*.

Uniform Resource Locator (URL)   An Internet standard naming convention for identifying resources available via various TCP/IP application protocols. For example, `http://www.microsoft.com` is the URL for Microsoft's World Wide Web server site, while `ftp://gateway.dec.com` is a popular FTP site. A URL allows easy hypertext references to a particular resource from within a document or mail message. See *Hypertext Transfer Protocol, World Wide Web*.

Universal Naming Convention (UNC)   A multivendor, multiplatform convention for identifying shared resources on a network. See *multitasking*.

UNIX   A multitasking, Kernel-based operating system developed at AT&T in the early 1970s and provided (originally) free to universities as a research operating system. Because of its availability and ability to scale down to microprocessor-based computers, UNIX became the standard operating system of the Internet and its attendant network protocols and is the closest approximation to a universal operating system that exists. Most computers can run some variant of the UNIX operating system. See *Multitasking, Internet*.

UseNet   A massive distributed database of news feeds and special interest groups maintained on the Internet and accessible through most Web browsers. See *Internet, World Wide Web*.

User Datagram Protocol (UDP)   A nonguaranteed network packet protocol implemented on IP that is far faster than TCP because it doesn't have flow-control overhead. UDP can be implemented as a reliable transport when some higher level protocol (such as NetBIOS) exists to make sure that required data will eventually be retransmitted in local area environments.

User Manager   A Windows NT application that administers user accounts and manages policies.

Username   A user's account name in a logon-authenticated system. See *Security*.

VDM   See *Virtual DOS Machine*.

VFAT   An extension of the FAT file system; VFAT allows long filenames up to 255 characters. Windows 95 and Windows NT use the VFAT file system.

Virtual DOS Machine (VDM)   The DOS environment created by Windows NT for the execution of DOS and Win16 applications. See *MS-DOS, Win16*.

Virtual Memory   A kernel service that stores memory pages not currently in use on a mass storage device to free up the memory occupied for other uses. Virtual memory hides the memory swapping process from applications and higher level services. See *Swap File, Kernel*.

Volume   A collection of data indexed by directories containing files and referred to by a drive letter. Volumes are normally contained in a single partition, but volume sets and stripe sets extend a single volume across multiple partitions.

Wide Area Network (WAN)   A geographically dispersed network of networks connected by routers and communication links. The Internet is the world's largest WAN. See *Internet, Local Area Network.*

Win16   The set of application services provided by the 16-bit versions of Microsoft Windows: Windows 3.0 and Windows 3.11 for Workgroups.

Win32   The set of application services provided by the 32-bit versions of Microsoft Windows: Windows 95 and Windows NT.

Windows 3.11 for Workgroups   The current 16-bit version of Windows for less-powerful, Intel-based personal computers; this system includes peer networking services.

Windows 95   The current 32-bit version of Microsoft Windows for medium-range, Intel-based personal computers; this system includes peer networking services, Internet support, and strong support for older DOS applications and peripherals.

Windows Internet Name Service (WINS)   A network service for Microsoft networks that provides Windows computers with Internet numbers for specified NetBIOS names, facilitating browsing and intercommunication over TCP/IP networks.

Windows NT   The current 32-bit version of Microsoft Windows for powerful Intel, Alpha, PowerPC, or MIPS-based computers; the system includes peer networking services, server networking services, Internet client and server services, and a broad range of utilities.

Windows on Windows (WOW)   The compatibility service that allows the use of Win16 apps under Windows NT. WOW serves as a 32-bit interface shell for 16-bit applications.

Windows Sockets   An interprocess communications protocol that delivers connection-oriented data streams used by Internet software and software ported from UNIX environments. See *Interprocess Communications.*

WINS   See *Windows Internet Name Service.*

Workgroup   In Microsoft networks, a collection of related computers, such as a department, that doesn't require the uniform security and coordination of a domain. See *Domain.*

Workstation   A powerful personal computer, usually running a preemptive, multitasking operating system like UNIX or Windows NT.

World Wide Web (WWW)   A collection of Internet servers providing hypertext-formatted documents for Internet clients running Web browsers. The World Wide Web provided the first easy-to-use graphical interface for the Internet and is largely responsible for the Internet's explosive growth.

WOW   See *Windows on Windows.*

Write-Back Caching   A caching optimization wherein data written to the slow store is cached until the cache is full or until a subsequent write operation overwrites the cached data. Write-back caching can significantly reduce the write operations to a slow store because many write operations are subsequently obviated by new information. Data in the write-back cache is also available for subsequent reads. If something happens to prevent the cache from writing data to the slow store, the cache data will be lost. See *Caching, Write-through Caching.*

Write-Through Caching   A caching optimization wherein data written to a slow store is kept in a cache for subsequent rereading. Unlike write-back caching, write-through caching immediately writes the data to the slow store and is therefore less optimal but more secure.

WWW   See *World Wide Web.*

Index

NETWORK PRESS® PRESENTS
MCSE TEST SUCCESS

THE PERFECT COMPANION BOOKS TO THE MCSE STUDY GUIDES

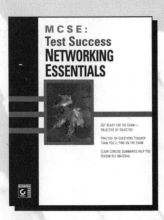

ISBN: 0-7821-2146-2
352pp; 7¹/₂" x 9"; Softcover
$24.99

ISBN: 0-7821-2148-9
352pp; 7¹/₂" x 9"; Softcover
$24.99

ISBN: 0-7821-2149-7
400pp; 7¹/₂" x 9"; Softcover
$24.99

ISBN: 0-7821-2147-0
352pp; 7¹/₂" x 9"; Softcover
$24.99

Here's what you need to know to pass the MCSE tests.

- Review concise summaries of key information

- Boost your knowledge with more than 400 review questions

- Get ready for the test with more than 200 tough practice test questions

Other MCSE Test Success titles:

- **Core Requirements**
  (4 books, 1 CD)
  [ISBN: 0-7821-2296-5] April 1998

- **Windows® 95**
  [ISBN: 0-7821-2252-3] May 1998

- **Exchange Server 5.5**
  [ISBN: 0-7821-2250-7] May 1998

- **TCP/IP for NT® 4**
  [ISBN: 0-7821-2251-5] May 1998